Other Webster/McGraw-Hill Titles in Home Economics

about the author

Elizabeth B. Hurlock is a lecturer, writer, and educational consultant. Dr. Hurlock was formerly Lecturer in Educational Psychology in the Graduate School of Education of the University of Pennsylvania. She was Assistant to the Adviser of Women Students and Departmental Representative for Undergraduates in the Department of Psychology of Columbia University. She is the author of many scientific and popular articles, of college textbooks, and of educational films on childhood and adolescence. Dr. Hurlock has served as Secretary-Treasurer and as President of the Division on the Teaching of Psychology of the American Psychological Association, as Secretary-Treasurer of the Division on Developmental Psychology, and as Representative to the Council of the American Psychological Association.

CHILD GROWTH

AND DEVELOPMENT

Fifth Edition

Elizabeth B. Hurlock, Ph.D.

Webster Division, McGraw-Hill Book Company
New York   St. Louis   San Francisco   Auckland   Bogotá
Düsseldorf   Johannesburg   London   Madrid   Mexico
Montreal   New Delhi   Panama   Paris   São Paulo
Singapore   Sydney   Tokyo   Toronto

Editors   Patricia M. Channon and Lynne Farber
Editing Supervisor   Linda Richmond
Design Supervisor   Joe Nicholosi
Production Supervisor   Salvador Gonzales
Photo Editor   Rosemary O'Connell

Photo Research   Suzanne Volkman
Illustrations   Vantage Art, Inc.
Frontispiece   William Hubbell/Woodfin Camp & Associates
Cover Design   Bennie Arrington

Cover Photo Credits   Front cover, clockwise from upper left: David
Greenberg/Photo Researchers; William
Hubbel/Woodfin Camp & Associates; Michael Philip
Manheim/Photo Researchers; Richard Nowitz;
Susan Johns/Rapho/Photo Researchers. Back
cover, clockwise from upper left: Richard Nowitz;
Bruce Roberts/Rapho/Photo Researchers; Jeffrey
Foxx/Woodfin Camp & Associates

Unit Opener Credits   x: Ginger Chih; 46: Dan Budnik/Woodfin Camp &
Associates; 142: HEW; 226: John Running/Stock,
Boston; 304: Bruce Roberts/Photo Researchers.

Library of Congress Cataloging in Publication Data

Hurlock, Elizabeth Bergner, date
    Child growth and development.

    Bibliography: p.
    Includes index.
    1. Children—Management. I. Title.
HQ769.H93   1978   649'.1   77-9484
ISBN 0-07-031437-3

Preface

Studying and learning about children leads the way to a better understanding of what they are all about. How do children grow and develop? What makes them different or alike? How do children change as they grow older? The answers to these and countless other questions are important in learning to live and work successfully with children.

This fifth edition of *Child Growth and Development* has been reorganized and revised—not only to make the text more meaningful to students, but also to create a better instructional medium for teachers. It has been entirely rewritten to include more basic and relevant information, to eliminate outmoded ideas, and to stress throughout the importance of family involvement in the care and guidance of children. Several new chapters have been added to expand the material covered in the previous editions and to introduce concepts that reflect changes in today's society. In addition, the totally new illustrative program has been selected on the basis of fair and equal treatment of males and females of all racial, ethnic, and economic backgrounds.

The following features have been incorporated into this new edition:

☐ The chapters have been reorganized to examine the various stages of child growth—starting with parents as they plan to have a child and proceeding through the early childhood years to the first grade.

☐ For Discussion, For Thought, and For Action questions have been strategically placed throughout each chapter to encourage student involvement in learning and understanding the practical aspects of the material in the text.

☐ Many charts have been added to include material of special interest or factual value. These not only provoke student interest but also summarize information in an easy-to-learn format.

☐ Career awareness has been injected into both the textual material and the illustrative program to spark student interest in opportunities in child care and development.

☐ Suggested Activities have been revamped along the lines of the new text material to give students greater insight into what is presented in each chapter.

☐ Metrication has been introduced with dual dimensions throughout the text.

☐ An extensive bibliography containing the most recent books and pamphlets on baby and child care has been totally updated.

It is hoped that students who use this text will feel confident that they are gaining the basic knowledge necessary in understanding children. In addition, it is also hoped that this text will go a long way in preparing students to make their own personal decisions about their future and about children who may be part of that future.

Elizabeth B. Hurlock

Contents

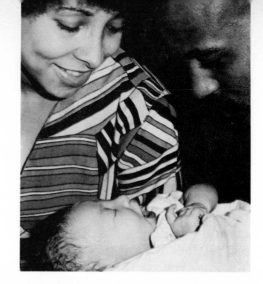

Unit Three THE EARLY CHILDHOOD YEARS   143

Unit Four THE CHILD IS AN INDIVIDUAL   227

Unit Five GROWING UP   305

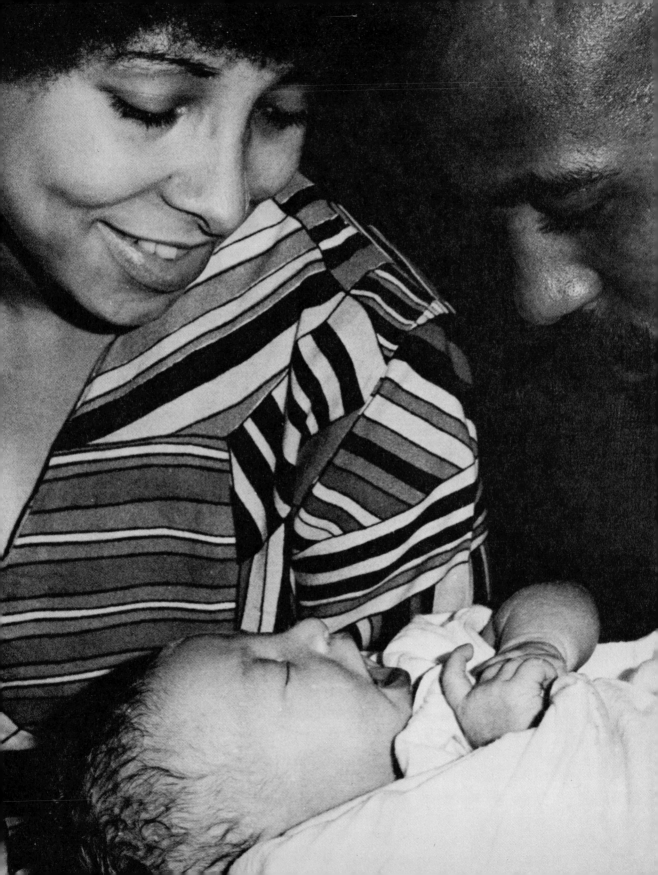

Unit One

HOW LIFE BEGINS

Most parents start getting ready for the arrival of a baby as soon as the doctor confirms the woman's pregnancy. This gives them seven or eight months—at the most—to make all their preparations. These days, when stores carry everything a new baby needs ready-made, this may seem to be plenty of time. It is enough time for meeting the baby's needs. But meeting the family's needs is another thing. This unit is about preparing families for a new baby. The earlier the preparation begins, the better chance a family will have to learn to accept, love, and understand its new member.

Chapter 1, "Planning and Preparing for Parenthood," discusses physical, psychological, and financial preparations that family members might make to help them adjust to the new baby. Health, attitudes, and expenses are taken up as major factors in family planning.

Chapter 2, "The Newborn Baby," explains how heredity and environment contribute to making babies what they are. This chapter describes typical newborn babies. Not only their appearance, but also their behavior and individuality are discussed.

Chapter 3, "The Baby in the Family," explains how other family members can and should make a baby part of the family. This chapter discusses changes that take place in the family when a baby joins. It also shows how everyone gains by sharing the responsibilities for the baby's care.

Chapter 1

Planning and Preparing for Parenthood

Some goals of this chapter are:
- [ ] To realize that people can decide whether they want to be parents and when they will have their children
- [ ] To understand why people should make physical, psychological, and financial preparations for parenthood
- [ ] To identify some of the immediate preparations for parenthood and realize their importance

Figures show that first babies usually arrive nine months to two years after marriage. Second, third, and later babies most often arrive a year to a year and a half after the last child's birth.

This means that couples have barely adjusted to their new roles as husband and wife and have hardly settled in their new home when they must begin to prepare for a new family member. And just as they are adjusting to one child, another is often on the way.

To Be or Not To Be a Parent

One of the most important preparations for parenthood is deciding whether one really wants to be a parent. In the past, marriage and parenthood went hand in hand. It was assumed that when people married they wanted and expected to have children.

Today, this is no longer true. With modern methods of *contraception*—means of preventing pregnancy—and the legalizing of abortion, people can decide not only *if* they want to be parents but also *when* they want to have their children.

For Discussion

When after marriage is it a good time to plan to have a first baby? What reasons can you give for and against having a baby during the first year after marriage?

There are some people who would like to be parents but who have second thoughts about bringing a child into the world. They may be concerned about contributing to overpopulation or losing their independence. Or, perhaps certain diseases, such as hemophilia or sickle cell anemia, run in the family.

If there are any potential medical problems, these should be looked into carefully before a couple decide to have children. Doctors are not always certain that a child will be affected by an unfavorable condition that may exist in either parent. In some cases though, accurate predictions are possible. In other cases, there is enough known from scientific research for doctors to advise people about the chances of their children's being affected.

In complicated or difficult cases, however, most feel that such advice should come from someone who specializes in the study of genes and heredity—a *geneticist*. Doctors and medical centers can refer a couple to a heredity clinic for counseling

A couple may choose not to have a child of their own and might want to arrange to adopt a child. Adopting a baby is far more difficult now than it was in the past. However, if there is evidence that the couple will make good parents, doctors and adoption agencies can usually find a child for adoption, either in this country or in a foreign country.

Long-Range Preparation for Parenthood

Even though a couple may not plan to become parents for several years, they can and should begin some preparation for the parental role. This preparation should include three important areas. They are: physical well-being, psychological health, and financial security.

Physical Preparation

Some physical conditions affect the kind of reproductive cells men and women produce and also affect the developing baby. These include glandular imbalance; chronic diseases, such as diabetes; anemia; and venereal diseases. A physical checkup and a talk with the doctor about regular health habits and medications is a wise precaution for people to take.

Sensible familyplanning includes physical, psychological, and financial preparations. Literature and guidance for planning a family are available in neighborhood health centers and planned parenthood agencies. Planned Parenthood

love is
a fourteen
letter word.

familyplanning

FOR FURTHER INFORMATION: PLANNED PARENTHOOD, 810 SEVENTH AVENUE, NEW YORK, N. Y. 10019

It is never too early to realize how your health and well-being as teenagers can affect your health and well-being as adults. Mimi Forsyth/Monkmeyer

For example, if the woman has never had German measles (rubella), she should report this to the doctor. A case of German measles in early pregnancy often has serious effects on the developing baby.

In the medical checkup, the doctor should examine the man's and the woman's reproductive organs to make sure that they are healthy. Some conditions that might cause *infertility*—the inability to have children—can be corrected. Some other conditions in the woman that might lead to miscarriages can also be determined. Often, steps can be taken to correct the conditions.

For Action

The next time you have a physical checkup, ask the doctor for guidelines to be sure you are doing everything possible for good health. Here are some suggestions about what to discuss with your doctor:

1. *Diet*. Because teenagers sometimes go in for fad diets, they may suffer from what doctors call "hidden hunger," or malnutrition. Your doctor can check your diet to see if it is good enough to meet your growth and health needs.

2. *Rest*. Burning the candle at both ends is common among students. They stay up too late at night and get little or no rest. Ask the doctor if you are getting enough rest and, if not, ask how much rest you should have.

3. *Drugs and Alcohol*. Many teenagers (and many older people, too) get into the habit of using laxatives for constipation, tranquilizers to calm them when they are worried, and "pep" pills to keep them awake and alert for late-night studying. Many also smoke marijuana once in a while. Some smoke it often. Report, truthfully, what drugs you use, and ask how drugs might affect a future child if you keep on using them.

4. *Smoking*. For many high school students, smoking is a symbol of being grown-up. Ask the doctor about the harmful effects smoking might have on your own health and on a child you may have in the future.

For Thought

Medical science has evidence of how the mother's activities during pregnancy affect a baby's physical and mental development. Cigarettes, alcohol, drugs, and malnutrition are likely to have damaging effects. Furthermore, it takes months for a person's body to recover from them.

Even if you are not yet thinking about becoming a parent, what are you willing to do to improve your health?

Psychological Preparation

An *attitude* is a feeling toward people, situations, and roles that affects the way a person reacts. Psychological preparation means developing attitudes. If a person's attitude toward something is favorable, the person will react positively and adjust well to it.

There are many factors that affect attitudes. They differ for different people and depend on a person's temperament, interests, and experiences. However, there are three factors that affect attitudes so often that they can be thought of as almost universal among people today. They are *knowledge* about a situation, *experience* in dealing with it, and *mental flexibility* toward it. See the chart below.

When preparing for parenthood, people develop attitudes toward the role of parent, the situations connected with this role, and the child to come. Like the parents, children in the family experience changes when a new baby arrives. They too need psychological preparation to help them cope with the new situation. An only child, who has been the center of family affection, may very well have mixed feelings about a new baby, who takes up so much of the parents' time and attention. A youngest child, who is likely to be pampered both by parents and by older brothers and sisters, may have to adjust to no longer being the "baby of the family." Older children, unless they have some knowledge about the baby, may also resent the newest family member.

For children, an attitude is mostly affected by knowledge and experience. Children tend to adjust well to new situations when given proper guidance.

How Common Factors Affect Some Attitudes toward a New Baby

Knowledge   A woman who knows that the physical changes and discomforts of pregnancy are only temporary will have a better attitude toward pregnancy than a woman who does not know such facts.

Previous Experience   People who enjoy doing things with, and for, children will look forward more eagerly to the arrival of their baby than those who have not had such positive experiences.

Mental Flexibility   Some people look forward to and accept change in their lives. They tend to make more favorable adjustments than people who fear or resent any change. Rather than restricting their social activities, new parents can make plans that include the baby.

How are the common factors that affect attitudes applied to life's different stages and role changes? For example, how would they affect your attitude toward a job after being a student for many years?

Financial Preparation

Having a baby is an added family expense. Saving some money regularly from the family income in preparation for the baby is a wise policy for a couple to follow.

Many women who work give up their jobs as pregnancy progresses. Even if a woman just takes a temporary leave from the job, the reduced income comes at the same time as the added financial burden. This often dampens the anticipated pleasure of parenthood.

An important factor in financial security is a medical insurance policy. Working people often have one through their job. It is wise to have an insurance policy that covers prenatal care and childbirth, including doctors' fees and hospital costs. If these are not covered by the policy, a clause should be added to include them, even though it adds to the cost of the payments. If this cannot be done, a separate policy should be taken out. These needs should be considered before a woman becomes pregnant. Very often, a new policy will not cover a woman who is already pregnant.

Immediate Areas of Preparation

All parents-to-be will have to make some preparation for the arrival of a baby. Those families that already have one or more children will prepare differently from those expecting a first baby. The preparations explained below are some of the most important.

Confirming the Pregnancy

A woman who has fairly regular menstrual periods and who has had sexual

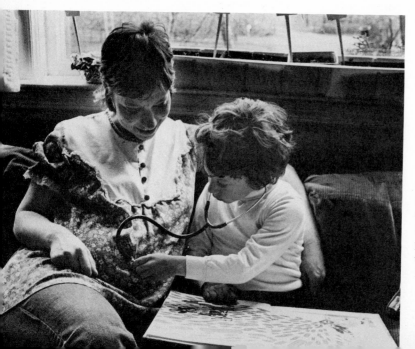

A mother's pregnancy can be quite a learning experience for children. By preparing children for a new brother or sister, parents can help them adjust to the new family member. Mimi Forsyth/Monkmeyer

Some Attitudes Affecting Psychological Preparation

Parents' Attitudes

Favorable

Wanting a child

Wanting a normal, healthy baby above anything else and being happy with a child of either sex

Accepting the temporary changes in the mother's figure during pregnancy

Accepting the normal discomforts of pregnancy

Regarding parenthood as personal fulfillment

Feeling that the satisfactions of parenthood make up for the responsibilities it brings

Realizing that the older children's jealousy and resentment toward the new baby is a temporary stage in their adjustment to the baby

Realizing that the new baby's helplessness is only temporary

Unfavorable

Not wanting a child

Wanting a child of a particular sex so much that it affects the parents' acceptance of a child of the opposite sex

Resenting figure changes during pregnancy

Resenting the child to come because of pregnancy discomforts

Regarding parenthood as the price for sex

Resenting the work and responsibility parenthood brings

Feeling irritation at the older children's jealousy and resentment toward the new baby

Feeling abused because the new baby must be waited on constantly

Wanting a "dream child" with all the characteristics the parents always desired in themselves

Children's Attitudes

Favorable

Realizing that the new baby cannot be treated as a toy

Wanting to help with the care of the new baby

Being glad to give up their crib, high chair, and some playthings to the new baby

Wanting to help prepare the clothes and nursery for the new baby

Wanting to talk about the new baby

Unfavorable

Resenting not being able to play with the new baby

Not wanting to help with the new baby

Not wanting to give up the crib, high chair, or playthings that they used as babies

Sulking whenever someone does things in preparation for the new baby

Being upset whenever the new baby is mentioned

The Anticipated Arrival Time of the Baby   Although doctors cannot tell exactly when a baby will arrive, the following method is used to get a rough idea: Count back three calendar months from the first day of the last menstrual period and add seven days.

Medical Checkups   When and how often the doctor wants to check the woman's and baby's progress during pregnancy should be discussed at the first examination. Checkups are made more often as pregnancy goes on.

The Cost of Prenatal Care and Childbirth   Costs vary greatly from community to community. Private doctors have higher rates than doctors in a clinic. Most health insurance policies cover at least part of these expenses.

Health Care during Pregnancy   After a complete physical examination, the doctor will prescribe a diet suited to the woman's needs and will specify the amount of rest and exercise she should have. Sometimes vitamins and calcium are also prescribed to supplement the diet. The doctor might suggest periodic checkups with a dentist.

Medicines during Pregnancy   Most doctors warn against taking *any* medicine during pregnancy without their knowledge and consent. If the woman is used to taking medicine, such as laxatives, aspirin, or tranquilizers, this should be reported to the doctor.

Telephone Consultations   When and where the doctor can be reached if any problems arise should be discussed at the first visit.

Choice of Pediatrician   Most doctors who take care of childbirth cases turn over the care of the baby to a pediatrician. If the mother-to-be does not know a pediatrician, her doctor can usually recommend one.

When Work Should Be Given Up   If the woman has a job, the doctor should be consulted about how long it will be safe and wise for her to go on working. This will depend partly on the kind of work she does and partly on her physical condition.

Circumcision   If parents want a boy baby to be circumcised, this should be told to the doctor so that the circumcision can be done before the baby is taken home from the hospital.

intercourse during the preceding month has reason to suspect that she is pregnant if she skips a menstrual period. If the next menstrual period is also skipped, she has reason to assume that she is pregnant. This is the time to consult a doctor, to make sure.

The family doctor or the woman's gynecologist may be prepared to take care of childbirth cases. However, a woman may be referred to an *obstetrician*, a doctor who specializes in pregnancy and childbirth. If the woman has been using a health center or clinic, she should go there, where an obstetrician will care for her throughout her pregnancy.

When the doctor's examination and tests show that pregnancy has begun, there are many things a woman may want to know. Doctors usually give their patients printed instructions about

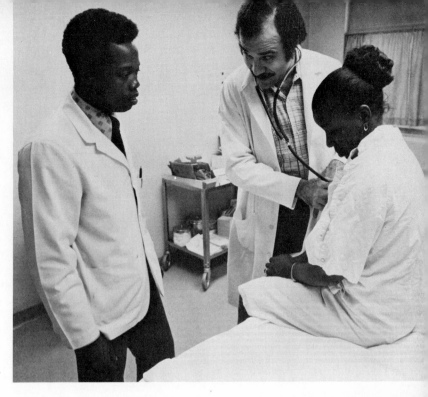

Seeing a doctor early in pregnancy can give a woman the assurance that all is well with her and the baby.   Cary Wolinsky/Stock, Boston

diet, rest, and exercise. They also usually give personal advice to fit each woman's needs. It is essential that the woman follow her doctor's advice very carefully.

Selecting a Pediatrician

If the family doctor is caring for the woman during pregnancy and childbirth, the same doctor will probably take care of the baby. However, shortly after the first visit to an obstetrician, the mother-to-be should consult a *pediatrician*, a doctor who specializes in the care of children. Since arrangements for the care of the new baby must also be made, it is important to visit the pediatrician before the baby is born.

Matters To Be Discussed with the Pediatrician

Fees   Some pediatricians charge a flat fee for the baby's first year. This usually includes an unlimited number of office visits and sometimes house calls.

Breast-Feeding versus Bottle-Feeding Most pediatricians favor breast-feeding. If a mother does not wish to breast-feed her baby or is unable to do so, she should discuss it with the doctor so that a formula can be substituted.

Provision for Day Care If the mother returns to work as soon after the baby's birth as she is well enough to do so, the pediatrician should be consulted about the care of the baby. The doctor should be able to recommend a caretaker or a carefully supervised and well-equipped day-care center.

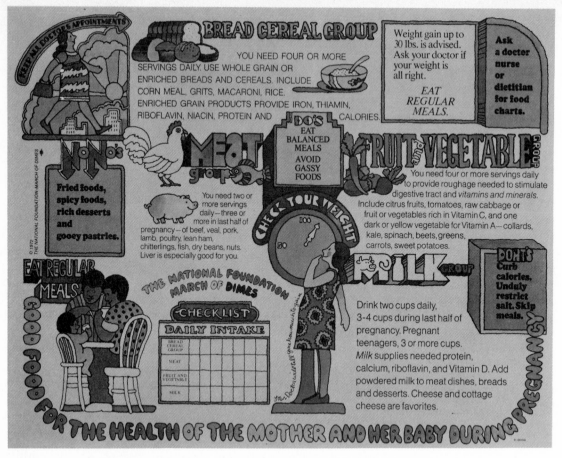

Doctors recommend special diets for pregnant women to be sure that they and their babies get all the nutrients they need. The National Foundation–March of Dimes

Choosing a Hospital

Doctors usually send their patients to the hospital where they are on staff. If her doctor is on the staff of more than one hospital, the mother-to-be may be able to choose where she will have her baby. If that is the case, the hospital's location and childbirth policies will probably determine the choice. Some hospitals let the father be in the labor and delivery rooms to share with the mother the experience of childbirth.

The practice of natural childbirth might be more welcomed in one hospital than in others. The type of anesthesia used for childbirth varies from hospital to hospital. This may be a concern for women who prefer one type to another.

Some hospitals let newborn babies be in the rooms with their mothers rather than in the nursery. This is usually called *rooming-in*. It gives the mother a chance to learn how to take care of the baby while she is in the hospital under the guidance of a nurse. On the other hand, with rooming-in, the mother has less time to rest and regain her strength before going home.

Budgeting Expenses for the Baby

No matter how careful parents-to-be are in spending money, they will find that having a baby is an expense that often taxes the family budget.

Besides the costs of medical and hospital care, there is the cost of equipment for the baby. Equipment for a new baby can be expensive. It is less costly when some of it is made at home, bought secondhand, or borrowed from friends and relatives. Money saved on equipment may be used for emergencies or for help at home after the baby is born.

New and inexperienced parents-to-be often want their children to have everything. They may get carried away by the store displays of baby clothes and nursery furnishings. It is easy for them to buy more than the baby will ever use.

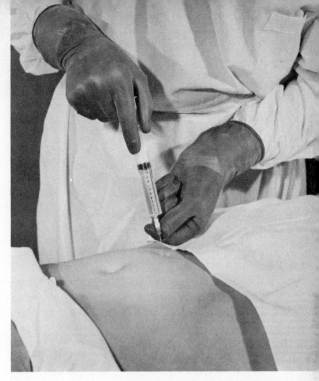

The removal of a small sample of fluid from the sac surrounding the fetus is called amniocentesis. By special medical tests, doctors can tell if the fetus is developing normally or is likely to have certain genetic defects. This procedure is used only in complicated or high-risk pregnancies. The National Foundation–March of Dimes

Essential Equipment for a New Baby

Clothing   3 to 4 cotton knit long nightgowns; 3 to 4 cotton knit shirts with short or long sleeves; 2 or 3 sacques; 1 cap; 3 to 6 dozen diapers (washable or disposable)

Bedding   2 or 3 flannelette-covered waterproof sheets to cover the mattress; 2 small waterproof pads to put under the baby; 2 mattress pads; 3 or 4 sheets; 1 cotton blanket for warm weather; sleeping bag for cold weather

Bathing Equipment   3 to 4 cotton flannel *receiving blankets* for use after the bath; 2 to 3 towels and washcloths;

baby soap, talcum powder, and lotion; diaper pail

Feeding Equipment   6 to 8 eight-ounce bottles and nipples; bottle and nipple brush; funnel to fill bottles

Medicine Chest   absorbent cotton; Band-Aids; rectal thermometer

Furniture   anything with sides, such as a carrying basket or carriage with a firm mattress for the infant; crib for after three months; folding carriage; chest of drawers; chair for mother to use while nursing; flat table for dressing baby

Hints in Selecting Equipment for a New Baby

Babies grow so rapidly in the months following birth that infant sizes in clothing are usually outgrown in four to six months.

Many articles of clothing (sweaters, caps, and booties), nursery furnishings (blankets, sheets, and lamps), and bathing items (towels, washcloths, and wrapping blankets) are given as gifts at baby showers or on the baby's arrival.

Babies have little need for dress-up clothes because they sleep most of the time.

Spring and summer babies have little need for warm clothing. Fall and winter babies have little need for warm-weather clothing.

Babies in the warmer parts of the country need very different clothing and bedding from those in the colder areas.

Bassinets are outgrown so quickly that they are an unneeded expense. A carrying basket or folding carriage can serve as a place for the baby to sleep as well as for transportation.

A large plastic dishpan is just as good for the baby's bath as an expensive Bathinette. This will be useful for less than a year. After that the baby can be bathed in the bathtub.

Because baby clothes, diapers, and sheets now come in no-iron materials, a limited supply of them will do when daily washing is a routine.

If the baby is to be breast-fed, little feeding equipment is needed.

Stores have ample supplies of baby equipment available; so parents should buy no more than the bare necessities. This will avoid duplicating gifts.

It is wise to put off buying equipment that is not needed right away, such as a playpen and high chair. This spreads out the expenses over a period of time.

When a new baby is the second, third, or later-born of the family, new equipment is usually not needed. However, it is a good idea to check the equipment used for the last baby, clean it up, and fix any damages to make it comfortable and safe.

Choosing a Name for the Baby

A child's name should be given careful consideration. When selecting a name, parents must keep in mind that the name they choose will be the *baby's* name, not theirs. It is the label by which the child will be known throughout life. Once it is legally registered a name cannot be changed without parental and court approval.

Parents-to-be should consider how the name they select will affect the child's personal and social adjustments. The name may be a source of constant teasing, embarrassment, or irritation for the child. Or it may make a favorable impression on other people and thus increase the child's self-confidence.

Because it is not possible to know whether the baby will be a girl or a boy, it is important to select a name for both. Most doctors can tell, as pregnancy goes on, whether there will be one or more babies. If more than one baby is expected, combinations of names have to be chosen. In the case of twins, for example, names should be chosen for a boy and a girl, two girls, and two boys.

What to Consider in Selecting the Baby's Name

When naming the baby after a parent, select a middle name or use a nickname to avoid confusing the child with the parent.

If the baby is named for a grandparent on one side of the family, the one on the other side may feel slighted. It is tactful to avoid this touchy situation.

Because children tend to nickname their playmates, select a nickname that will not annoy or embarrass the child when growing up.

Children like names that are not too different from those of their playmates and not too hard to pronounce or spell.

Avoid unpopular names that might cause the child to be teased or made fun of.

Be sure that the first and middle names sound good with the family name.

Remember that the name will last throughout the person's life. What may seem cute or charming for a small child may be inappropriate or silly for an adult.

Arranging for Help

Few women are strong enough to do their usual household duties right after they return home from the hospital. Many new fathers arrange to be at home to help out when the baby arrives. Other new parents may get help from neighbors, friends, and relatives. If the family budget can stand the strain, a nurse can be hired to help with the new baby. Or a student can help after school with the dinner and cleaning to relieve the new mother of some work.

When there are older children, arrangements must be made for their care when the mother is in the hospital. If the father is unable to care for them, a friend or relative might be able to do so. If not, parents have no choice but to hire outside help. Here again is an expense that adds to the cost of having a baby.

Whoever will care for the children during this time should arrive before the mother leaves for the hospital. By doing this, the helper can become familiar with the family routine, learn where things are kept, get to know the children, and help with some of the housework. Equally important, the mother will not worry about being away from the children if she knows they are in capable hands.

Arrangements for help should be made several months before the baby is due. This is not easy when friends and relatives have their own families, homes, and jobs to take care of and when domestic help is scarce. The matter is also complicated by the fact that the exact date for the arrival of a baby is difficult to predict. An early or late arrival may mean that the help will not be available. That is why two sets of plans should be made.

Learning To Be a New Parent

While some new parents are lucky enough to have a friend, relative, or paid caretaker to help them with the baby's care, most are not. They have to face this responsibility alone. It is often a terrifying experience for a couple to be parents of a first baby.

Hospitals and health-care centers give infant-care courses to expectant parents to prepare them for their new responsibilities. Richard Watherwax

To avoid being unprepared, parents-to-be should try to take a course in infant care. Such a course is offered by the prenatal clinics of most hospitals and is open to anyone who wants to enroll. In the course, people are shown how to feed, bathe, clothe, and diaper new babies as well as how to place them in comfortable positions.

A trained infant nurse teaches the course, using a doll that resembles a newborn baby. Every student in the

In natural childbirth classes, women learn to exercise muscles that are used during delivery of the baby. An increasing number of fathers-to-be participate in helping to deliver the baby. Long Island Jewish–Hillside Medical Center

class has a chance to care for the "baby" under the watchful eye of the nurse. Such a course gives new parents confidence about handling their babies. Books or pamphlets, written by doctors and nurses telling how to take care of a new baby, are also helpful to new parents.

Being Ready

At a routine checkup late in pregnancy, the doctor is able to determine the size and position of the unborn baby in the mother's body. On the basis of this examination, the doctor forecasts the approximate date of the baby's arrival. It is a good idea, at this time, for the mother-to-be to pack a bag for her stay in the hospital. She can also make some last-minute preparations for the baby or arrange for someone else to make them while she is in the hospital.

As pregnancy reaches its final stages, the doctor explains in detail what the warning signals of birth are and tells the woman exactly what to do when they begin. The mother-to-be knows that her baby is on the way because of periodic pains known as *labor*. As a rule, babies rarely arrive in the world without warning, even in the easiest birth. If everything is ready, the woman will have no cause to fear that the baby will arrive before she can reach the hospital.

Highlights of Chapter 1

☐ Parenthood changes the usual pattern of family life. Preparation for it physically, psychologically, and financially should begin as early as possible.

☐ When pregnancy has been confirmed, an obstetrician should be chosen for the care of the mother and a pediatrician for the care of the baby.

☐ Clothing and equipment for a baby is an added expense for new parents. Careful shopping can reduce some of the strain on the family budget.

☐ Arrangements for help during the mother's stay in the hospital and on her return home should be made as early as possible to ease the mother-to-be's anxiety.

☐ How soon before the baby's arrival the woman should give up her job depends partly on her health and partly on the nature of the work she does.

☐ Names are lifelong labels. Careful thought should be given to the choice of a name for a baby.

☐ Taking a course in child care before the baby is born gives the new parents confidence in handling and caring for the infant.

☐ Few babies arrive at the scheduled time. Therefore, all arrangements for going to the hospital and for the care of the home and family should be made well in advance.

Suggested Activities

1. From the March of Dimes headquarters in your area, get literature about birth defects—what causes them and what measures can be taken to prevent them.

2. Visit an employment agency and ask what the wages are for a person who does domestic work on a daily or weekly basis. Then find out from the employment office in your school what students charge for after-school and weekend work in a home, helping with cooking, cleaning, and the care of young children. On the basis of this information, estimate the cost of hiring help for a week or more when a mother returns from the hospital with a new baby.

3. Do a comparison study of babies' equipment made now and the same type pieces made ten years ago. What safety features are now considered a "must" that were unthought of then? Discuss why safety features should be a main consideration when purchasing babies' equipment—new or secondhand.

4. If a pregnant woman's health is good and there are no problems, when should she stop working? Would it be better for her to leave some types of jobs sooner than she would leave other jobs? In giving your answer, think about factory jobs, office jobs, and jobs that bring the woman into contact with the public.

5. Ask the librarian at the public library to suggest books that give names for boys and girls, with their origins and meanings. Make a list of possible names for a girl baby and for a boy baby. Give reasons why you made the selections you did.

Chapter 2

The Newborn Baby

Some goals of this chapter are:
- [ ] To understand how the hereditary traits and sex of a child are determined at conception
- [ ] To realize that newborn babies must make major adjustments to their new environment
- [ ] To be familiar with the characteristics common to every newborn baby
- [ ] To understand what prematurity and postmaturity are and how they affect the baby's adjustments to life

Biologically, life begins at the moment of conception. Birth is merely a break in the pattern of growth and development that has been going on for about nine months. In relation to a person's life span, nine months seems to be a pretty short time. However, during these nine months before birth, growth and development are more rapid than at any other time in life. To realize how rapid the growth is, think of a cell so small that it can be seen only under a microscope. Then compare it with an average baby who, at birth, weighs about 7 pounds (3.2 kilograms) and measures 20 inches (50 centimeters).

While growth is taking place, so is development. A round cell is formed at conception. A tiny human being with head, trunk, limbs, and all the external and internal organs is delivered at birth. Like growth, development is so rapid that by the end of the second month after conception, all the important parts of the body have begun to take shape. In only a few more months they take on their full shape and are ready to function. Even if the baby arrives in the world several months before the due date, the development of the body is so advanced that the baby can live, although in need of medical aid.

What Happens at Conception?

At the moment of conception a sex cell of the father, called a *spermatozoon* (plural, *spermatozoa*), unites with a sex cell of the mother, called an *ovum* (plural, *ova*), and fertilizes it.

Within the sex cells of every man and woman are twenty-three pairs of chromosomes. A *chromosome* is a thread-like structure that has strings of tiny particles called *genes*. The genes are the true carriers of heredity. They are the physical substances passed on from parent to child. The parents' genes, in turn, have come from their parents, grandparents, and other more distant ancestors.

It has been estimated that there are between 80,000 and 120,000 genes in each sex cell. Some of the genes are responsible for determining physical traits, such as height, hair color, and size and shape of the nose. Other genes determine mental traits, such as intelligence, artistic talent, and temperament. Some of the genes are *dominant*—they produce the trait in every generation. Other genes are *recessive* and produce traits that skip several generations.

The Hereditary Package

In order for the spermatozoon to fertilize the ovum, both sex cells must be ripe, or mature. As the sex cells mature, the twenty-three pairs of chromosomes divide, or split. A mature cell contains only twenty-three single chromosomes,

Curly hair, olive skin, a turned-up nose—each is only a part of a person's hereditary package. Genes are responsible for determining all the physical characteristics of everyone. Freda Leinwand/McGraw-Hill

in which there are between 40,000 and 60,000 genes. When fertilization takes place, the chromosomes of the mother's and father's sex cells combine. These chromosomes contain the genes that make up the person's entire hereditary package.

The genes of the newly formed being are a combination of the mother's and father's genes. After conception, genes cannot be changed or traded for different ones.

For Discussion

There is an old saying, "That child is a chip off the old block." What does this mean? Does it refer to the person's hereditary traits? Does it mean that the person looks or behaves like a parent? Or is the "old block" a grandparent or some other ancestor?

Girl or Boy?

There are many legends and myths about how parents can produce a child of the sex they desire. It has been said that if a mother eats large amounts of sugar during pregnancy, she will have a girl, but if she eats a great deal of meat, she will have a boy. Others have believed that the month of the year in which the child is conceived determines its sex.

Scientists have disproved all these theories. It is now known what determines the sex of a child, but there is no sure way to control it. Scientists, however, are working at it. Sex, like all other traits, is entirely a matter of chance. The chances are slightly more favorable to the male sex than to the female sex. There are between 105 and 106 boys born for every 100 girls. To date, no one can give reasons why this is so.

At conception, every person receives twenty-three chromosomes from each parent. These forty-six chromosomes make up a child's inherited traits. The mother and the father contribute equally to the child's heredity.

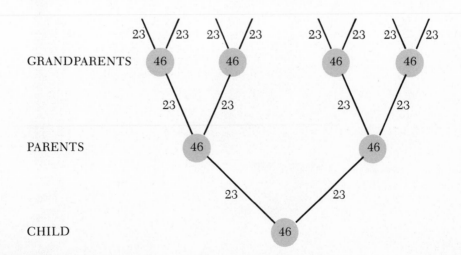

GRANDPARENTS

PARENTS

CHILD

The sex of a child is determined by the type of sex chromosome in the spermatozoon. Twenty-two of the pairs of chromosomes match each other. The twenty-third pair is made up of two sex chromosomes, an X and a Y. One-half of all mature spermatozoa carry the X chromosome. The other half carry the Y chromosome. By contrast, all mature ova carry the X chromosome.

In any fertilized ovum, there is always an X chromosome from the ovum and either an X or a Y chromosome from the spermatozoon. If two X's combine, the child will be female. If, on the other hand, an X and a Y combine, the child will be male.

Number of Babies

Usually, human mothers produce one baby at a time—a singleton. Sometimes they produce two or more. Multiple births can be twins (two babies), triplets (three babies), quadruplets (four), quintuplets (five). The larger the number of babies, the less often such a birth occurs. However, multiple births are occurring more often now than in the past. This is due to fertility drugs that some women take to help them conceive.

There are two different types of multiple births, *identical* and *nonidentical*, or *fraternal*. In the case of twins, identical twins come from a single ovum which splits into two parts shortly after fertilization. Nonidentical twins come from two ova released during the same menstrual cycle. Each is fertilized by a different spermatozoon.

Because identical twins come from the same fertilized ovum, they have the same chromosomes and genes. As a result, identical twins are similar in ap-

How the Sex of a Baby Is Determined

The father's mature sperm contain either an X or a Y chromosome. There are equal numbers of each.

The mother's mature ova all contain an X chromosome.

X

Y

X

If a sperm with an X enters the ovum:

X
X   = XX = GIRL

If a sperm with a Y enters the ovum:

Y
X   = XY = BOY

pearance and abilities and are always of the same sex.

By contrast, nonidentical, or fraternal, twins can be of the same sex or of different sexes. Chromosomes are not the same in two different ova or spermatozoa. Therefore, nonidentical twins are more likely to be different than alike in physical and mental makeup.

Larger multiple births—triplets, quadruplets, and quintuplets—may be either identical or nonidentical. Triplets, for example, may have come from two fertilized ova, one of which has split during the early stage of development. In such a case, two of the triplets will be identical and the third, nonidentical.

Before birth, children of a multiple birth are crowded in the mother's uterus. They are developing in a sac that is meant to accommodate only one baby. As they grow larger, this crowding hampers their development. The walls of the uterus can expand only so far. Very often multiple-birth babies are born *prematurely*, or ahead of schedule. They are also smaller at birth than most singletons.

Factors Affecting the Baby

After conception the baby begins to grow and develop. For the most part, it is a natural process over which one has very little control. However, some factors that do affect the baby can be controlled to some degree.

The Prenatal Environment

Many things having to do with the baby's growth and development between conception and birth are referred to as *prenatal*, or before birth.

The baby's prenatal environment is the mother's body. If the mother is in good physical condition and eats a well-balanced diet, chances are that the baby will grow and develop normally.

Unfortunately, not all babies have an environment that provides for normal growth and development. There are certain unfavorable conditions in the mother's body that are known to affect the baby. Smoking stunts the baby's growth, even for several years after birth. However, there is not enough proof to show that the stunting continues to adulthood. If the mother is addicted to drugs, the baby will be also. After birth, the baby will go through the shock of drug withdrawal.

The time when unfavorable conditions are most likely to upset normal growth and development is during the first three months after conception. During this time, physical features are forming. If the mother catches rubella when the eyes and ears of her baby are forming, they may not develop normally. If she catches rubella afterward, the eyes and ears will not be damaged. However, another part of the body which might be developing at that time, such as the heart, may be damaged.

Rubella is only a temporary condition in the mother that affects a developing baby. Long-lasting conditions, such as malnutrition or severe emotional stress, can also seriously damage the baby. They may cause some physical or mental defect or cause damage to the baby's nervous system.

Some unfavorable conditions bring about a *miscarriage*—the forcing from the mother's body of the developing baby before it is ready to be born.

Development of the Unborn Baby during Pregnancy

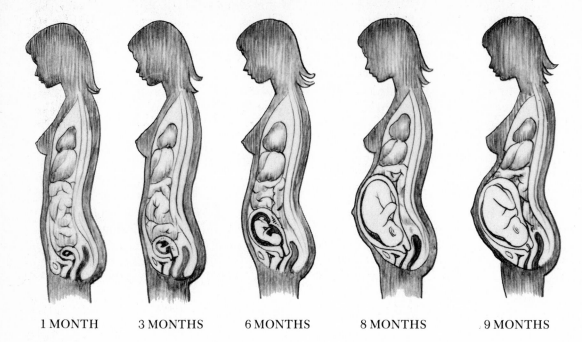

| 1 MONTH | 3 MONTHS | 6 MONTHS | 8 MONTHS | 9 MONTHS |

Others cause malformations of different parts of the body. What will be wrong depends on the part that is developing when the unfavorable condition occurs.

Birth

Of all different kinds of birth, the most favorable for the baby's adjustment to life is the normal, spontaneous birth. This is because it is far less likely that the baby will be harmed in any way during the birth. The chart opposite defines the various types of birth.

Because of the baby's position, breech and transverse births are difficult. They are associated with problems that affect the baby, the mother, or both.

Caesarean births present more problems than normal, spontaneous births.

Unfavorable Conditions in the Prenatal Environment

Malnutrition of the mother	Diseases that are constant, such as diabetes, tuberculosis, or cancer
Vitamin and glandular deficiencies	Certain temporary diseases, such as rubella and the venereal diseases
Excessive use of alcohol	Severe and constant stress on the mother
Excessive smoking	
Use of drugs, especially narcotics and tranquilizers	

Kinds of Births

Normal or Spontaneous The baby emerges from the mother's body head first.

Breech The baby's buttocks or legs come out first, followed by the trunk and then the head. There is usually a need to use instruments. The mother needs heavy medication.

Transverse The baby's body lies crosswise in the uterus. Unless the position can be changed, the baby must be brought into the world with instruments. The mother needs heavy medication.

Instrument When the baby is too large to pass through the mother's birth canal, or when the position of the baby makes normal birth impossible, the baby must be brought into the world by the use of instruments.

Caesarean Section When normal childbirth might be difficult, doctors may decide to operate on the mother. Her abdomen and uterus are cut open to bring the baby into the world. Julius Caesar is supposed to have been born this way.

Precipitate The birth is very speedy. There is no need for the use of instruments or time to medicate the mother.

However, when Caesarean births are planned, these problems can be lessened. In emergency cases, it is usually the condition requiring the Caesarean birth that leads to problems, not the operation itself. If the Caesarean section takes too long, the baby as well as the mother becomes anesthetized. This makes it difficult for the baby to take the first breath, leading to a lack of oxygen. If this goes on for too long, the baby may suffer some brain damage.

In precipitate birth, the baby emerges very fast from the mother's body. Like babies delivered by Caesarean section, babies born precipitately often have difficulty in starting to breathe. As a result, they may suffer brain damage.

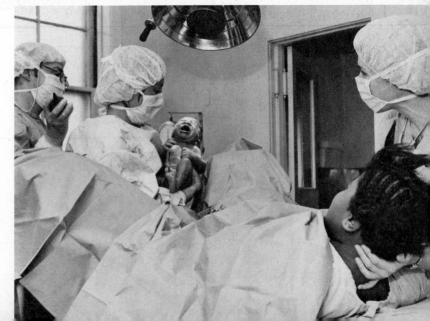

Being awake during delivery gives women the chance to witness their babies' first breath of life. The National Foundation–March of Dimes

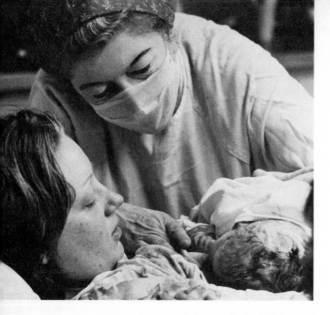

Many women choose to have their babies at home with the help and guidance of a midwife.
Richard Watherwax

Until recently, it was not known whether medication given to the mother to ease the pain of childbirth had any effect on the baby. It was assumed that if there was any effect, it would wear off quickly, as it does with the mother. Today, there is evidence that medication can have more than a temporary effect on the baby. This is true only when certain medicines are used in large doses. To avoid this, many doctors encourage women to prepare for natural childbirth. They give the women exercises to strengthen the muscles used in labor. This gives the woman some control over the labor pains and makes medication less necessary.

In small amounts, medication given to the mother has only a temporary effect on the newborn baby. It may make the baby less active, or dazed, for a day or two. If too much medication is used, or if it is a kind that can affect the brain

tissue of the baby, it may result in permanent brain damage. This will make normal development impossible.

Adjustments after Birth

The period right after birth is called the "period of the newborn." The baby is called a "newborn baby" or an "infant." The word "infant" suggests the extreme helplessness of all newborn babies.

After living in the mother's body for about nine months, babies go through quite a change at birth. Adjusting to life outside the mother is a challenge for them. It takes a week or two after birth for babies to adjust to their new world. In the process, babies often lose weight and may even seem less healthy than they were right after birth.

The first adjustment a newborn baby must make is breathing. The lungs are not used while the baby is in the mother's uterus, even when they are well enough developed for breathing. The birth cry is nature's way of inflating the lungs to start the breathing process. Normally, crying occurs right after birth or as the baby's head emerges from the mother's body. When crying does not happen on its own, the doctor often holds the baby up by the feet and slaps the buttocks. Should this also fail to bring about the birth cry, the lungs are inflated artificially with oxygen.

Of all adjustments infants must make, taking food through the mouth is the hardest for them to learn. Even though sucking and swallowing are reflexes, provided by nature to meet this new need, they are not always well developed at birth. Also, the reflexes are not well coordinated. As a result, babies often suck and swallow at the same

Adjustments to Life

Temperature Infants spend about nine months in a constant temperature of around 100°F (38°C). Newborn babies must suddenly adjust to temperatures that change from time to time. These range from 60 to 80°F (16 to 27°C).

Breathing Before birth, oxygen is supplied to the developing baby through the umbilical cord that attaches the baby to the wall of the mother's uterus. This oxygen comes from the mother's bloodstream. With the cutting of the umbilical cord after birth, the baby must get oxygen from the air. The birth cry is nature's way of inflating the lungs and starting up the breathing process.

Taking Nourishment Before babies are born, food for growth and development comes from the mother's bloodstream through the umbilical cord. After birth, babies must develop their sucking and swallowing reflexes to get the food they need.

Elimination Waste products from the developing baby's body pass through the umbilical cord into the mother's circulation. The mother then eliminates them in the normal way. After delivery, the umbilical cord is cut. At this time, the baby begins to eliminate wastes, itself.

time. They may choke on food and spit it up. Thus, they miss out on the nourishment needed for growth.

A newborn must make these adjustments in order to live. The first two days after birth are the infant's critical days. Infant deaths take place most often at this time. The second day after birth is especially dangerous. Unless adjustments are made, either normally or artificially, the baby can very easily die. On the other hand, if the adjustments are made, the chances of living increase quickly with each day.

All newborns should have their eyes disinfected moments after birth. Their hearing can be tested a few hours later with a special instrument.
Left: Roy Pinney/Monkmeyer; right: Monkmeyer

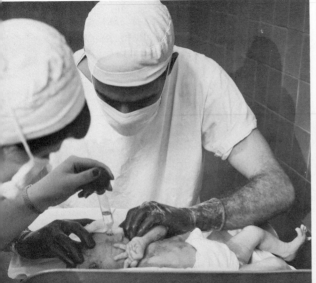

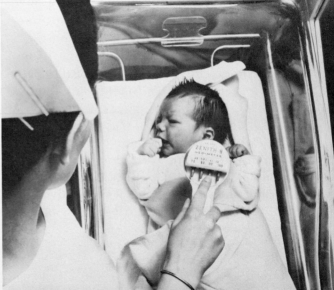

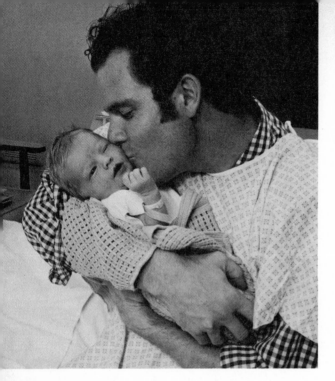

Studies have shown that babies respond to tender, gentle affection during their early adjustments to life. HEW

Characteristics of the Newborn Baby

Unlike the pictures of babies on birth announcement cards or in baby books, a real baby at birth is anything but beautiful. The head may have been *elongated* (made longer and narrower) during the birth; the skin is blotched; the eyes are uncoordinated; and the head seems too big for the tiny body.

The average American baby born today measures, at birth, about 20 to 21 inches (50 to 52.5 centimeters) in length and weighs from 7 to 7$\frac{1}{2}$ pounds (3.2 to 3.4 kilograms). Boys, as a rule, are slightly longer and heavier than girls. There are greater variations in weight than in length for both boys and girls. Some premature babies weigh only 3 or 4 pounds (1.4 to 1.8 kilograms); other babies, born normally, may weigh 12 to 14 pounds (5.4 to 6.4 kilograms). The baby's body is top-heavy. The head of a baby is about one-fourth of the whole body length. An adult's head is one-seventh of the total body length.

The newborn baby has almost no neck. The shoulders are narrow and sloping. The abdomen is large and protruding, especially after feeding. The arms and legs, in proportion to the rest of the body, are short and thin, and the hands and feet are very small. The toes and fingers have well-developed nails even when the baby is born a month or two ahead of the expected time. Quite often there is a heavy growth of fine-textured hair on the baby's head, back, and arms. This is prenatal hair that disappears soon after birth.

Babies' bones are made up mostly of cartilage or gristle. They are soft and flexible. The muscles are soft, small, and uncontrolled. The leg muscles are less developed than those in the arms. Babies' skin is soft, and their coloring is often blotchy. Babies are often chubby. Soft fat covers most of their bodies.

For Action

Visit several stores that sell baby-shower and birth-announcement cards. Study the pictures of babies on these cards.

1. Do the pictures look like the newborn babies you have seen in person or in photographs?

2. If you had never seen a newborn baby in real life or in a photograph, how would you feel when you saw one after getting a mental picture of newborns from these cards?

For Action

Make arrangements to visit a hospital nursery for newborn babies. Stay for at least half an hour so that you will have some time to observe the infants.

1. Look carefully at several babies. Do you think the description on page 26 of why babies look the way they do is accurate?

2. What part of the face is most responsible for making newborns look the way they do?

3. When the babies have their eyes open, watch how they look at people or objects. Does the poor eye coordination affect their expression?

4. Watch the babies move. Notice how little control they have over their heads, arms, and legs.

5. Try to listen to the infants' crying. Can you figure out what they are trying to tell the nurses, or what they want or need?

6. Compare the appearance and behavior of several of the newborn babies. Do you notice enough similarity to be willing to say that all newborns are alike? Or do they all show individuality?

Knowing ahead of time how a newborn baby looks is very important for parents-to-be. Otherwise, they may be shocked when they see their baby for the first time. It also helps them understand why their baby may be one of the homeliest in the hospital nursery. Many of the others were born earlier and are already beginning to look better.

Behavior of the Newborn

Because their muscles are soft and their nervous systems undeveloped, newborn babies have no control over their movements. They are completely helpless. When picked up, they seem in danger of falling apart. They cannot turn their bodies, sit up, reach for an object, or even coordinate their eyes very well. Sometimes one eye may turn one way and the other eye another way. This not only gives them a funny expression, but it also means that they cannot see clearly.

For Discussion

What evidence is there that the common phrase, "the helpless newborn infant," is correct? In what ways is a newborn infant helpless? What is responsible for this?

When newborn babies move one part of their bodies, they move all over. This is known as *mass activity* and is very energy-consuming. Even the simple act of sucking, for example, is accompanied by waving arms, kicking legs, and twisting and turning of the head and the body.

Most parents-to-be know that newborn babies are helpless. They are willing to wait on their babies hand and foot. What many do not know is that this helplessness is temporary. Within a few weeks after birth, helplessness begins to decrease as the nervous system develops, as muscles strengthen, and as bones harden.

Though these newborn twins look and behave so much like each other, their individuality will increase with each passing day. The National Foundation–March of Dimes

For Discussion

Why do newborn babies react differently to different people? They may cry when handled by someone who has not taken care of them before. How do newborns know that they are being handled by a strange person, and why do they cry?

Parents can easily get into the habit of thinking of their babies as helpless just because they were helpless as infants. They may get into the habit of doing things for their babies rather than giving them a chance to learn to do things for themselves when their bodies and minds are ready.

All babies have their own characteristic cry. It may be harsh and piercing or low and moaning. They cannot change the tone of their cries. This makes it hard for people to know what is bothering infants. However, their cries do vary in strength. The cry is low in

Conditions Contributing to the Newborn Baby's Helplessness

Body Movements   When newborns move, they move all over in mass activity. Infants are unable to do specific things such as reaching, grasping, or turning.

Vocalization   Even though crying normally begins at birth, the tonal quality is very undeveloped. At this point, the only way babies can let people know that they want or need something is by crying. Infants often make low, sighing sounds that seem to have no meaning.

Sense Organ Development   The most important sense organs—the eyes and ears—do not work very well at birth, even though they appear to be well developed. At times the eyes do not coordinate well because of weak eye muscles. The middle ear is sometimes stopped up with fluid from the prenatal sac. Newborns' senses of smell, taste, and touch are well developed compared to the other senses.

State of Daze   For several days after birth, new babies are in a dazed state. They do not really know where they are, and nothing is seen clearly.

pitch when they are tired and high when they are rested.

Well-meaning advice about letting babies "cry it out" may at times be all right for older babies. However, it can be dangerous advice for helpless newborns. Babies cry to let us know that something is the matter with them. Therefore, it is wrong to ignore the signal. Furthermore, when they cry, they cry all over. If left to "cry it out," they will use up energy that is needed for growth.

Besides their cries, infants make low, sighing sounds, such as "eh-eh" or "ah-ah," which are sometimes called "cooing." These sounds are very important. They are the basis upon which speech develops.

Individuality of Infants

No two newborn babies are exactly alike, not even identical twins or triplets. Both in looks and behavior, babies differ from one another.

Some newborn babies are small and scrawny. Some are large and plump. Some babies have elongated heads; others have well-shaped, rounded ones. In the case of multiple births, one baby tends to be larger and better developed than the others.

Babies are just as different in behavior as in appearance. Some are quiet and content; others are nervous, highstrung, and fretful. Some cry often; others seldom cry. Some infants are dazed; others are alert and aware of what is going on around them.

These differences, which give newborn babies individuality, are due to many factors. Basically, babies are different because of differences in heredity, in prenatal environment, in the amount of time spent in their mothers' bodies, and in the kind of birth they went through.

With each passing day, an infant's individuality becomes more obvious. Because no two babies begin life exactly alike, no two will ever grow up to be carbon copies of each other.

Prematurity and Postmaturity

A baby who is born nine months after conception is a *full-term* baby. A *premature* baby is one who arrives ahead of the expected time. A *postmature* baby comes into the world after the expected time.

No one knows exactly why babies arrive early any more than they know why their arrival is delayed. However, it is thought from medical evidence that both prematurity and postmaturity are the result of the mother's glandular condition. There is little proof that a premature birth comes from a fall or from a severe emotional shock. Until the exact cause of prematurity is known, doctors will be unable to control it. The most they can do now is try to prevent brain damage and keep the babies alive artificially until they are able to take over the functions needed for survival.

The premature baby's development seems to lag behind that of a full-term baby. However, the lag is usually less than it seems. This is because the premature baby is being compared to babies of the same age who were not prematurely born. For example, babies who are born two months early have had seven months to develop instead of the usual nine months. When they are

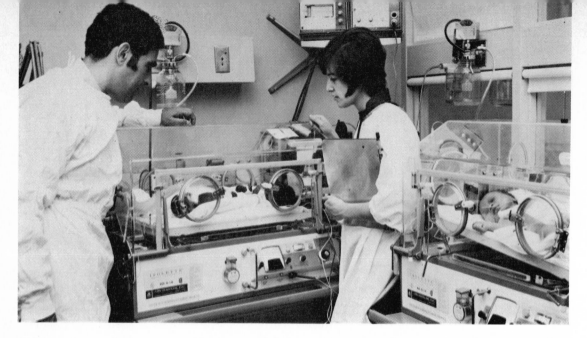

Babies who are born prematurely may need help in adjusting to life. Such babies are placed in incubators until they are able to survive on their own.
Long Island Jewish–Hillside Medical Center

six months old, they have had only thirteen months since conception to develop. Full-term babies have had fifteen months to develop.

However, the effects of prematurity do not last long. By the time premature babies are a year or two old, they are usually up to the standards of full-term babies. They have completely overcome the developmental lag.

Unless there is brain damage, the most serious long-term effects of prematurity come from poor parental attitudes. Many parents are too worried about, and protective of, their premature babies. They do not realize that doctors would not send a premature baby home if the baby had not yet developed enough to be treated like a normal, full-term baby.

In America today, relatively few babies are postmature because doctors can bring on a baby's birth. During the last part of pregnancy, they can tell if the baby is getting so large that it may cause problems. Regardless of the position in the mother's body, a very large baby may take too long to pass through the birth canal. The baby may be brain-damaged during the birth. This damage may be only slight, but it is too great a risk to take. It is also possible that a large baby may harm the mother. A Caesarean section may be performed so that the postmature baby does not pass through the birth canal.

If postmature babies are not brain-damaged, there is no long-term effect on their development. However, they may seem big for their age for a year or two after birth. Often, more is expected of them than they are ready to do. They may, for example, seem big enough to start walking, but their brains, nervous systems, bones, and muscles may not have developed enough.

Determining Prematurity and Postmaturity

Length of Pregnancy Many women do not know just when pregnancy started because their menstrual cycles are irregular. As a result, length of pregnancy is not the best way to determine prematurity or postmaturity.

Birth Weight The average American baby today weighs 7 to 7½ pounds (3.2 to 3.4 kilograms). Boys usually weigh slightly more than girls. A boy baby who weighs 5½ pounds (2.5 kilograms) or less and a girl baby who weighs 5 pounds (2.3 kilograms) or less are considered premature. Those who weigh more than 7 pounds (3.2 kilograms) are called postmature. However, heredity and many other factors affect body weight. They should be considered when judging whether the baby is premature or postmature.

Body Length The average American baby measures 20 to 21 inches (50 to 52.5 centimeters) at birth. Those who are several inches shorter are considered premature. Those who are several inches longer are considered postmature. However, body length, like body weight, varies with the background of the baby.

Developmental Status The newborn baby's physical and nervous-system development should be at the point where the infant can adjust to living independently. The abilities to breathe and to take food are tested right after birth. Full-term and postmature babies adjust quickly. Premature ones may have difficulty. If there is any question, the newborn baby is quickly put into an incubator, where these needs can be met.

The total helplessness of newborns is so temporary that a noticeable difference can be seen in just a few weeks. Erika Stone/Peter Arnold

Highlights of Chapter 2

☐ Birth breaks the pattern of growth and development that has been going on for about nine months.

☐ Three important things happen at conception: determination of the baby's hereditary package, the baby's sex, and whether the baby will be a singleton or one member of a multiple birth.

☐ There are six kinds of births. Each affects the baby differently.

☐ Development after birth is slowed down for a time as the infant adjusts to the new environment.

☐ All newborn babies are helpless because of the undeveloped state of their nervous systems, muscles, and sense organs.

☐ From the moment of birth, newborn babies show individuality in the way they look and act.

☐ Prematurity and postmaturity, in themselves, have only temporary effects on newborn babies.

Suggested Activities

1. Consult some up-to-date newspaper or magazine articles on the progress scientists have made in controlling heredity and the sex of a child. Report your findings to the class.

2. Observe how active babies are when they cry or when they are fed. How long does it take before they become exhausted from all their activity?

3. What is an incubator? Do some research to find out when it is used and how it works. Report your findings to the class.

Chapter 3

The Baby in the Family

Some goals of this chapter are:
- [ ] To identify ways all family members can share in the adjustment to, and the care of, a baby
- [ ] To give reasons why adjusting to a new baby's schedule is one of the hardest adjustments family members must make
- [ ] To describe ways family members can help a baby feel like a part of the family

Bringing a new baby home from the hospital should be a joyous time for all family members. Unfortunately, this is not always true. In fact, sometimes it is a time of chaos.

Perhaps the baby arrived earlier than had been planned. The equipment for the new baby may not be in place. The house may be in disorder. The father may not be able to take time off from work to help. The older children may demand attention and become troublesome when they do not get it right away. On top of all this, the new baby who was as "good as gold" in the hospital may now cry all the time, no matter what. The importance of preparing for a new baby may never be fully realized until the baby is brought home.

Not all problems, of course, can be prepared for. This is true even in families that have faced the home-from-the-hospital situation several times before. But if the major problems are foreseen and met before the baby's birth, the less important ones can be solved more easily as they arise. The emotional tension of adjustment can then be reduced.

For Discussion

How would you prepare a child for the arrival of a new baby in the family? Why should the preparation for a preschool child be different from that for a school-age child? How would it be different?

Preparation Begun Too Late   If parents wait until the new baby arrives before sending older children off to a day-care center or to nursery school, the children may feel that their parents want them out of the way. As a result, the children may resent the baby and dislike nursery school as well.

Belief That Preparation Is Needed Only for the First Baby   Each baby's arrival changes the pattern of family life and the roles of every family member.

Unrealistic Expectations   Children who are expecting a playmate may be disappointed when they see that the baby is too small to play any games with them.

Theoretical versus Practical Preparation   When a father-to-be is told that he will have to take on added home duties as well as care for the new baby, he may agree that this is logical and reasonable. But unless he has some practice doing the new chores and helping with baby care before the baby's arrival, he may not be able to deal with the real situation.

Adjustments Must Be Made by All

In every size family, the pattern of life changes with the arrival of any new member. If the new member is a grandparent, the family makes adjustments by considering the feelings and rights of the grandparent. The family members may also try to do all they can to make the grandparent feel welcome. In turn, the older person is usually able to make some adjustments to fit into the family's life pattern.

However, to make a new baby feel welcome, *all* adjustments must be made by the other family members. Babies are too immature, physically and emotionally, to adjust to any pattern of life except the one that fits their developmental level. They are also too involved with their own body functions, such as eating and sleeping, to be able to make any other adjustments. For example, new babies cannot conform to a family's schedule of meals because their stomachs are too small to hold enough food to satisfy them for more than a few hours at a time.

If psychological preparation has been realistic and understandable, all family members know that a new baby will bring changes into their lives. They are also willing to adjust to these changes in every way they can.

Role Changes

The arrival of a baby in the family means role changes for every family member. Couples who are free to come and go as they please, with no responsibilities except to each other, will find parenthood quite different. The couple are now responsible, morally and legally, for a helpless, totally dependent person.

Parental roles involve many responsibilities. As children grow up, the parents' responsibilities change to meet the needs of the child at that age, but the roles stay the same.

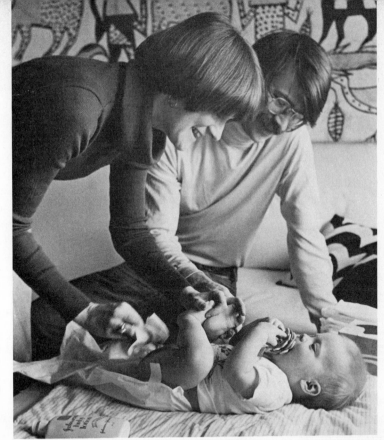

Preparing for the baby's arrival will make some adjustments easier. However, role changes cannot be truly experienced until the baby is brought home from the hospital. Robert Capece

For Discussion

Often role changes mean new labels for the people involved in these changes. For example, when a couple become parents they may begin to address each other as "Mommy" and "Daddy" instead of by their names. How might the new labels affect their attitudes toward themselves and each other?

As long as they live, many parents feel the responsibility of caring for the needs of their children. While the children are young, this takes the form of feeding, bathing, and dressing them. As they grow older, it takes the form of providing the guidance and supervision they need to do these things for themselves. Even when children become

Some Roles of Parents

Caretaker of physical needs	Teacher of values, attitudes, and skills
Giver of affection	Provider of a stimulating environment
Playmate to child	Comforter in times of trouble
Model for the child to imitate	Admirer of child's achievements
Disciplinarian	Stimulator of child's abilities

adults, some parents still feel the responsibility of caring for their children's well-being.

For Thought

Study carefully the roles parents must play if they are to meet the needs of their children. Consider these roles, one by one, and ask yourself how well prepared you feel to carry out these roles.

Then, think of how you could prepare yourself to carry out the roles successfully. For example, how would you fulfill the role of provider of a stimulating environment?

Parents play the role of comforter when a young child is frightened or hurt. They comfort an older child who feels alone and hurt by being left out of games or a grown child who feels discouraged by losing a job. As needs change with the child's age, so must the way the parent's role is expressed.

Children in the family, too, experience role changes when the new baby arrives. "Only" children are now the eldest. Parents may ask for their help. If they are old enough, they may be given some responsibility in looking after the baby. Being prepared for their new roles makes children, like adults, better able to handle them.

Sharing family responsibilities will give parents more time to enjoy each other and their children. Richard Nowitz

In preparing older children for the new baby, parents should give them small duties and responsibilities. This will teach the children to be helpful to others as well as teach them to take care of themselves. By the time the baby arrives, the children will be used to helping and will be able to do more for themselves.

All role changes—whether a new job or a new status in the family—are hard to adjust to. All cause some emotional tension. It takes time to adjust to and to be willing to accept the new roles. That is why psychological preparation should begin long before the new baby's arrival.

Sharing Responsibilities

Even the most organized and efficient person needs help at one time or another in taking care of a baby. When other children are still very young, help is needed all the time.

Chores and responsibilities can be shared rather than left for just one parent to do. The father can prepare

---

How Family Members Can Help with the Care of a Baby

What the Father Can Do

Feed the baby (if the baby is bottle-fed)
Change diapers and dress the baby
Bathe the baby
Prepare the baby for sleep
Take the baby for outings
Watch the baby while the mother is resting or busy with other duties
Amuse the baby
Find out what the baby's cries mean
Supervise and help older children with self-feeding and self-dressing

What Young Children Can Do

Help with the baby's bath
Brush the baby's hair
Powder the baby
Bring the baby's clean clothes or diapers for changing
Play with the baby
Carry and hold the baby's bottle, bibs, and other little items during feedings
Help push the baby carriage
Help dress the baby
Select toys and hand them to the baby

What Older Children Can Do

Amuse or help younger children while parents are busy with the baby
Find out why the baby cries
Feed the baby (if the baby is bottle-fed)
Later, assist the baby with self-feeding
Change the baby
Watch the baby for a short time while the parents are out, depending on the child's age
Play with the baby
Take the baby out for a short ride in the carriage

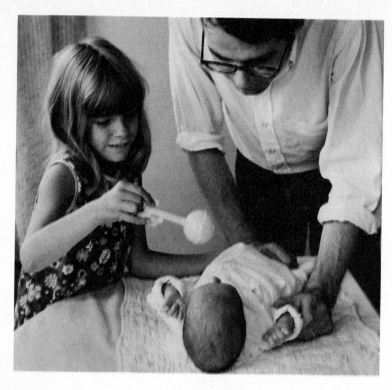

Men no longer feel that child care is "women's work." The care of the baby is the responsibility of the whole family.
Michal Heron/Monkmeyer

some meals, or can supervise and play with the other children, while the mother feeds the baby. Or he can feed the baby, if the baby is bottle-fed, while she prepares the family meal. The father can do the marketing, or he can take charge of the baby and the other children while the mother does it. It is not so important what each parent does as long as they help each other carry the burden of the baby's care.

Many parents believe that young children are more of a bother than a help when it comes to doing things in the house. So, instead of giving them small tasks that they are able to do, parents send the children off to play by themselves.

Not expecting to be asked to help care for the baby is psychologically bad for family members. It suggests that they are not able to do these jobs. It also suggests, even when not true, that the mother is more interested in the new baby than in them.

Babies gain the most from cooperative family care. Being a part of the family early in life makes them feel loved and wanted. Babies can learn early that they are just one unit in the family rather than the most important unit.

When babies are taken care of by the father and brothers and sisters, as well as by the mother, they learn to adjust to different ways of being handled and to different people. This helps the babies later as their social horizons broaden to include people outside the home. They will be better able to adjust to new people than will children who from earliest babyhood were cared for by the mother alone.

For Discussion

How would you encourage the older children in a family to share in the care of the new baby? Would this make them less likely to be jealous of the new baby? What else can be done to create favorable attitudes in the children toward the new baby?

The Baby's Schedule

One of the most difficult adjustments family members must make to a new baby is fitting their lives into the baby's schedule. Babies are unable to adjust to a pattern of living that fits the needs of older children and adults. They must be on a schedule that meets their needs at that time.

There is no set schedule that will fit every need of every baby. During the baby's first year, the schedule tends to be rigid and tight. By the second year, the schedule is more flexible and can usually fit into the family schedule. By then, everyone probably has similar schedules, except for bedtime.

Schedules are only rough guidelines. They can, and should, be modified to

Young children gain a sense of pride when allowed to help with the baby. David S. Strickler/Monkmeyer

Suggested Schedule for Babies

Birth to Six Months

6:00 to 6:30 A.M.	Feeding	5:00 to 5:30	Playtime, alone
6:30 to 9:30	Sleep		
9:30 to 10:00	Exercise and bath	5:30 to 6:00	Exercise and play
10:00 to 10:30	Feeding	6:00 to 6:30	Feeding and preparation for bed
10:30 to 1:30 P.M.	Sleep (outdoors when possible)	6:30 to 10:00	Sleep
		10:00 to 10:30	Feeding
1:30 to 2:00	Playtime, alone	10:30 P.M. to 6:00 A.M.	Sleep
2:00 to 2:30	Feeding		
2:30 to 5:00	Sleep (outdoors when possible)		

Six Months to One Year

7:00 to 7:30 A.M.	Breakfast	3:00 to 5:00	Fruit juice, ride in carriage or stroller or play indoors
7:30 to 7:45	Preparation for morning nap		
7:45 to 9:30	Sleep	5:00 to 5:30	Exercise and play
9:30 to 10:30	Bath, exercise, and orange juice	5:30 to 6:00	Supper and preparation for bed
10:30 to 12:00	Play in crib or playpen		
12:00 to 12:30 P.M.	Dinner	6:00 P.M. to 7:00 A.M.	Sleep
12:30 to 3:00	Nap		

meet the needs of every baby. All babies vary from time to time in their needs. If babies do not waken and cry at the usual feeding time, it means that they are not hungry then. On the next day, they may be hungry at the usual time. These variations should be expected and accepted as normal, not as a cause for concern or worry.

Parents who have already had children are usually far less schedule-conscious than are first-time parents. A schedule is good to follow, partly because it is better for the baby and partly because it reduces confusion in the pattern of family life. But, when something important comes up, it is a good idea to make shifts.

For Action

List some recreations you and your family enjoy and are used to doing during your free time. Pretend a baby just joined your family. Which of these recreations would have to be given up, for a time at least? Which activities could still be carried out, even while the baby was very young? What other recreations would you select to replace the ones you had to give up?

By the baby's first birthday, even first-time parents realize that schedules need not be as strict as they may have thought. They realize, also, that a baby must learn to adjust to changes. If kept on too strict a schedule, the baby will be upset by even the slightest change. Later on, this will make good personal and social adjustments difficult.

For Discussion

How much variation can be made in a young baby's schedule over weekends or on holidays without upsetting the baby? What part of the schedule can be varied with the least harm to the baby? What parts should be strictly followed? Is it possible to decide these things without knowing the particular baby concerned?

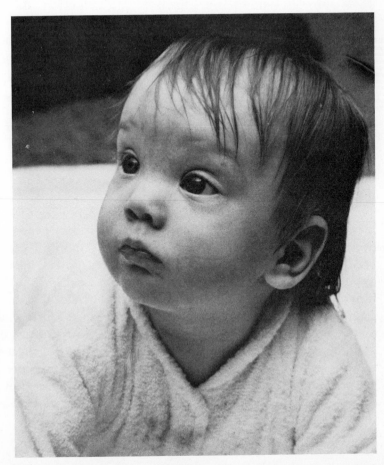

When babies become aware of their environment, they show an interest in everything around them. They are especially interested in the people who are familiar to them.
Erika Stone/Peter Arnold

Talk to Them   Even though babies may not understand what is said, all family members should, from time to time, talk directly to babies. They, in turn, will "talk back" in their babyish way. Babies should also be encouraged to coo and babble when the family group is talking. This gives them a feeling of belonging.

Play with Them   Babies love to play simple games. Play peek-a-boo, swing a ball for them to hit with their hands, and count their fingers and toes while they watch.

Keep Them with the Family Group   When the family is together as a group, babies can be there too. The babies can watch what is going on, and the family members can talk or play with them.

Let Them Help   When babies grow older, they want to contribute to what others are doing. It gives them a feeling of achievement and of belonging. For example, when the table is being set, they can carry the napkins.

The Baby as Part of the Family

When infants are first brought home from the hospital, family members want to hold and touch them, talk to them, and run to them whenever they cry. This is enough to make very young babies feel that they belong in the family. However, before babies are a year old, this is no longer enough. As they spend less and less time asleep, babies have more time to become aware of their environment and the people in it. They hear and see other family members doing things, and they want to do them, too.

All babies should be given a chance to become a part of the family as soon as they are ready. Babies often show this readiness by crying for attention when alone and by being pleased when accepted as part of the group. Their developmental readiness to become part of the family is shown when babies use "comforters" to take the place of the af-

fection and attention they want from people. Thumb-sucking or an attachment to a special blanket or stuffed toy is often a sign of a baby's readiness to join in family activities.

The family members are responsible for providing the baby with chances to become part of the family. The chart above gives some ideas of how they may go about it.

Beware of Pampering

Giving too much attention to any family member often results in pampering or spoiling. Babies are the ones most often spoiled. It starts very early in their lives.

At first, babies cry to let someone know they need something, such as food, a diaper change, or company. When babies are pampered, cries come to mean that they want more attention than they have been getting. It often gets to the point where attention is given to them at the expense of other family members.

No matter how large the family, all babies do get some pampering. Babies are cute, and people enjoy pampering them. Family members gladly respond to their helplessness by going to them whenever they cry. Pampering a baby may give people pleasure, but it is bad for the baby. Babies who are pampered come to have a false idea of their importance. They learn to expect more than their share of time and attention from others. When they do not get this, they become angry and resentful.

For Discussion

Which family members are most likely to pamper a baby—parents, older children, or relatives? Can pampering be controlled? How can you control pampering without hurting the feelings of those who are doing it?

Babies can never be loved too much! Family members should realize, however, that pampering and spoiling babies is *not* loving them. Barbara Pfeffer/Peter Arnold

Danger Signals of Pampering

Crying after needs have been met

Showing signs of triumph when they have gotten the attention they want

Fussing and crying when they are not the center of attention

Doing things to annoy others

Expecting others to do for them things that babies and toddlers can do for themselves

Too much pampering lays the basis for poor social adjustments as the baby grows older. Other people, both adults and children, cannot be expected to do the pampering that family members have done. Instead, outsiders may feel that pampered children are "spoiled brats," a label that may hurt social relationships for many years.

To determine whether or not a baby is becoming spoiled, the parents must first figure out where to draw the fine line between meeting needs and meeting wants. If *needs* are met, this is not pampering. If, on the other hand, a baby's *wants* are unreasonable and are being met too often, the baby is being pampered.

Highlights of Chapter 3

☐ Bringing a new baby home from the hospital may be a time of chaos unless enough preparation has been made.

☐ The pattern of family life changes when a new member becomes part of the family.

☐ The arrival of a new baby usually causes role changes for every family member.

☐ Care for a baby should be shared by all family members.

☐ Family members who are not allowed to help with the new baby may feel left out. They may even begin to resent the baby.

☐ The baby's schedule must be different from the schedules of other family members.

☐ When babies spend less time sleeping, they have more time to become aware of their environment and the people in it.

☐ Because babies are helpless, family members enjoy doing things for them.

☐ Too much attention given to the baby may lead to pampering the baby.

Suggested Activities

1. Make a list of things to do to prepare the home and the family members for the new baby. Which of these things can be done by the older children, and which must be done by adults?

2. Research the kinds of things young children can do while the parents are busy with the care of a new baby. Besides helping, what can children do to keep from feeling neglected and pushed aside by the new baby?

3. Map out a schedule of your family's daily activities. How would that schedule fit the schedule most babies must follow during the first year? Can the schedules be set up to satisfy everyone?

4. How can a person tell the difference between a baby's needs and wants? Why is it important to be able to do this? If it is not done accurately, how will it affect the baby?

5. Conduct a survey to find out how the people you know feel about men's taking a more active role in the care of babies than they did in the past. Compare answers of older and younger people, and of males and females. Report the results to the class.

Unit Two | THE BABYHOOD YEARS

Babyhood is a time when the newborn becomes less helpless and more independent. It is the first two years of life.

During the first year of babyhood, the child is still considered a baby. For the first six to nine months, the baby's physical growth and development are still very rapid. During the second year, the baby's physical growth and development slow down, while mental growth and development progress rapidly. At this time, the baby is a toddler.

With control over their muscles, babies are now able to explore their environment and learn new things about it. Troublesome as this may seem to parents, it is a very important part of growing. Babies must know about the world if they are to become a part of it.

Chapter 4, "How Babies Grow and Develop," discusses babies' physical growth and development and how it affects their behavior and attitudes toward other people and themselves.

Chapter 5, "Physical Care of the Baby," describes the care needed for good health, growth, and development during the babyhood years.

Chapter 6, "Learning Body Control," shows how babies learn to control the different parts of the body. As time passes, it becomes possible for them to do things that just a few months before had to be done for them.

Chapter 7, "Learning to Communicate," describes the stages a baby goes through before being able to speak.

Chapter 8, "Some Common Babyhood Problems," covers the most important problems babies must face in going through stages of development. It also gives some suggestions for ways parents can help the babies adjust.

Chapter 9, "Caretakers for Children," gives a brief overview of career and job opportunities in caring for children. It also describes how baby-sitting introduces teenagers to working with children.

Chapter 4

How Babies Grow and Develop

Some goals of this chapter are:
- [ ] To be aware of the difference between patterns of growth and patterns of development
- [ ] To understand the effects that body proportions have on behavior
- [ ] To understand how the developing nervous system and sense organs add to independence
- [ ] To realize how a baby's minor illness can develop into a major one if not properly cared for

Twice during the entire life span there are periods of rapid physical growth. The rest of the time, growth is at a slower and more even rate until it comes to a complete halt.

The first period of rapid growth starts as soon as the fertilized ovum becomes attached to the wall of the mother's uterus. The rapid growth continues for six to nine months after the baby's birth. The second growth spurt is later in life when the child's body is changing into an adult body. This is known as the *puberty growth spurt*. It begins around the age of 11, reaches a peak when the child's sex organs start to function, and then slows down. It usually lasts for about four years. By comparison, the *baby growth spurt* lasts for less than two years.

As shown in the chart on page 50, there are several important things to

During the growth spurt, the baby needs some extra TLC.
Erika Stone/Peter Arnold

know about growth spurts. They affect the pattern of life for the person who is going through them, even if only for a short time.

Interrelationship of Physical and Mental Growth

Studies of physical and mental growth have shown that they are interrelated. This means that when physical growth is rapid, mental growth is too. When one is slow, both are slow.

Health and nutrition affect both physical and mental growth. In babyhood, for example, poor nutrition does not only stunt physical growth. It also affects the developing brain. This, in turn, hurts mental development.

Important Effects of Growth Spurts

During rapid growth, the body needs extra food. This results in a ravenous appetite. As growth slows down, so does the need for food. The baby's appetite then decreases.

Rapid growth saps energy. The baby tires more easily than when growth is at a slower rate.

To get over the tiredness caused by rapid growth, the baby needs more rest and sleep than are needed when growth is at a slower rate.

Rapid growth is not limited to one part of the body. However, different parts of the body grow rapidly at different times and at different rates. They never grow at exactly the same time and never at the same rate.

Bones and muscles grow at different times and at different rates, making coordination of the body impossible. This results in the mass activity that is a trait of the baby and the awkward movement of the toddler.

Physical growth is easier to watch and control than mental growth. For the sake of both, serious attention should be given to good nutrition and health care during the important years of babyhood. These years are the base on which the rest of the life is built.

Pattern of Growth

Growth is never smooth and even. When the baby is growing in height, weight increase may be small. When the internal organs, such as the heart and stomach, are going through a growth spurt, outside features stay pretty much unchanged. This is the pattern of growth that all babies follow. However, there are differences in the rate of growth for different babies.

The pattern of growth is slightly different for boys and girls. These differences show up soon after birth. Boy infants lose more weight after birth than girls. Once they adjust to life outside the mother's body, boys then gain a little more in height and weight than girls.

American babies gain more weight than babies do in other countries. This can be explained by the diet and medical care they get. These are usually better than those of babies in many other parts of the world.

Patterns of Growth in Height and Weight in Babyhood

	Height		Weight
Birth	20 in (51 cm)	Birth	7 lb (3.2 kg)
4 months	24 in (61 cm)	4 months	14 lb (6.4 kg)
1 year	28-30 in (71-76 cm)	1 year	21 lb (9.5 kg)
2 years	33-37 in (84-94 cm)	2 years	25-28 lb (11.3-12.7 kg)

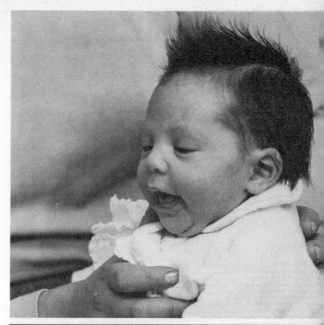

The infant's total helplessness gives way to growing independence during the babyhood years. Erika Stone/Peter Arnold

For Thought

How would it be if the rate of growth during the first year of life went on until the person was fully grown? Think of how tall or how heavy a person would be if growth went on at that rate for sixteen to eighteen years. If you tripled your weight every year, as a baby does during the first year of life, how much would you weigh at 16? Thinking in these terms should help you see why growth slows down very rapidly after the early months of life.

In babyhood, weight gain comes mostly from an increase in fat tissue. This is caused by the large amount of fat in milk—the main part of the baby's diet. Later, as foods other than milk become part of the diet, weight increases come more from bone and muscle tissue than from fat tissue.

There is no scientific proof that fat babies are healthier than thin babies. The facts show that they have as many illnesses as thinner babies. In addition, fat babies tend to be somewhat slow to develop motor skills. This is because any extra weight increases the top-heaviness that is a trait of all babies.

Pattern of Development

Growth always comes with changes in body proportions as parts of the body develop in their own way. A baby's

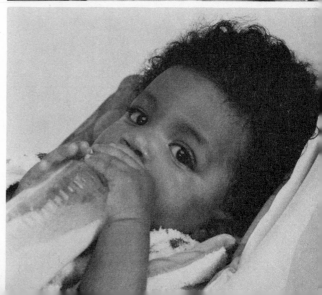

looks change greatly during the baby-hood years.

At birth, babies are top-heavy. Throughout babyhood, their heads keep on growing, but at a slower rate than the rest of their bodies. By the time babyhood ends, babies are no longer so top-heavy.

The parts of the body that are least developed at birth, the trunk and limbs, grow and develop fast during baby-hood. The trunk becomes longer and the shoulders broader; the stomach flattens. The body gradually takes on a more definite shape than when the baby was born.

Compare the baby's body proportions to those of the adult. The baby's head is about one-fourth the entire body; the adult's is about one-seventh. Christy Park/Monkmeyer

For Discussion

How does knowing about growth spurts and their effects on behavior change people's attitudes toward a baby's behavior? Does it make it easier for them to accept a baby's behavior? Does it lessen their worry about whether the baby is developing normally?

Body Proportions

All newborn babies vary in body build. Some seem long and spindly; others seem short and chubby. But body types do not show up until the body proportions change during the baby-hood years. Before babyhood ends, babies have developed their specific body type. Differences in body build become even clearer during childhood.

Significance of Body Proportions

The baby's body proportions have far-reaching effects. As long as babies are top-heavy, they are helpless. They are too clumsy to sit, stand, or walk. This is due mainly to poor balance caused by top-heaviness.

Small hands and small feet also add to clumsiness. A baby's hands are not large enough or strong enough to hold anything heavy. And since it takes more effort to do things with small hands, babies give up quickly when they try to feed themselves or hold toys.

Small feet, likewise, quickly tire when the full weight of the body is put on them. Therefore, babies fall when they try to stand or walk. As a result, they do not want to keep on doing these things for more than a short time.

Changes in body proportions also have an important effect on the baby's looks. As different parts of the body change their size and shape, babies get better looking. They begin to look more the way adults expect.

The Baby's Bones and Teeth

The bones of the newborn infant are soft—more like cartilage or gristle than like bones. Throughout babyhood, the bones harden very slowly. This hardening is called *ossification*. It begins shortly after birth and ends as the child nears puberty, around the age of 11 or 12.

The softness of the baby's bones is very noticeable in the spots called *fontanels* on the baby's skull. The largest and easiest to see of these fontanels is the one on the top of the baby's head. The four pieces of bone that make up the top of the skull have not yet grown together there.

The fontanels are nature's way of giving the brain room to grow. During the early months of life, the need to protect the brain is not as great as it will be later, when the baby becomes more active. Between twelve and eighteen months after birth, the fontanels close. Within two years, they are well hardened.

There are two important facts about the bones of babies. First, breaks in bones mend quickly and readily. Second, the bones easily become misshapen. Babies who spend too much time lying on their backs, for example, may develop flat heads. When the baby can sit and stand, poor posture may cause curvature of the spine. This curving

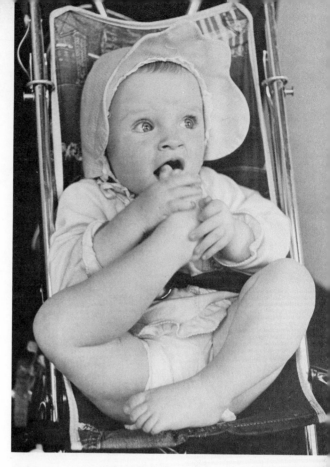

Babies can put their bodies into some pretty awkward positions because their bones are so soft. Tom Carey/Monkmeyer

spine could become set as the baby grows older if posture is not corrected at an early age.

Teeth

Every human being normally has two sets of teeth, the temporary or "baby" teeth and the permanent teeth. There are twenty baby teeth and thirty-two permanent teeth. Because the baby teeth are temporary, they are of lesser quality than the permanent teeth. They are usually soft and small, with small, shallow roots. Unless the diet of the baby and young child is good, the teeth

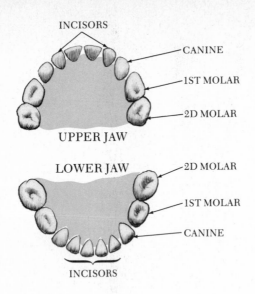

INCISORS

CANINE

1ST MOLAR

2D MOLAR

UPPER JAW

LOWER JAW

2D MOLAR

1ST MOLAR

CANINE

INCISORS

may decay before they are replaced by the permanent teeth.

Teeth start to develop in the baby's jaws during the third or fourth month of prenatal life. They do not start to appear until the baby is 5 to 6 months old. Then they usually come in at a rate of about one tooth a month until the baby is 2 to 2¹/₂ years old. This is known as *teething*, or cutting teeth.

Approximate Ages at Which the Baby Cuts Teeth	
Order of Appearance	**Age**
Two middle-lower incisors	6 to 8 months
Four upper incisors	8 to 12 months
Two lateral-lower incisors	12 to 14 months
Four first molars	12 to 15 months
Four canines	18 to 20 months
Four second molars	24 to 30 months

Teething starts at different ages and with different degrees of difficulty. The age depends partly on heredity and partly on the baby's health and diet.

The age at which babies cut their teeth has been found to be far less important than the *sequence* (order) in which the teeth appear. Sometimes teeth do not appear in the usual sequence, as when the upper teeth come in before the lower. This is likely to throw the jaw out of position, affect the lower part of the face, and cause the permanent teeth to be out of line. Dentists are not sure what causes the sequence to be irregular, and they have no way to prevent it.

Sometimes teething brings on fever, digestive upsets, loss of appetite, sleep loss, earaches, and colds. Babies differ greatly in the amount of discomfort or actual pain they have while teething. Even those who have little discomfort do not feel their best.

There are four important things to remember about teething. First, it almost always affects the baby's mood. It is not at all uncommon for a baby who has been as "good as gold" during the first year of life to turn into a fretful, irritable, hard-to-manage toddler. This may be only temporary, but the baby may develop the habit of being fretful and disagreeable unless steps are taken to make teething easier.

Second, all teething is likely to have some effect on babies' physical well-being. They cannot be expected to eat or sleep as well as they normally do. They may also have less energy than normal.

Third, most babies try to ease the discomforts of teething by thumb-sucking. Many people believe that this should be stopped because it will distort the shape of the mouth by causing the front teeth to stick out. But there is little proof that this will happen unless thumb-sucking becomes a habit. Most dentists suggest that babies who are teething be given teething rings to chew on and that their gums be rubbed to ease the pain. Unless the doctor or dentist says so, no medicine should be used for the pain or when rubbing the gums.

Fourth, the baby's diet is important not only for healthy baby teeth, but also for healthy permanent teeth.

Baby teeth should never be pulled out. The jaw may shrink where the tooth was, and the permanent teeth may come in crooked. If a tooth is knocked out by accident, the baby should be taken to the dentist at once.

The Nervous System

The nervous system starts to develop soon after conception, but it is far from fully developed at birth. This is another reason why the newborn infant is helpless. After birth, the nervous system develops at a rapid rate. This makes it possible for babies to begin to control the muscles of their bodies and to learn, thus helping them become more independent.

Some people believe that because the baby's brain is large, it is well developed and functions at a fairly high level. This is far from true. While the brain is proportionally larger than the other parts of the body, its internal development is not yet complete. However, the brain also begins to develop internally right after birth. The *cerebrum*

Babies chew on just about anything they can hold in order to ease the pain caused by teething. A teething ring is made especially for this purpose. George Roos/Peter Arnold

makes up the major portion of the brain. It controls sensory experiences as well as body movements, memory, and learning. The part of the cerebrum that controls body movement develops earlier than the part which controls learning. During their first year, babies begin to crawl and walk, and later they learn to speak. The *cerebellum* is a small portion of the brain that controls posture and balance. It too develops during the baby's first year, making it possible for them to keep their balance while sitting, standing, and walking.

Sensory Experiences of Babies

Vision   The baby's eyes are well developed at birth, but the muscles that attach the eyes to their sockets are weak. Until these strengthen, within two or three months after birth, things cannot be seen clearly. Color vision appears a month or two after birth.

Hearing   The liquid from the prenatal sac drains out of the middle ear several days after birth. When this happens, the baby's hearing becomes very clear.

Skin Sensations   The baby's skin has the same number of sense organs for touch, pain, and temperature as an adult's, but the skin is thinner. As a result, the baby feels touch, pain, and temperature more keenly than an adult does.

Smell   The baby has as many cells for smell inside the nostrils as an adult but does not have the hair that lines the inside of the adult's nose. As a result, odors can get to the smell cells easily. The baby has a keen sense of smell.

Taste   The baby's taste buds are on the surface of the tongue, as is true of adults. They also line the insides of the cheeks. This makes the baby very sensitive to all tastes. Much of the taste comes from smell, and the baby's sense of smell is very good. This increases the baby's keen sense of taste.

The Baby's Senses

Even though all the sense organs are present at birth, they are not all well developed and functioning at that time. However, they develop rapidly during the early months of life. They are, in many ways, different from the sense organs of adults. As a result, babies' sensory experiences are different from those of adults. See the chart above.

Illness in Babyhood

How babies grow and develop depends greatly on how healthy they are. Babies who are often sick or have long illnesses tend to be slow both in growth and in development. This is because their strength and energy are sapped by illness. If their health gets better as they grow older, they may catch up to the level of other children. However, the chances are that they will never completely reach their fullest possible growth.

For the first four to six months of life, babies are comparatively immune to disease. From then on, they are likely to have a growing number of respiratory and gastrointestinal illnesses. Babies have more respiratory illnesses during the winter months and more gastrointestinal illnesses when the weather is hot.

In spite of new medical methods, immunization, and new drugs, there are still many deaths among babies under 1 year old. One major reason for this is that many parents do not realize how quickly a baby's minor illness can become serious. Because an adult gets over minor illnesses quickly, many parents think that a baby will also.

Unfortunately, this is far from true. In babyhood a slight temperature in the morning may reach alarming heights by the afternoon. Therefore, whenever a baby is feverish, refuses to eat, or cries more than usual, the parents should telephone the doctor and report these facts. If the doctor cannot tell what the trouble is over the telephone, the baby should be taken to the doctor's office or to the clinic.

In the case of a serious illness, a baby may have to go to a hospital. This is usually an upsetting experience for a baby as well as for the parents. Many hospitals have places for parents to stay with their babies. Hospitals want parents to help with the care of the babies. If parents are not allowed to stay in the hospital to which the doctor sends the baby, the mother or father should spend as much time there as possible. This will reduce the tension that makes the baby's illness worse and slows recovery.

To keep babies from becoming ill, they should often be taken to the doctor's office or the clinic for checkups. During the first year, most doctors want to check a baby every month or two. By the second year, the checkups are usually every three to four months.

Immunization

There are some diseases that are so serious that doctors feel babies should be immunized against them to help the babies build resistance to the diseases. While immunization may not prevent the disease completely, the case may not be nearly as bad. It can also prevent complications that often accompany the disease, or these may be greatly reduced.

The immunization puts into the bloodstream some of the disease germs themselves or other germs that will kill

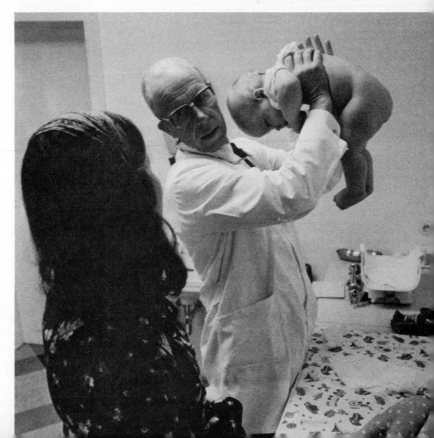

Even if they seem to be perfectly well, babies should be seen by a doctor for periodic check-ups. Cary Wolinsky/ Stock, Boston

When Babies Should Be Immunized

Diphtheria, Pertussis (Whooping Cough), and Tetanus (Lockjaw) Immunization against these three diseases is given in one combined shot, the DPT shot. The first shot is given when the baby is 3 months old, followed by a second at 4 months, and a third at 5 months. When babies are a year old, they are given a Shick test to determine their immunity to diphtheria. Between the ages of 12 and 18 months, and again at 4 years, a booster DPT shot is given. Between the ages of 12 and 14 years, the child is given a booster for diphtheria and tetanus, but not for pertussis.

Poliomyelitis (Infantile Paralysis) There are two ways to immunize against poliomyelitis: The Salk vaccine is injected into the bloodstream, and the Sabin vaccine is given orally in liquid or pill form. Most doctors prefer the Sabin vaccine because it gives a better, longer lasting immunity. It is given when the baby is 2 months old, followed by two more pills six or eight weeks apart. A booster is then given at 15 months and again at 4 years.

Measles The baby is immunized against measles between the ages of 8 and 9 months and again at 12 years. Should there be an epidemic of measles in the neighborhood, or should a family member get measles before the baby has been immunized, the doctor usually immunizes the baby at once. This might keep the baby from catching it or keep the case from becoming a bad one if the baby already has it.

Rubella (German Measles) Unless there is an epidemic in the neighborhood or a case in the family, doctors usually prefer to immunize babies against rubella when they are 1 year old.

Mumps Immunization to prevent mumps is usually given when the baby is 1 year old and again when the child is 12 years old. This is especially important for boys. If a boy catches mumps when he is an adolescent, he may become sterile.

---

the disease germs. An immunization is almost always accompanied by a reaction. It may last for a few hours or days. After receiving a DPT shot, for example, the baby may have fever, loss of appetite, broken sleep, and fretfulness. These reactions usually start several hours after the shot has been given. They clear up in a day or two.

Besides immunization against diseases, some babies are immunized for allergies. When babies develop skin rashes, watery eyes, or stuffy noses, and vomit, sneeze for no known reason, or breathe heavily, they should be given skin tests to find out if they have allergies. If they are allergic to some food or foods, such foods will be taken out of the diet. If, on the other hand, the tests show the trouble to be something such as dust or pollen, babies can be immunized against the source of trouble.

Colds and respiratory illnesses are very common among babies. In spite of this, no satisfactory way has been found to immunize babies, or anyone for that matter, against colds.

All children need a record of immunization when they go to school or college or get a job. It is wise for

For Action

Study the list of diseases against which babies are usually immunized. Find out whether you have been immunized against them, when this was done, what doctor or what clinic immunized you, whether you had booster shots, and when they were given.

If no records have been kept by your family and no one is sure about your immunizations, do the following things:

1. Contact the doctor or the clinic you now go to and ask to have your full immunization record sent to you.

2. If you have not been immunized for some diseases, speak with your doctor about having the immunizations now. It is especially important for girls to be immunized against rubella and for boys to be immunized against mumps.

parents to keep their own records besides those kept by the doctor or clinic. Parents should record for every child the dates for the immunizations and for the booster shots as well as the name and address of the doctor or clinic where they were given.

For Discussion

Note that smallpox is not listed with the diseases for which babies are immunized. Find out why this is so. When would a person be immunized against smallpox?

Minor Physical Defects

No human being is physically perfect. Some physical defects are hereditary. Some may be the result of a poor condition in the prenatal environment. Others are caused after birth by diseases or accidents.

Some physical defects are easily noticed. They can be quickly spotted by the doctor or parents. Some are not so easily found by doctors because they do not see the baby all the time, as parents do.

Doctors are on the alert for any physical defects. They realize that finding them early makes it easier to completely correct them. However, unless doctors see babies often and under varying conditions, they will not know of some defects that could be corrected. It is therefore the responsibility of parents to tell the doctor of any suspicions they may have of a defect in the baby. The doctor will know what should be done to correct it.

Far too many parents believe the baby will outgrow the defect. They may notice, for example, that the baby's eyes coordinate poorly. They believe that this will go away as the eye muscles strengthen. Even when this lack of coordination continues, they still wait for the baby to outgrow it. Later, when the doctor finds the weakness, it may have to be corrected by surgery. In some cases, the parents' suspicions of a defect may be unfounded. Their worry will be reduced if the doctor says that the baby will outgrow the defect or that it can be corrected.

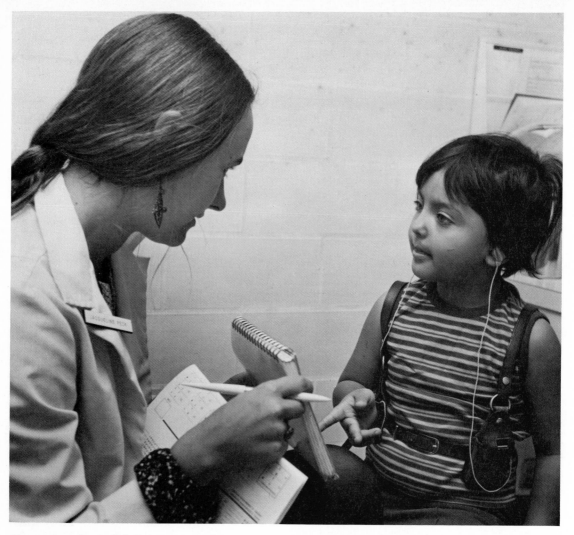

Correcting physical defects at an early age will help children in their learning and in the development of their abilities. The National Foundation—March of Dimes

Correction of defects is important for a number of reasons. First, any defect, even minor, can and often does interfere with a baby's normal pattern of growth and development.

A physical defect may interfere with movement, which is important to normal growth and development.

Second, as babies grow older, overweight or excessive thinness may keep them from playing games that children of their age enjoy.

Third, any defect, no matter how minor, makes children self-conscious if playmates talk about it and if this makes them feel uncomfortable.

Common Physical Defects in Babies

Allergies to various foods and particles in the air can cause hives, sneezing, nausea, heavy breathing, swelling of the eyes, and running of the nose.

Anemia often causes lack of energy and pale skin.

Birthmarks may be flat or raised, as in the case of "strawberry" marks. Birthmarks sometimes go away as the baby grows older, but they may get larger as the body grows and the skin expands to cover a larger surface.

Blueness of skin when crying or moving energetically may mean the baby is not getting enough oxygen.

Poor hearing shows itself in the baby's failure to react to sounds or in always turning the head to one side when people speak.

Poor teeth are shown by spots or early decay.

Poor tonsils often lead to bad sore throats and high fever whenever the baby has a cold.

Poor vision is a problem if the baby is unable to coordinate the eyes. The baby might also squint when looking at some-thing or bump into things more than usual.

Earaches are often accompanied by severe pain, high fever, and slight breaks in the eardrum whenever the baby has a cold.

Enlarged adenoids make it hard for the baby to breathe with a closed mouth. Later, the child's voice may take on a nasal tone.

Excessive fat of a flabby type, even when the diet is moderate and fairly free from fattening foods, needs attention.

Excessive thinness in spite of a good appetite and a well-balanced diet may be a sign of trouble.

Eye infections cause redness around the lids and frequent sties.

Heavy breathing whenever moving or crying should be looked into by the doctor.

Orthopedic (bone) defects are shown by turning ankles when standing, flat feet, or misshapen feet.

Skin eruptions, such as hives, rashes, and boils, are often caused by an allergy.

Is the Baby Thriving?

All parents worry about whether their babies are thriving or in good health. Some parents judge this by gains in the baby's size, especially weight. They become "scale watchers" and weigh the baby every day to see how much is gained. If the baby does not gain or even loses a few ounces, they become upset, thinking that something is wrong.

Other parents use behavior to judge if the baby is thriving. If the baby is cheerful, alert, and friendly, they figure that all is well. Some parents depend on the doctor's periodic checkup to be sure that all is well.

No one standard is enough to judge whether the baby's growth and development are following the normal pattern. Instead, a number of standards should be used. These fall into two groups: appearance and behavior.

Should the baby fall short on these, growth and development are not going as they should. This may be caused by

The way the baby looks and acts in various situations helps parents know whether the baby is healthy, happy, and thriving. Tim Egan/Woodfin Camp & Associates

the kind of physical care the baby is getting. It could be the wrong diet or too little rest. It may have an emotional cause. The environment may be too exciting for the baby at that age. This could interfere with sleeping and eating. Or maybe the baby is getting too little stimulation. This causes boredom and lack of interest.

Because parents can rarely be objective in figuring out the cause of trouble in their babies, they should get advice from the doctor. They should not wait for the condition to get better by itself.

It is important to know that a steady gain cannot be expected. Even thriving babies have short-term setbacks due to colds, teething, or temporary overexcitement. So deciding whether the baby is thriving should not be done on a day-to-day basis or even week to week. If, at the end of the month, there is evidence that growth and development are ahead of what they were at the beginning of the month, there is plenty of reason to believe that all is well.

For Discussion

In judging whether babies are healthy and thriving, do you think their appearance or their behavior tells you more about their physical state? Do you feel that you could judge well by using one set of standards alone, or do you feel that you should use both?

Standards for Thriving

The Baby's Appearance

Eyes Bright and shiny; the baby looks happy most of the time.

Hair Glossy; becomes thicker as the baby grows older.

Limbs Straighten and begin to be covered with a thin layer of firm fat; well-developed muscles.

Skin Smooth and elastic with a clear complexion.

Teeth Well-shaped, firm, and white.

The Baby's Behavior

Activity Always in motion, even when asleep; as babies grow older, they become more active.

Appetite Looks forward to mealtimes, is hungry, and eats well.

Crying Always with a reason; not fussy.

Digestion Free from constant digestive upsets, such as gas, colic, and vomiting.

Sleep Sound; baby awakens bright, cheerful, and alert.

Excitement Is curious and excited about anything new and different; wants to explore it.

Joy of Living Usually in a good mood; laughs and babbles; smiles often.

Highlights of Chapter 4

- ☐ The two growth spurts during a person's life span affect personal and social adjustments.
- ☐ Physical and mental growth are closely related.
- ☐ Body proportions change greatly during babyhood. This makes sitting, standing, and walking possible.
- ☐ Babies' bones are soft. Shortly after birth they begin to harden. This hardening process is called *ossification*.
- ☐ Teething is an uncomfortable time for babies. As their teeth come in, babies may be fussy.
- ☐ Rapid development of the nervous system and sense organs in babyhood is partly responsible for changing babyish helplessness into toddler independence.
- ☐ Illnesses develop suddenly and minor physical defects appear during babyhood. Noticing and treating an illness early and correcting a defect can reduce its damaging effects.
- ☐ Babies should be immunized against the common childhood diseases.
- ☐ To decide whether babies are thriving, their appearance and their behavior should be considered.

Suggested Activities

1. Visit a drug store and ask to see teething aids, such as medicine to rub on gums, medicine to take orally, and teething rings. Note the varieties of each. Ask the druggist which are sold most and why they are thought to be best for soothing the discomforts of teething.

2. Watch the standing, walking, sitting, and sleeping postures of several babies. Compare the older babies with the younger ones.

3. Make a list of physical defects, such as poor hearing, poor vision, and slightly crooked teeth. Choose several from the list on page 61, and add some others. Next to each defect, note how it can be corrected.

4. Which two of the appearance standards and which two of the behavior standards do you think tell the most about the baby's state? Would you be willing to judge babies by these four standards alone, or would you feel safer using the longer list given on page 63?

Chapter 5

Physical Care of the Baby

Some goals of this chapter are:

- [ ] To be aware of all the factors that must be considered when feeding babies
- [ ] To know about the kind of clothing needed for babies of different ages, and why
- [ ] To be able to give reasons why the amount of sleep a baby needs varies depending on age, health, and activities
- [ ] To be able to describe how a baby should be bathed and discuss the importance of safety in the bath
- [ ] To know the importance of care of a baby's teeth
- [ ] To understand why fresh air and exercise should be part of the daily care of a baby

In no area of child study are there more opinions than in the physical care of a baby. Some parents believe in the age-old methods and see everything new as "faddish." Others accept all the latest methods, more because they are new than because they are better than some of the older, tried methods. Still other parents would like to use the newer methods but do not because relatives and friends say they may harm the baby.

Until new ways of caring for children have been tried and judged, it is a good idea for parents to question their use and discuss such matters with the baby's doctor.

Feeding the Baby

The newborn baby is usually fed for the first time within twelve hours after being born. Most newborns are able to suck right away, but only for a short time—five or ten minutes at the most. Sucking is very hard work for infants (see pages 24–25). They tire very easily and get little food. Newborns often lose weight for a day or two after birth because of this. As they gain strength, babies suck for a longer time and are able to get more nourishment.

For Discussion

Why is it important for new methods of baby care to be tried, judged, and approved before using them? Would this be more important for some areas of baby care, such as feeding, than for others, such as bathing? If so, explain why.

Breast-Feeding versus Bottle-Feeding

Before the baby is born, the mother usually decides whether or not she will breast-feed the baby. Should she decide not to, she is given a shot right after the baby's birth to hold back the flow of milk to her breasts. If she decides to breast-feed, it is done from the beginning, even though milk does not flow right away. *Colostrum* is the food the baby gets from the breast at first. It has more protein than mother's milk but less carbohydrates and fats. This is why breast-fed babies often lose more weight than others during the first few

Breast-feeding is an experience only a mother can share with the baby. The father, as well as other family members, may have the chance to meet the baby's most basic needs when the baby is bottle-fed. Left: Erika Stone/Peter Arnold; right: Thomas Hopker/Woodfin Camp & Associates

days after birth. Colostrum also gives the baby immunity to a number of illnesses.

Some mothers who would like to breast-feed their babies do not have enough milk for the babies' needs. In such cases, doctors often recommend bottle-feeding the infants as well as breast-feeding them. Sometimes this is done by taking turns breast-feeding and bottle-feeding. In other cases, the mother can start the baby's meal by breast-feeding and finish up by bottle-feeding until the baby's needs have been met.

Most doctors agree that there are advantages and disadvantages to breast-feeding. They also feel that the advantages outweigh the disadvantages. The advantages and disadvantages of breast-feeding for the baby and the mother are shown in the chart below.

In spite of the advantages of breast-feeding, it should not be done if the mother's or father's attitude toward it is not good. Studies have shown that children who were bottle-fed as infants are just as healthy, happy, and well-adjusted as those who were breast-fed. The love the baby receives during a feeding period is far more important than the method of feeding.

The Baby's Formula

Even a breast-fed baby sometimes gets some milk from a bottle. This is not just

---

Advantages and Disadvantages of Breast-Feeding

Advantages	Disadvantages
To the Mother	**To the Mother**
The baby's sucking stimulates her breasts and helps speed the return of her uterus to its former size and condition.	Breast-feeding keeps her more housebound than bottle-feeding does.
Breast-feeding saves the time, energy, and cost of making a formula.	Breast-feeding often leads to a temporary gain in weight.
Breast-feeding is psychologically valuable. The mother feels that she is giving something that no one else can.	Breast-feeding may, in some cases, make her feel uncomfortable, tired, nervous, and irritable.
To the Baby	**To the Baby**
Breast-feeding takes away the possibility of getting contaminated milk.	Breast-feeding does not always supply the same amount of milk. At times, there may not be enough.
Breast milk has ingredients that cannot be completely copied by a formula.	If the mother becomes tense, nervous, or overtired, the amount and quality of her milk will be affected.
Digestive upsets and constipation are rare among breast-fed babies.	Breast-fed babies often become so used to being fed by one person that they have a hard time adjusting to being fed by other people when breast-feeding ends.
The active sucking needed to draw milk from the breast stimulates the development of the lower part of the baby's face.	

milk, but a formula made of milk, water, and a sweetener. It is made to be as much like breast milk as possible. Some doctors prefer fresh milk; others prefer evaporated or powdered milk. Everyday granulated sugar is used most often, but some doctors prescribe brown sugar or corn syrup as the sweetener.

The amount of each ingredient in the formula depends on the baby's age and weight. The amounts of water and sweetener are gradually lessened as the baby gets older. When babies are 6 or 7 months old, they are able to take milk alone.

No one formula is just right for all babies. If a baby has a hard time digesting fresh, evaporated, or powdered milk, lactic acid or sour milk may be used in the formula instead.

To ease the work of formula-making, many doctors recommend the use of prepackaged formulas and throw-away bottles. This takes away the need to sterilize the bottles and boil the formula. However, this is more costly than the old-fashioned way of making a formula.

Burping the Baby

While they are feeding, babies usually swallow air. It happens whether they feed from a bottle or from the mother's breast. It is most likely to happen if the baby cries during feeding.

The baby can be burped in two ways. You can sit the baby upright on your lap and gently rub the stomach or back until the burp comes. Or, you can hold the baby upright in your arms with the head resting on your shoulder. Gently pat the baby's back until burping occurs. Robert Capece

The swallowed air takes up room in the stomach, making the baby uncomfortably full. Unless something is done to remove the air, the baby may get stomach pains and may spit up some of the undigested milk. Removing the air is known as *burping* or *bubbling*.

If babies slow down while eating, even though they have eaten little, it usually means that they need to be burped. All babies, at least until they are 3 months old, should be burped after a feeding period. Often they need to be burped in the middle of a meal. After 3 or 4 months of age, babies help with the burping. By 5 or 6 months of age, they will have learned how to burp by themselves.

Amount of Milk Needed
During the early months of life, nourishment comes mainly from milk. The best way to judge whether babies are getting enough is by their weight gain over a period of a week and by how they act between feedings.

The weekly gain in weight for babies under 2 months of age should be, roughly, between 4 and 6 ounces (113 and 170 grams). From then until they are 6 months old, they should gain 6 to 8 ounces (170 to 227 grams) weekly.

When babies wake up and cry a half hour or more before their next feeding, and when they gulp food once it is given to them, it could mean that they are not receiving enough.

For the first six months of life, the amount of milk babies should get at each feeding goes from about 1 ounce (28 grams) during the first week to 4 to 6 ounces (113 to 170 grams) at 2 months, and 5 to 7 ounces (142 to 198 grams) be-

tween 4 and 6 months. After that time, babies will need less milk. By that age they will be eating other foods.

Schedule of Feeding
It takes time for a baby to learn to be hungry at a certain hour. These days, doctors advise using a flexible feeding schedule during the early weeks of life. A schedule that meets the needs of one baby may fall far short of meeting the needs of other babies. As a result, attitudes toward feeding schedules are more relaxed now than they were twenty-five years or so ago.

This does not mean that doctors want to do away with feeding schedules. Nor do they suggest feeding babies whenever they cry.

Babies need guidance and help in learning to eat according to a schedule. Like all learning, this takes time. Doctors advise parents to encourage babies to *want* to eat at scheduled times. What these scheduled times are will vary according to the baby's age and general health. The chart on page 40 gives some ideas for feeding times during the baby's first year of life.

Weaning
In the strictest sense of the word, *weaning* means getting a baby used to drinking milk from a cup instead of sucking milk from the breast or bottle. In the broader sense, it also means getting the baby used to taking food by biting and chewing instead of only by sucking. Today it is believed that weaning should begin no later than 6 months of age.

To make weaning an easy adjustment for a baby, doctors recommend that it be

When weaning is delayed beyond the age of 6 months, it becomes one of the major feeding problems of babyhood.

Taking food in a new form and in a new way is a major adjustment for a baby. It can be made with least emotional strain for the baby if it is done gradually.

The longer babies are allowed to get food in a liquid form and with one taste, the more they will fight against learning to bite and chew foods with different tastes.

While milk is the "perfect food" for babies, it has little of certain elements, especially iron. Normal growth and development will not take place unless the baby gets those elements from other foods.

done gradually—step by step. Beginning around the age of 2 or 3 months, babies should start taking food in new forms and by new methods. At the beginning of the meal, when babies are extra hungry, they should be given the milk from the nipple. Otherwise, they are likely to swallow more air than usual in their hurry to satisfy their hunger. Later in the meal, when their hunger is partly satisfied, babies can drink from a cup or be fed with a spoon.

If weaning is started before the ninth month, it usually does not take more than a month to finish.

Introduction of New Foods

Before the end of the baby's first year, the baby should be eating foods other than milk. Only one new food should be introduced at a time. It should be given to the baby at each meal for several days. There are two reasons for this: first, the baby becomes used to the taste and feel of the new food more quickly, and second, it gives parents a chance to see if the food agrees with the baby. If a certain food causes vomiting, skin rashes, or diarrhea, it should be taken out of the diet, at least at that age.

Since babies do not have teeth when some new foods are introduced, the foods must be strained or sieved so they do not have to be chewed. To make the new taste and feel easier for the baby to adjust to, doctors recommend that the food be mixed with milk. Gradually, the milk can be lessened and then left out. As the baby's teeth come in, the food can be mashed instead of sieved. Later, it can be chopped in small pieces, to encourage the baby to chew.

Most of the foods needed for a baby can now be bought in a ready-to-heat form. These prepared foods come in baby and junior types. Baby food is sieved, and junior food is chopped. The change from baby to junior foods is usually made around the age of 9 months.

For Action

Ask the parents of babies you sit for or relatives, friends, or neighbors who have young children how they introduced new foods to their babies. Find out about how old the babies were when each new food was tried.

New foods should be introduced gradually into the baby's diet during the second half of the first year. It may seem strange, but a baby has to learn to eat and get used to different types of food. Nancy Hays/Monkmeyer

Suggested Ages for Introducing New Foods

Orange Juice   Between 1 and 3 months of age, the baby should be given a small amount, diluted with water. Gradually more is given and the water left out.

Cereal   Between 1 and 4 months of age, precooked cereal is mixed with formula and given in small amounts. Gradually more cereal is given, and milk takes the place of the formula.

Fruits   As soon as the baby becomes used to cereals, stewed fruits and mashed ripe bananas can be introduced into the diet. Later, a piece of peeled apple or pear can be given to the baby as a between-meal snack.

Vegetables   A week or two after fruits are introduced into the diet, strained vegetables, mixed with the formula, can be given.

Meat   Between 2 and 6 months of age, strained meat, mixed with the formula or milk, can be given. Later, the meat can be chopped into small pieces. Meat soups, made with barley, rice, or pureed vegetables, can be introduced at the same time as meat.

Potatoes, Noodles, and Rice   When soft and in small pieces, they can be given from 6 months of age on.

Eggs   When the baby is 4 to 6 months old, the sieved yolk of a hard-boiled egg can be put on meat or vegetables. By 9 months, a whole egg, soft-boiled or scrambled, can be given.

Puddings   As interest in milk gets less, puddings made of milk can add to the milk in the diet.

Fish   Between 10 and 12 months of age, boiled or broiled fish with all bones removed can be given.

Finger Foods   As soon as teething begins, toast or zwieback can be given to encourage biting and chewing.

Sample Meals for Babies

6 to 12 Months

Breakfast Orange juice; cereal; egg yolk; milk.

Dinner Meat or meat soup; sieved vegetable; pudding or gelatin dessert; milk.

Supper Cereal; potato, noodles, or rice; stewed fruit or pudding made with milk and egg; milk.

Between Meals Fruit or tomato juice; toast or zwieback with butter or margarine.

12 Months to 2 Years

Breakfast Orange juice; cereal; whole egg; toast; milk.

Dinner Meat, fish, or meat soup; potato, rice, or noodles; vegetable; stewed fruit, pudding, or both; milk.

Supper Cereal; fruit or pudding made with egg; milk.

Between Meals Fruit or tomato juice; piece of fresh apple, pear, or banana; toast or zwieback with butter or margarine.

As new foods are introduced into a baby's diet, meals begin to look more and more like those of older children and even adults. As a result, the baby can be fed with the rest of the family. Not only the food, but also the feeding schedule becomes more like the family's. The chart above gives some sample meals for babies. If prepared foods are used, one-half jar of each kind is usually enough at first. Later, the baby will need a full jar at each meal.

Vitamins

From the time babies are 2 weeks old, they are given a vitamin preparation of vitamins A, C, and D. This is given with a dropper. When babies are old enough, they can take it from a spoon. The preparation is almost tasteless compared to the fish-liver oil once prescribed for babies. Few babies fight against it, and few have bad reactions. The vitamin preparation is usually given when orange juice is given, in midmorning. The time and amount will be decided by the doctor.

Clothing the Baby

Gone are the days when babies were buried in layers of clothes and blankets. Our great-grandmothers would say that today's babies would "catch their death of cold" the way they are dressed.

Modern heating in the American home is partly the reason for this change. Also partly responsible are advances in knowledge. People used to think that the baby lived in an abnormally hot environment in the mother's body for nine months before being born. We now know that the temperature in the womb is about the same as the mother's body temperature (about 98.6° Fahrenheit, 37° Celsius). And, of course, the baby is naked.

Even in the hospital during the first days of life, today's babies are not wrapped in blankets except when taken from the nursery to the mother's room for nursing. They may have a light blanket laid loosely over their bodies and legs, but that is all.

After they leave the hospital, today's babies have the least possible binding clothing and covering. The reason for this is that babies must use their muscles if they are to develop normally. The more freedom the babies have, the better the chance that they will use their muscles.

Of course, when babies are taken out-of-doors in the cold of winter, they must be bundled up, as adults are. But the rest of the time they do not need the binding clothes and blankets of babies of the past.

Clothes for the Infant

The most important item of clothing for a young baby is the diaper. Some are made of soft, absorbent cloth. Many are easy to wash and need no ironing. Others are made of paper and are thrown away when soiled.

The washable diapers are folded to fit the baby's body. After being put between the baby's legs, the front and back parts of the folded diaper are pinned together on either side of the baby's shirt. When it is important to keep baby's clothes dry, waterproof panties can be used to cover the diaper.

For added warmth, the shirt and diaper can be covered with a sacque or kimono-style garment. It opens down the back and is fastened by tapes. Another favorite covering for the baby is a one-piece stretchy jumpsuit. For very hot weather, these coverings will not be needed.

In cold weather, young babies can be dressed in buntings when taken outdoors. A bunting is an all-in-one garment opening down the front with a zipper. It looks like a bag with a hood to protect the baby's head, neck, and ears. When the weather is cool, a sweater and lightweight cap are enough outer clothing. Since a baby's legs are completely covered by a blanket, socks or booties are usually not needed. Baby clothes are made of materials that need no ironing.

Clothes for the Older Baby

By the time babies are 5 or 6 months old, they have outgrown the clothes they wore as infants. They are also now ready for clothes that meet the needs of a more active life. Diapers and shirts will still be worn. For sleep, pajamas are better than sacques and kimonos. While awake, clothes that do not get in the way of movement are better than wrappers. Shoes and socks are not

---

Why Babies Should Not Be Overdressed

The fewer clothes babies wear, the easier they are to put on and the less frustrated babies will be.

Babies must be free to move different parts of their bodies to exercise their muscles. Any clothing that gets in the way of these movements will slow growth and control over the different parts of the body.

Because the sweat glands of babies do not work very well, being overdressed is likely to cause prickly heat and other skin rashes. The fewer the clothes, the more contact the skin has with the air to prevent or lessen the rashes.

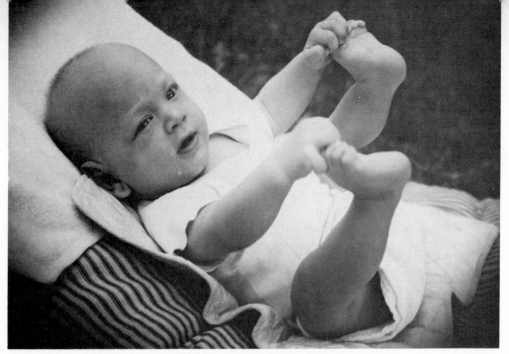

A change in clothing needs occurs with each stage babies go through.
Above: Tom Carew/Monkmeyer; left: George Zimbel/Monkmeyer;
right: Erika Stone/Peter Arnold

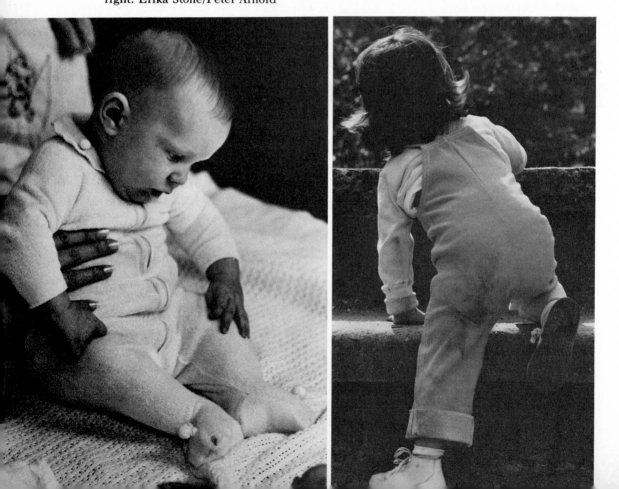

needed until the baby walks outdoors, unless the floors are cold. Babies can get a firmer grip and strengthen their muscles if the feet are not hampered by socks and shoes.

For outdoor clothing during cold weather, the baby wears a snowsuit instead of a bunting. Like the bunting, this is an all-in-one garment that zips up the front. Unlike the bunting, the snowsuit has sleeves with mittens at the ends and feet attached to leggings. For cool weather, sweaters over their indoor clothes give babies enough protection.

Clothes for the Toddler

During their second year, babies are beginning to walk. They are also being toilet trained. Training panties replace a diaper for daytime wear. Diapers, though, are still used at night and for naps. The training panties should be covered with waterproof panties until the baby is fully toilet trained. It is a good idea to leave off the waterproof panties at times when it is not serious if the toddler does become wet. Feeling the wet panties, especially as they become cold and clammy, gives toddlers an added reason to make it known when they have to go to the toilet.

For play, toddlers wear clothes that let them move easily, such as shirts with shorts, pants, or skirts. They are usually made of cotton knit or synthetic fabric that is easy to wash and needs no ironing. In cool weather, overalls and sweaters are worn. In very cold weather, a snowsuit is needed. During the hot weather of summer, sunsuits with only the training panties under them can be worn.

Shoes with flexible soles and soft tops are worn until the toddler has mastered the skill of walking. Then the baby needs a stronger shoe for support. To avoid blisters, socks should be worn, even in hot weather. Many doctors recommend that toddlers go barefoot in the house or on grass or sand to encourage the development of the foot and leg muscles.

The best sleeping clothes for toddlers are pajamas made of thin cotton material for summer and of warmer cotton flannel for winter. There are also bathrobes that toddlers can wear over their pajamas for added warmth if they play before bedtime.

Because playsuits are colorful and often gaily decorated, toddlers do not really need special dress-up clothing. At this age children are still unaware of what their clothing looks like. When parents want their children to look special, clean clothes are all that is needed to give the children a dressed-up look.

Sleep for Babies

The amount of sleep babies need is closely related to the rate of growth. Newborn babies sleep about 80 percent of the time. Their rapid growth goes on for several weeks after birth. As growth begins to slow down toward the middle of the first year of life, less sleep is needed. The 1-year-old sleeps only about 50 percent of the time. This sleep pattern remains almost unchanged through the second year.

As babies' stomachs enlarge, they are able to take more food at each feeding. As a result, they sleep for longer periods than they could earlier. Except for morning and afternoon naps, the 1-year-old will be awake from six or seven o'clock in the morning until six or seven in the evening. This is also true for the toddler.

Doctors take a far more relaxed attitude toward the amount of sleep babies should have than they did in the past. They stress that sleep must be tailored to each baby's needs.

Naps
Beginning around 6 months of age and going on through their first year, babies usually nap about an hour in the morning and one to two hours after the noon meal. Most babies are so busy during their waking hours that they accept naps without rebellion.

However, as they near their second birthday, many babies begin to fight against the morning nap and cry when put to bed. If they resist for several days, the morning nap can be omitted and a longer afternoon nap taken. Crying is often more tiring than not having a nap. When babies are tired, they will sleep until rested.

The Baby's Bed
Infants need a cozy, safe place for sleeping. However, there is no need for parents to buy a bassinet, as it serves for only a couple of months before it is too small for the baby. A large carrying basket, a carriage, or a section of the crib can be used until the baby is 2 to 3 months old and needs more room for sleeping comfort.

Doctors agree that pillows are not needed and, in fact, can be harmful. They can throw the baby's head out of line, causing a slight curvature in the neck. Even more important, babies could smother if pillows accidently got over their faces. Babies are not strong enough to push the pillows away. Top sheets and bedspreads are not needed either. What is needed is an easy way to protect the mattress pad that keeps the mattress dry. A fitted, no-iron sheet over the mattress and pad can be changed often if it becomes wet.

Sleep Position
Doctors favor a stomach position for the sleeping baby. It has advantages other sleep positions lack. However, babies should also be placed on their backs and sides for part of the sleep time.

There are reasons for changing the baby's sleep position. First, the baby's bones are so soft that they are easily misshapen if too much pressure is placed on them for too long a time. Second, shifting of the sleep position results in a deeper and more restful sleep. Between their fourth and sixth months, babies can move their bodies by rolling. They will then be able to find the most comfortable sleep position by themselves.

Safety in Sleep
In the past, babies were snugly wrapped in blankets to protect them, not only from drafts and cold, but also from being smothered by their bedding. Today, sleeping bags are often used instead. They are made of different materials for hot and cold weather. Sleeping bags cover the baby's entire body except for the head. They should be large enough to let arms and legs move freely inside.

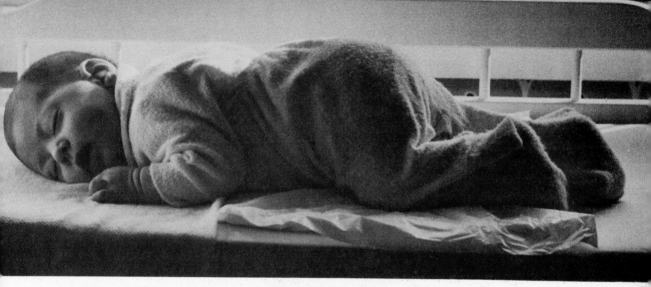

One of the most relaxing sleep positions for babies is lying on their stomachs.
Erika Stone/Peter Arnold

For Action

Visit the nursery department of a store, and ask to see the safety devices the store has for babies' cribs. The three most widely sold are sleeping bags, safety belts, and blanket clips. Examine each of these carefully, and read the instructions that go with them to see exactly how they work.

By the time a baby is 16 to 18 months old, the sleeping bag is usually not needed. Babies then have enough coordination and muscle strength to keep themselves from getting caught in their blankets.

The Baby's Bath

Infants should not be bathed in a tub until the tied-off umbilical cord falls off. This usually happens one or two weeks after birth. Until then, babies are sponged off with warm water and rubbed with baby oil.

A large plastic or enamel dishpan is good enough for the baby's first bathtub. Warm water is poured 2 to 3 inches

Advantages of Sleeping on the Stomach

Babies can stretch to their full length. This helps them straighten their legs and use their lungs to full capacity.

Pressure on bones of the skull, which are still soft, is prevented. This lessens the possibility of babies having a flat spot at the back of their heads.

There is less chance that babies will gag or choke on food that may be burped up during sleep.

Babies are encouraged to lift up their heads and chest with the aid of their hands and arms. This strengthens their back muscles.

Babies are far less likely to kick off their coverings.

(5 to 7.6 centimeters) deep in the pan. A diaper or towel placed on the bottom of the tub keeps the baby from slipping.

It is never safe to leave babies even for a minute while they are in a tub. Before beginning the bath, everything should be ready for it. This means having a sponge or washcloth, soap, towel, baby oil, powder, and clean diapers nearby.

For Discussion

Suggest some of the experiences babies might have to make them afraid of their baths. Which of these can be prevented and how? Why is it serious for babies to be afraid of being bathed in a tub even though they can be kept clean without being placed in a tub?

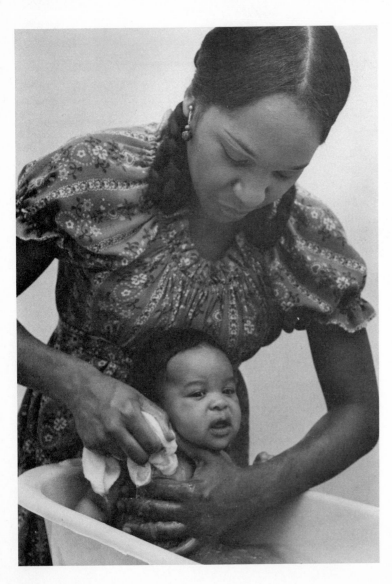

Until babies can sit up by themselves, they need firm, gentle support while being bathed.
Erika Stone/Peter Arnold

78

Why Babies May Fear Their Baths

The Water Temperature Is it too hot or too cold? Did the person who is bathing the baby test it by using an elbow or just by putting a hand in the water?

Slipping in the Tub Was a rubber mat, diaper, or bath towel put in the bottom of the tub where the baby was being bathed to prevent slipping?

Soap in the Eyes Was the baby's face washed with soap and water or just water? Most doctors recommend not using soap on a baby's face.

Soapy Water over the Face during a Shampoo To remove the shampoo, the baby's head should be tilted back when the head is rinsed. Make sure that none of the soapy water gets on the face or into the eyes.

Being Held Too Tightly Parents, afraid of harming babies during a bath, hold them more tightly than is needed. This angers and frightens the babies.

Getting Water in the Mouth If babies get some water into their mouths, they may choke and become frightened.

Many doctors recommend that young babies be bathed in a tub several times a week. Between tub baths, sponge baths are enough. Babies' faces should be washed with water, but not soap, and the hair shampooed only once or twice a week. If the baby's head has little hair, it can be washed daily when the face is washed.

By the time babies are 6 or 7 months old and can sit up with only a small amount of support at their back, they are ready for a regular tub bath. There should be only 2 or 3 inches (5 to 7.6 centimeters) of water in the tub. Babies should never, under any conditions, be left alone in the tub. Older babies usually have a daily bath and a shampoo two or three times a week. Soap still should not be used on their faces.

Some babies develop a fear of the bath and cry whenever they see the preparations for it. This fear may come from many causes, several of which are listed in the accompanying chart. If fear of the bath develops, it is best to stop bathing the baby for a time. After several weeks, the tub bath can be tried again at the end of the sponge bath. Most babies, especially if they are under a year old, will have forgotten the unpleasant experience that caused the fear. If the fear is still strong, talk the matter over with the baby's doctor.

Besides a daily bath, older babies should get used to having their faces and hands washed before and after every meal, before going to bed, after toileting, and after play. Most young babies accept this in a matter-of-fact way. As they grow older and are expected to do some of the washing themselves, they often fight against washing their hands and faces. This is why it is good to develop the habit before the resistance starts.

Care of Baby Teeth

Doctors and dentists urge parents to have their baby's teeth checked as early as the second year and at least once a

Care of Gums   Even before the first tooth cuts through the gums, rubbing the gums will help keep them healthy and prevent some of the discomfort of teething. This should be done until the baby is old enough to take it over.

Brushing the Teeth   As soon as the first tooth appears, it should be brushed. It is never too early to teach babies about brushing their teeth.   There are soft-bristled toothbrushes and mild-tasting toothpastes made just for children. Brushing is recommended after every feeding and before babies are put to bed for the night.

Diet   While the baby teeth are completing their development and cutting through the gums, the permanent teeth are also developing in the gums behind them. A good diet now is even more important than it will be after teething is over. A good diet is a well-balanced diet. Often vitamins are prescribed by the doctor. Even the best diet, however, can be spoiled by eating too many snacks between meals.

year after that.   Tooth decay can develop very quickly.   If children are to have good permanent teeth, care must be taken of their baby teeth.   See the chart above.

For Discussion

Why are many babies, especially during the second year, given lollipops, candy, cookies, and ice cream between meals when it is so widely known that eating sweets between meals is bad for the teeth? What would you suggest giving instead?   Would these serve the same purpose as sweets?   Give reasons for your answer.

If babies have trouble cutting teeth, the doctor should be told before anything is rubbed on the gums to ease the pain and before any medicine is given. Doctors often recommend rubbing the baby's gums with warm water or baby oil. This keeps the gums soft and helps the teeth pierce through the gums more easily.   Only when the discomfort is so great that it leads to restless sleep, loss of appetite, and fever do most doctors say any other treatment is all right. They do, however, suggest giving teething babies zwieback, toast, and raw apples to eat to massage their gums. Chewing on safe rubber toys or teething rings can also ease some of the discomfort of teething.

Going Outdoors

Unless it cannot be avoided, babies should not be taken outdoors until they weigh at least 10 pounds (4.5 kilograms).   Most babies weigh 10 pounds (4.5 kilograms) by the time they are 3 weeks old.   However, if babies are 3 weeks old and weigh only 8 pounds (3.5 kilograms), they should not be taken outdoors unless the temperature is 60° Fahrenheit (16° Celsius) or over.

Babies can get fresh air indoors as well as outdoors.   The windows and doors of the room can be opened and the room aired while the baby is not there. After the windows are closed, the baby can be returned to the room.

The amount of time babies spend outdoors in a carriage begins with fifteen to twenty minutes. It is then increased gradually to several hours, depending on the weather.

Whenever the weather is good, someone should try to take the baby for a short ride in the carriage. This has a psychological as well as physical value. By the time they are 6 months old, babies become bored and fretful unless they have some stimulation. One way to get it is from a change of scene. When babies are old enough to stay awake when outdoors, they are able to be propped up in a carriage, a carrying basket, or a carrying pack worn by an adult. From this position, babies have a chance to see new sights.

Toddlers, even more than babies, need psychological stimulation. Outings can be walks to different parts of the neighborhood where they can see new things and new people.

Exercises for Babies

Because they are always moving, babies exercise many of their muscles on their own. They turn their heads, kick their legs, wave their arms, and move their fingers. But such activity does not exercise *all* muscles. Babies cannot exercise their trunk muscles until they can sit or stand. Nor can they exercise their ankle and feet muscles until they are able to stand up. Therefore, good physical care of the baby should include daily exercise periods.

Besides their getting sunshine and fresh air, babies are surrounded by a world of wonders when outdoors. Erika Stone/Peter Arnold

Exercise periods for babies should begin around the third week of life. By then, they have completely recovered from birth and have adjusted to their environment. At first, exercise periods of ten to fifteen minutes should be given. This should be increased gradually to about one-half hour.

For their exercise period, babies should be completely naked, even without diapers. Only when they are doing exercises with an adult should babies be taken out of the crib or playpen. Babies never should be on a raised surface unless someone is with them all the time. The playpen is a safe place for the exercise period when the babies are able to roll, by the third or fourth month.

Part of each exercise period should be for free movements of the head, arms, and legs. Babies should be encouraged to make these movements by holding objects for them to look at from different positions. Half of the exercise period should be for exercises that need the aid of an adult. Suggestions for exercises that help develop different parts of the baby's body are given in the chart on page 83.

When babies reach the age of 6 or 8 months, they try to pull themselves to a sitting position by holding onto the bars of the crib or playpen. Several months later, they try to pull themselves to a standing position. This helps babies develop the muscles they formerly

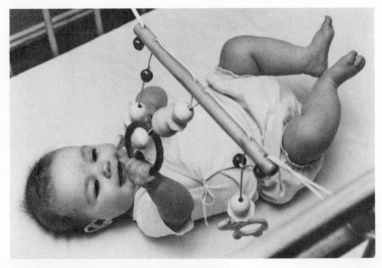

Gym sets for cribs enable babies to exercise muscles while they amuse themselves. Babies need help in exercising muscles they cannot exercise alone. Left: Lew Merrim/Monkmeyer; below: Kenneth Karp

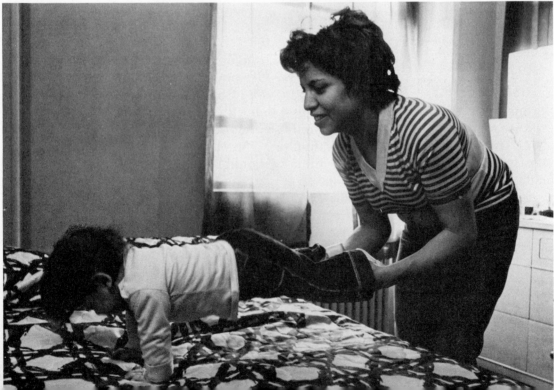

could not exercise for themselves. However, the daily exercise period should be kept up through the growth years of childhood, at least for those children whose chances for active outdoor play are limited. Children who spend much time in active neighborhood play, such as running, climbing, bike riding, and ball playing, do not need a home exercise period.

For Discussion

Which muscles are hardest for babies and toddlers to exercise for themselves? Why is it important for someone else to help babies exercise these muscles? Refer to the accompanying chart for suggested exercises for different parts of the baby's body.

Exercises for Babies

For Back Muscles   While the baby is lying on the back, let the baby grip your hands firmly. Gently pull the baby to a sitting position and slowly let him or her return to the first position. Repeat 5 times and gradually increase to 10 times. When the baby is 6 or 7 months old, hold the feet and let the baby walk on the hands, like a wheelbarrow. Do this until the baby gets tired.

For Trunk Muscles   While the baby is lying on the back, grasp each hand firmly with yours and pull the baby slowly first to the right and then to the left. Repeat 5 and later 10 times. After the baby can sit, have the baby lie on the stomach with hands on the floor at shoulder height and push up the trunk by raising the head and body. When the baby can stand firmly, as he or she nears the second birthday, have the baby put her or his hands on the sides of the waistline and slowly bend the trunk back and forth and from right to left.

For Leg Muscles   Hold each of the feet, just above the ankles, and gently push both legs up to the stomach. Then straighten the legs one at a time. Repeat these exercises 5 times and gradually increase to 10 times.

For Feet and Ankle Muscles   Take hold of the baby's right foot and gently move it from right to left, backward and forward, 5 to 10 times. Repeat with the left foot.

For Arm Muscles   Holding each of the baby's hands, slowly bend the arms so that the hands touch the shoulders. Repeat 5 to 10 times. Then pull the arms across the chest so that the right hand touches the left shoulder and the left hand, the right shoulder. Repeat 5 to 10 times.

For Finger Muscles   Hold a dangling object in front of the baby. Let the baby grasp it and then take it away, repeating 5 to 10 times. Hold each of the fingers, one at a time, with your thumb and forefinger, and gently bend it forward toward the palm 5 to 10 times.

Highlights of Chapter 5

☐ There are advantages and disadvantages to both breast- and bottle-feeding.

☐ The amount of milk a baby needs and the schedule of feeding change as the baby gets older.

☐ Weaning means learning to take food by biting and chewing instead of only by sucking. It is usually accompanied by a gradual reduction in the amount of milk a baby drinks.

☐ The amount and type of clothing babies need change as the babies change from being fairly inactive infants to being active toddlers.

☐ The amount of sleep a baby needs is related to the rate of growth and the pattern of feeding.

☐ Recommended ways of bathing a baby and caring for the teeth stress encouraging the baby to cooperate.

☐ Fresh air is basic to good health in babies.

☐ Exercises to strengthen all body muscles should begin early in life and be used throughout the growth years of childhood.

Suggested Activities

1. Find out how some of your friends and relatives feel about breast-feeding babies. Try to choose males and females of various age groups. Record their answers and discuss in class what is responsible for the different attitudes.

2. What are some reasons for differences in the amount of food a baby takes at each feeding and in the amount of time spent in sleep from day to day? Should changes be made so that, if possible, there are no variations? Give reasons for your answer.

3. Visit the baby department of a store, and look at the different clothes needed for babies. Compare the styles and kinds of clothes for babies of different ages. What type of clothes are hard to move in? Which leave the baby the most freedom of movement?

4. Display different articles of baby clothing. Discuss what makes them easy or hard to put on and take off the baby. For example, some baby T-shirts open down the front and overlap, with snaps to close them, instead of having to be put over the baby's head.

5. Examine toothbrushes and tooth powders, or pastes, that dentists recommend for babies and young children. Compare them with brushes and pastes recommended for adults. Discuss why there are differences in the size, shape, and feel of brushes and in the flavors of the powders and pastes.

Chapter 6

Learning Body Control

Some goals of this chapter are:
- [ ] To recognize the normal pattern of body control and learn the usual ages at which different parts of the body can be controlled
- [ ] To describe how skills can be learned and what factors add to the development of skills
- [ ] To identify some of the important skills of babyhood and know when they can usually be learned

At birth, babies are so helpless that they could not survive if they were not always cared for by others. They cannot move their bodies from the positions in which they have been placed. They cannot grasp anything placed within their reach. They cannot put food into their mouths. They cannot see anything clearly. However, before the first birthday, all of this is changed. By that time, babies can do many things for themselves, if given the chance.

Pattern of Body Control

Studies of large numbers of babies have shown that control over different parts of the body develops in an orderly way as a baby matures. Body control follows the laws of developmental direction—going from head to foot and from trunk to arms and legs.

In some babies, the pattern of body control unfolds more rapidly than in others. But because the patterns are always similar, it seems clear that body control comes mainly from maturation and not from learning.

The chart on page 86 shows the approximate ages at which different parts of the baby's body come under control. Note how much later the baby gains control over the legs and feet than over the trunk muscles. This is because standing and walking call for the ability to balance the body *as well as* the ability to control the muscles. As long as the baby is top-heavy, balance is difficult.

Approximate Ages of Gaining Body Control

Head Control

1 month: follows objects with eyes for a short distance

2 months: raises head when lying on stomach

3–4 months: coordinates eyes on same object in any direction the object moves

3–4 months: controls the lip muscles to smile, spit, and form simple sounds

5 months: raises head when lying on back

5 months: holds head up when sitting with support

6–8 months: holds head up when sitting without support

Trunk Control

2 months: turns body from side to back

4 months: turns body from back to side

6 months: turns body completely around

6 months: pulls body to sitting position with help

6–9 months: sits unsupported for several minutes

Arm and Hand Control

3 months: brings hands together in front of body

3 months: grasps rattle placed in fingers

4–5 months: reaches for and grasps stationary object

5 months: accepts one object placed in hand

5–6 months: reaches for and grasps dangling object

6 months: passes a toy from one hand to the other

6–7 months: carries object to mouth

7 months: accepts two objects handed to her or him

8–9 months: picks up object with thumb used in opposition to fingers

10 months: accepts three objects handed to her or him

12–15 months: scribbles with pencil or crayon

Leg Control

7 months: crawls (lies on stomach and pushes body forward by pulling with arms and pushing with legs)

9 months: creeps (pushes body forward on hands and knees)

10 months: stands with support

12 months: stands without support

12 months: walks with support

14 months: walks without support

18 months: walks like an adult, with knees bent

18 months: climbs steps on hands and knees

Babies' muscles are so developed at birth that they are ready for use. However, the babies have to learn how to control them before the muscles can be of any real use. This muscle control develops very rapidly during the baby's first year.
Erika Stone/Peter Arnold

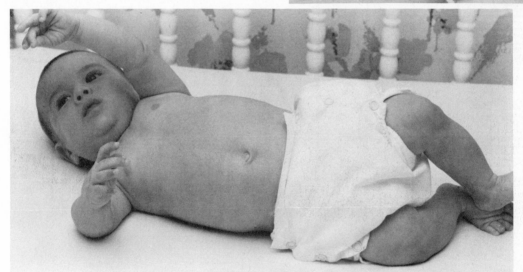

The baby will fall when trying to stand without extra support. As the legs grow longer and the feet bigger, they are better able to balance the head and trunk.

There are two reasons why it is helpful to know at what ages to expect different areas of body control. First, it warns parents and others responsible for the baby's care that the time has come to take safety measures. Before babies can roll, it is safe to put them on a bed or table while they are being dressed. But, when they can roll from side to back or back to side, the days of safety are over. Babies must then be protected from falling. When babies can grab objects held before them, anything dangerous must be kept out of reach.

Second, knowing when to expect different areas of body control leads to

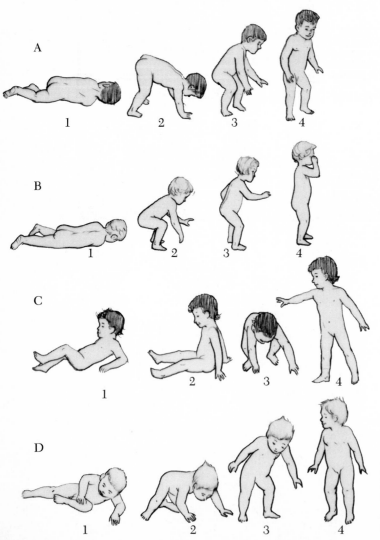

How Four Different Babies Get Up (Adapted from M. B. McGraw: *Growth: A Study of Johnny and Jimmy.* Appleton-Century-Crofts)

greater understanding of the baby's readiness to learn skills. Because the hands and arms come under control earlier than the legs and feet, it means that the baby can learn hand skills before leg skills.

Similarities in Patterns of Body Control

The ways in which babies gain body control also show the role of maturation. For example, babies start to stand up by rolling their bodies so that they can push themselves to a sitting position or to an all-fours position. Next, with the aid of their arms, they push themselves into an upright position. The drawing at left shows how four babies go from lying down to standing. Note how similar their patterns are.

When babies first stand or walk, they try to balance themselves. Their legs are placed wide apart, knees are stiff, toes are pointed outward, and arms are held straight or pulled up tightly to their bodies. Gradually, babies relax this wooden-soldier posture. They then stand or walk with toes pointed forward, knees slightly bent, arms and hands relaxed at the sides of their bodies, and heads held upright instead of forward.

Skills

A *skill* is a series of movements that has been learned through practice. It calls for the coordination, or working together, of nerves and muscles. When a skill is well learned, it becomes a *habit*; the person does not have to think about it.

Body control and skills are not the same thing. Body control is usually lim-ited to the coordinated movements of the body that come with maturity. Skills, on the other hand, are the coordinated movements of the body that come from learning. Babies are not born with skills; they must learn them. On the other hand, all babies are born with the ability to control the body. This unfolds during the early months of life. Body control is the groundwork on which skills will be built later.

The major part of babyhood is spent in the unfolding of important natural traits. Thus, the baby will not be ready to learn many skills until babyhood is nearly over. However, babies are then ready to learn the basics for such skills as dressing, feeding, and bathing themselves; amusing themselves; and communicating with others. These are the skills that will help babies become independent.

It is important that the groundwork for skills be well laid in babyhood. Then the skills learned later will make it possible for the child to do things with the least effort and wasted motion. Although poor skills can be replaced if the child learns them over, this is a long and hard task. It is also discouraging for a child to unlearn what he or she has tried so hard to learn.

How Skills Are Learned

Skills can be learned by trial and error, in which babies do things on their own. The baby tries one thing and, if it does not work, tries another and still another. Finally, by chance, the baby hits upon an act that works. In self-feeding, for example, the baby may grasp a spoon in one way and try to carry the food to the mouth. If the baby can get enough food to satisfy hunger in this way, she or he will repeat the act over and over again until it develops into a habit. On the other hand, if more food is being spilled than is getting into the baby's mouth, the baby may try holding the spoon in a different way.

Trial-and-error learning is the least efficient way to learn. Training—or learning with guidance—is the most efficient way. *Training* does not mean, as the term may suggest, a classroom lesson or a sports workout led by a coach or trainer. Training of babies happens in a natural, relaxed way in the everyday course of events in the home or child-care center. An adult trains a baby by watching, gently guiding the baby's hand when needed, leading the baby through the desired pattern almost as if it were a game, and sharing enjoyment of the baby's newfound skills. Training should not be a grim chore or a stern responsibility.

Nor does training mean that the person teaching the baby the skill does all the work and the baby waits to be molded into a new form. It is a cooperative effort between the baby and the trainer. If this effort is to have good results, nine essentials must be present. They are explained in the accompany-

---

Essentials for Learning Skills

Readiness to Learn This is shown when the baby has real interest in the activity and when the baby's efforts bring improvement.

A Strong Desire to Learn Without this, the baby will not put forth the effort needed for learning.

Encouragement Interest begins to drop when the newness of a task wears off and when learning becomes hard. Thus, the baby's desire to learn must be kept alive by encouragement.

Chances to Practice To learn a skill, it must be done over and over again until the nerves and muscles are trained to work together. Many chances to practice will strengthen these coordinated movements.

A Good Model "Practice makes perfect" only when the practice is a copy of a good model.

Practice until the Skill is Well Learned How long this practice will have to go on depends on how hard the skill is. When the skill can be done without thinking, there has probably been enough practice.

Guidance in Copying the Model Babies need someone to guide their movements and to help them copy a model until they get the "feel" of the right movements. Then guidance can be relaxed.

Supervision of Practice When learners repeat, over and over again, the movements they have been taught to make, close supervision is needed to make sure that they will not repeat mistakes. This supervision is most important during the early stages of learning.

Few Distractions In the early stages of learning a skill, learners must give undivided attention to what they are doing. Anything that distracts them slows down the learning and leads to errors. The harder the skill, the more harmful any distractions will be.

ing chart. Some of these essentials are supplied by the learner and some by the trainer. In any case, not one can be left out if the results are to be of value to the baby.

It is important that a baby learn one new skill at a time and master it before beginning to learn a new one. For instance, the baby should master the skill of using a spoon before trying to learn to use a fork. And the use of the fork should be mastered before the use of a knife is tried.

For Discussion

How might stressing the importance of training babies carefully in some skills frighten parents and others responsible for the baby's care? What can happen if the parent becomes very nervous, worried, or determined that the baby must learn skills "just so"?

Unless this training method is followed, the baby may become confused. Once a skill has been well learned, however, it is so natural that the movements of that skill are not likely to be mixed up with the movements of a new skill.

Mastering only one skill at a time lengthens the learning time. It may mean that parents must spend more time teaching skills than some feel is needed. However, since babies can keep their minds on a task for only a short period, the time parents really spend is not as great as it may seem at first. It is simply spread out over a long period.

For Discussion

Many students say that they can study better with their radios turned on than they can in a quiet room. Is this similar to a baby's trying to learn a skill when there are distractions? In what ways do these learning situations call for the learner's attention?

Some Important Skills of Babyhood

There are some skills that are important to a baby because they lessen the helplessness that babies find so frustrating. Among these are skills for taking care of physical needs, such as self-feeding, dressing, bathing, cleaning teeth, combing hair, and learning to amuse oneself by playing with toys.

There are also some skills that are fairly unimportant to the baby but that will become more and more important in early childhood years. Among these skills are the social-help skills, which make a person able to help others. Among the social-help skills are helping the parents with household chores or helping playmates in cooperative play.

There are other important skills that the baby is not ready to master. However, the basics for these skills can be learned in babyhood. Among these are the skills needed to control the organs of elimination.

Eating Skills

In the first four or five months of life, the baby's eating is infantile. This means that food must be sucked into the mouth and swallowed without chewing.

For this reason, food must be in a liquid form.

One of the greatest problems in changing to more mature forms of eating comes when liquids are drunk instead of sucked. In early attempts to drink, the baby will most likely suck in air. This will cause choking or even vomiting. The hungrier the baby is, the greater will be the likelihood of gulping liquids and sucking in air.

Learning to drink can best be mastered if a cup replaces the nipple at the end of a feeding period. The baby's hunger is so nearly satisfied then that there is less likelihood of gulping. This learning is aided by the use of a training cup with holes that allow the liquid to come through a little at a time. After the baby gets the feel of drinking, a regular cup can be used in place of a training cup.

Biting seems to be a natural form of behavior that takes place even before the teeth cut through the gums. Before the biting can work well, however, the baby must learn how large a bite to take. If the parent sometimes holds onto the food—a piece of apple, toast, or zwieback—it will help the baby learn. However, since it is important for babies to learn to feed themselves, the baby should be allowed to hold the food most of the time. The parent should watch closely, and if the baby takes much too large a bite, the parent can quickly remove it from the mouth before the baby chokes on it.

Because babies do not know exactly how to go about chewing they may spit, hold food in the mouth, or chew only with the front teeth. However, after a while they learn to use gums and tongue as well as their few teeth to mash the food. It is a messy period, and parents need a lot of patience. If the baby has a lot of trouble with chewing, it may be best to go back to a soft diet for a little while.

Babies also need to learn how to swallow the chewed solid foods. Swallowing liquids is a natural reaction, but

One of the first skills a baby is interested in learning is self-feeding. Richard Nowitz

swallowing solids, even after chewing, must be learned. Sometimes it helps the baby if the head is tilted back slightly so the food can rest on the throat. This stimulates the throat muscles. Also, a swallow of milk will help wash down the chewed food. This should be done only until the baby gets the feel of swallowing.

Self-Feeding Skills

Babies' readiness to feed themselves is shown by the way they try to hold the bottle and by the way they carry the spoon to their mouths even when there is no food in it. The period between 6 and 18 months of age is a very important time in developing self-feeding skills. At this time, babies have a strong desire to learn to feed themselves.

An important introduction to self-feeding is finger-feeding. Babies who are given a piece of toast, apple, or zwieback have the feel of carrying food up to the mouth. They will make marked headway with eating utensils, such as spoons and forks, if given a chance to learn and guidance in how to hold and use them.

Babies differ in their readiness to learn the skills of self-feeding. Therefore, it is impossible to give exact ages at which any one baby can be expected to use the different eating utensils. However, studies of babies have given average ages for these different activities. They are shown in the accompanying chart.

Self-feeding skills are difficult skills. Because of this, only the groundwork

---

Approximate Ages for Using Eating Utensils

Cup   If the cup has two handles, the 6-month-old baby will grasp each handle with one hand. If it has only one handle, the baby will grasp the handle with one hand and use the other hand to support the cup. The baby will then carry the cup to the mouth and will suck on the rim of the cup, tilt it, and try to get the liquid from it. By 18 to 20 months, most babies drink with very little spilling.

Spoon   At 6 months, the baby plays with a spoon by sucking, banging, and throwing it. A month or two later, the baby can be shown how to carry it to the mouth and how to turn it slightly to get the food from the spoon into the mouth. By 18 months, babies can feed themselves with little spilling.

Fork   By 18 months, the baby should begin to use a fork for all except soft, semiliquid foods. At first babies will spear the food and carry it to their mouths with much spilling. Few babies can use their forks without spearing food and much spilling before they are 3 years old.

Knife   Shortly before the age of 2, the toddler can use a knife to spread butter or jam on crackers or bread and to cut soft food, such as potatoes or fish. Cutting meat is not usually mastered before the child is 5 or 6 years old.

Glass   By the second birthday, the baby is ready to use a glass in place of a cup for drinking. At first, the baby will hold the glass with both hands. As the hands become larger and stronger, the child will gradually shift to the use of one hand. This will not be much before the age of 5 or 6.

can be laid before babyhood ends. But if this basis is good—if the baby learns to hold a spoon well—the feeding tasks will become habits early in childhood.

Two aids to learning self-feeding will make the task easier for babies. First, because babies' attention wanders easily, they should have their meals in a quiet place, whenever possible, with only a parent or other adult to help by guiding their learning. The part of the meal in which the baby will be fed by another person can be given when others are around, but the parent should try to keep the baby from being too distracted. Starting the baby's meal ten or fifteen minutes before the rest of the family eats often works well.

Second, it is easier to learn eating skills if the utensils are suited to a baby's strength. Small spoons, forks, and knives, made of stainless steel or plastic are lighter than adult-sized utensils or those made of silver. If they are exactly like adult utensils, only smaller, the baby can learn the right way to use them from the start. If baby utensils with curved handles are used, the child may later have to relearn skills. Plastic cups and glasses are lighter than those made of glass and are easier to hold.

For Discussion

What type of eating utensils are most suitable for babies? Why would it be practical for the baby to begin self-feeding with spoons, forks, and knives made like adult ones, rather than with utensils with curved handles?

Self-Dressing Skills

The time between 18 months and $2\frac{1}{2}$ years is the most important for learning self-dressing skills. This is the time when most babies are very eager to learn to dress themselves.

The accompanying chart gives the ages at which most babies are able to learn the skills needed for self-dressing. Note that undressing comes before putting on clothes, because it is easier. Note also that by the time babyhood ends, only the basics of most of the dressing skills have been learned. However, if good groundwork has been laid, mastery of the skills can be finished fairly quickly during early childhood.

There are three ways to make learning self-dressing skills easier. First, the baby should have few distractions

Approximate Ages for Self-Dressing Skills

Undressing Skills   Around 1 year of age, babies start to pull off cap, booties, mittens, and socks. By the age of 2, they can take off all clothes, including diapers.

Dressing Skills   Between $1\frac{1}{2}$ and 2 years, babies try to put on shirts, sweaters, socks, and caps but get tangled up. At 2 years, they try to put on all clothes but do well only with shirts, sweaters, and caps.

Fastening Skills   Between 1 and $1\frac{1}{2}$ years, babies fumble with buttons and zippers. By 2 years, they can push buttons through their holes and pull down zippers.

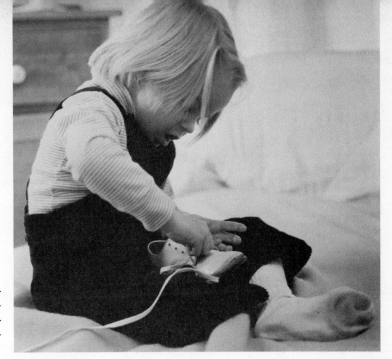

Before babies can dress themselves, they become master artists of undressing and undoing. Suzanne Szasz/Photo Researchers

while learning. Second, clothes should be chosen that have aids to self-dressing in mind. Zippers, for example, can be used instead of buttons or snaps, and the clothing can open down the front instead of down the back or side. Third, until the major tasks are mastered, the parent can help with the dressing, taking over the hard parts, such as getting the arms into a snowsuit, while giving the baby the easier task of zipping it up.

Self-Bathing Skills

The skills involved in self-bathing are easier to master than those of self-feed-ing and self-dressing. However, some of these skills cannot be mastered until the baby grows more. Babies' arms, for example, are so short that it is hard, if not impossible, for them to reach their backs. They even have trouble reaching the center of the neck.

The accompanying chart gives the approximate ages at which babies take part in various ways in their bathing. Chances to try, desire to learn, guidance, and supervision help determine when and how well these skills will be learned. Because bathing is fun for babies and because they like to splash

---

Approximate Ages for Self-Bathing

6 Months to 1 Year   Splashes water, grabs for bathing equipment, sucks sponge and soap, and plays with toys.

1 to 1½ Years   Runs sponge or washcloth over face and center of body.

1½ to 2 Years   Washes face and front of body; rinses off soap; tries to wash hair, toes, and ears, but needs help with back and neck. Dries self in front fairly well but needs help with back.

Though babies need supervision during their bathtime, they enjoy the freedom of doing some things for themselves. Robert Capece

If babies want to brush their own teeth, they should be encouraged to do so, even if an adult has to help them finish. Robert Capece

water, they have a strong desire to take part in bathing.

Self-Grooming Skills

Babies are most often fascinated by the feel of a hairbrush and comb and want to try them. Even before they reach their first birthday, they try to brush and comb their hair the way they have seen their parents do. During the second year, because they are often mixed up by the reversed image in the mirror, they are more likely to mess up their hair than to brush and comb it.

Most babies want to try to brush their teeth, and they grab for their toothbrushes. At first, they suck the powder or paste from the brush and chew on the bristles. By the middle of the second

year, they settle down to cleaning their teeth, but they put most of their efforts on the front teeth, forgetting about any teeth they may have in the back part of the gums. Not until they are close to 6 years old can children be expected to be responsible for the care of teeth without adult help.

Play Skills

Most babies are given toys, but few are shown how to use them. Left to their own, babies will figure out ways to play with simple toys, such as rattles, strings of beads, stuffed animals, and dolls. These exploratory activities need little skill or guidance.

Most of babies' play needs only simple skills. As more complicated activities and toys are introduced, the baby will enjoy them more if the person caring for the baby shows some of the new skills and play possibilities that the baby might not think of. In the case of a tricycle, for example, the toddler will push it around until shown how to sit on the seat and use the feet to move the pedals. This is not likely to be needed, however, if the toddler has ever seen older children at play.

Most games are too complicated for even toddlers to learn. However, playing peekaboo and covering the face with a handkerchief to play hide-and-seek should be encouraged. These games lay the groundwork for the cooperative play of early childhood. They give the baby a good attitude toward give-and-take activities.

Social-Help Skills

Social-help skills are used when one person helps another. Most parents feel a baby's help gets in their way. So they do not teach the baby social-help skills or encourage learning them. Instead, they send the baby off to play with toys while they carry out the tasks alone.

If babies enjoy helping with household chores, they will be more eager to learn the skills needed to be a real help when they grow older. Just as important, a good attitude toward helping others will help make the child a cooperative member of the play group.

Many toys help develop muscles needed for different skills. When parents show their babies how to use toys correctly, they may make skills easier for babies to learn later. Erika Stone/Peter Arnold

Although most housekeeping skills are too hard for a baby to learn, there are some simple ones that can be learned with guidance. Babies, for example, can hand parents clothing that has been laid out to be put on after the bath. They can hand the parent the brush when it is hair-brushing time. Once they can walk well enough, babies can carry napkins to the dining table, carry shoes from the center of the bedroom floor to the closet, and carry dirty clothes to the hamper.

For Discussion

Studies of babies have shown that they are able to learn only the basics of social-help skills. If this is so, would it not be better to wait until they are older before trying to teach them these skills? If not, why not?

Skills Involving the Organs of Elimination

Control of the organs of elimination means holding back waste products that are trying to leave the body. To make this possible, the controlling muscles must be both strong and well-coordinated.

Because there is no given age at which babies are ready to learn these skills, each baby's readiness must be judged separately. One way parents can do this is to keep a daily record, for at least a week, of the times when urination and bowel movements have taken place. If the baby is ready for training, the record will show a fairly regular pattern from day to day. The following chart gives the ages at which many babies are ready for different parts of the training program. Not all babies reach the stages given in this chart at the same time. Babies who reach the different stages of toilet training early are not necessarily brighter than those who reach the same stages later. Note also that the skills needed to control the organs of elimination are still far from being mastered when babyhood ends. This means that only the groundwork of these skills, like many others, have been laid in babyhood. Mastery of

Approximate Ages of Gaining Control over the Organs of Elimination	
Bowel Control	**Bladder Control**
6 months: beginning of control of bowel movements	15–16 months: beginning of bladder control
18 months: awareness of coming of bowel movements	18–24 months: gives some sign of desire to urinate
18–24 months: gives some sign that a movement is near	2–2$\frac{1}{2}$ years: goes to toilet to urinate; dry during day except for mistakes due to being excited, tired, or ill
2 years: control achieved except for mistakes due to being tired, excited, or ill	3–3$\frac{1}{2}$ years: dry at night except for a few mistakes
2–2$\frac{1}{2}$ years: goes to toilet alone for bowel movement	

these skills is an important task for the early childhood years.

A baby who is ready to learn must be given the chance to learn. This means that someone must take the baby to a toilet at the times when urination or bowel movement usually take place. The baby needs to be shown how to use the toilet. Some doctors recommend turning on the faucet so that the baby can hear the sound of running water, or making sounds as if pushing to eliminate the waste products from the body in a bowel movement.

Learning the skills needed to control the organs of elimination is a long, hard process. Any aid that can be given will speed up the learning process. There are four aids that have been found to be most helpful.

First, the baby should not be distracted. Giving the baby a toy to play with while on the toilet seat, for example, will take the baby's mind off the reason for being there.

Second, equipment suited to the baby's size and stage of development makes the training easier and less frightening. Being put on an adult-sized toilet, with feet dangling in the air, may frighten even a baby who is safely strapped onto the toilet seat. On the other hand, a low toilet chair with a potty under it is less frightening because the feet can be placed on the floor.

Third, when one is upset, all muscles become tense. This includes the muscles needed for elimination. If the skills of control over the organs of elimination are to be learned, muscles must be in a relaxed state so that the baby can control them. If babies are scolded or

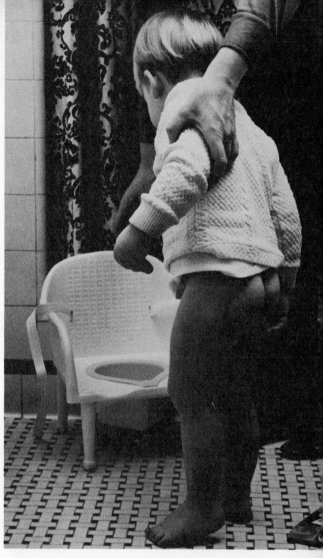

Toilet training is made easier for most babies when a baby-sized toilet seat is used to increase their comfort and security. Erika Stone/Peter Arnold

punished while on the toilet for not doing what is expected, or if they are upset because their play was interrupted, they will suffer from the emotional tension that makes the learning of these skills impossible.

Fourth, parents should understand that the learning process will be long, with many setbacks and periods of no progress. Then they may have a more relaxed attitude toward toilet training. This will encourage the baby to be relaxed—which is essential to learning any new skill.

Handedness

During the first three or four months of life, all babies are *ambidextrous*—they use both hands with no preference for one or the other. By the middle of the first year, however, signs of hand preference begin to appear. It is at this time that the hands have grown larger and stronger. Babies can now do more with one hand alone than they could earlier when they had to use both hands to hold onto any object.

The hand that does most of the work, the *dominant* hand, is aided by the other hand, the *auxiliary*, or helping, hand. In holding a cup, for example, the baby holds onto the handle with the dominant hand and helps hold the cup steady with the auxiliary hand. One hand will become dominant when the baby uses it more often than the other hand to pick up or hold objects.

Preference for using the right or left hand is most often based on which is most comfortable to use when handling objects.
Erika Stone/Peter Arnold

Highlights of Chapter 6

- ☐ The pattern of gaining body control follows the laws of developmental direction.
- ☐ *Body control* means coordinated movements of the body resulting from maturation. Skills are coordinated movements resulting from learning.
- ☐ Trial and error is the least efficient way of learning skills; training is the most efficient.
- ☐ In learning skills, there are nine essentials, each of which plays an important role in the learning process.
- ☐ The learning of skills in babyhood stresses learning to eat in a mature way, self-feeding, self-dressing, self-bathing, and self-grooming.
- ☐ Only the groundwork of play skills and social-help skills can be learned before babyhood comes to an end.
- ☐ Control of the organs of elimination is well advanced by the time the toddler is 2 years old.
- ☐ Skills in doing things with the dominant hand and the auxiliary hand can begin to be learned during the second year.

Suggested Activities

1. Watch several babies who are just starting to walk and several who have been walking for three or four months. As they walk, compare the position of their feet, how they hold their arms, how much movement there is in their legs, and how they hold their heads.

2. Watch a toddler eating in a quiet room and the same toddler when eating at the family table. Time the child in both settings to see how much watching others slows down the time needed to eat the meal.

3. Show a baby how to hold a spoon and how to button a shirt. Then watch how he or she copies you. How well does the baby do after seeing it only once or twice?

4. Go to the toy department of a store and look at the toys recommended for babies under 6 months of age, for those from 6 to 12 months, and for those between 1 and 2 years. Ask yourself what babies can do with each toy to amuse themselves and how it encourages the development of skills. For example, what can babies do with a rattle to amuse themselves, and how much does a rattle encourage practice in the coordination of hand and arm muscles?

Chapter 7

Learning to Communicate

Some goals of this chapter are:
- [ ] To identify the common forms of communication and explain which are most useful
- [ ] To know what the prespeech forms of communication are and why they are essential
- [ ] To understand the four tasks a child must master to be able to speak

Although the words "speech" and "communication" are often used as if they meant the same thing, their meanings are actually somewhat different.

Communication is an interchange of thoughts, feelings, and emotions. *Speech* is the expression of thoughts, feelings, and emotions in words said aloud. It does not mean that the person who hears these words must understand them.

There are two essentials in communication. First, the person trying to communicate something—sending a message—must be able to put thoughts or feelings in a form that can be understood. Second, the person receiving the message—seeing or hearing it—must understand what is meant. If not, communication has not taken place.

For example, a baby who is hungry and wants others to know will try to communicate the need for food in any way possible. A baby who is very young communicates only by crying. However, if the communication is to serve its purpose, those who take care of the baby must be able to understand what the cry means. If not, it will communicate nothing.

Communication

Speech is by no means the only form of communication people use, but it is the best form for many purposes. Within a group of people who speak the same language, speech is more widely understood than any other means of communication. However, there are many other ways in which people can communicate. Of these different forms, the ones that can be best understood, and that are most widely used, are gestures; face and body movements that show different emotions; touch, such as picking up a baby; sign language, as used by the deaf; arts, such as music, dance, and painting; and written symbols for words. All these forms of communication can be thought of as language. Speech is just one form of language.

When adults communicate with a baby, they often use gestures and emotional expressions to catch the baby's attention. The baby is able to respond to such communication at a very early age. Above: Frostie/Woodfin Camp & Associates; below: Alice Kandell/Rapho/Photo Researchers

For Discussion

How many different forms of language can you think of? Consider written words, spoken words, gestures, art, etc. Which of these forms do you use in everyday life? Which do you find most useful and direct?

Learning to speak is one of the hardest skills a person must master. There are two reasons for this. First, in order to speak a person must be able to control the voice mechanism as well as the muscles of the tongue and lips. All must work together to make sounds that are meaningful words. Second, the speaker must know the meaning of the words used if they are to communicate what is meant.

Understanding
The first task in communication is understanding others' messages.

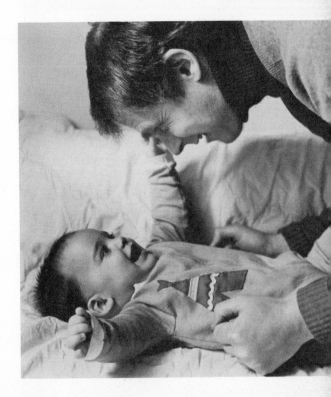

Aids in Learning to Understand

Try to get the baby's attention when you speak by using a facial expression or gesture. If the baby does not look at you, the connection between your words and your expressions or gestures will likely be lost.

Be sure that your form of communication is simple, yet meaningful. Words of approval and pleasure can be strengthened with a smile and a hug. Try to speak clearly.

Repeat words you know the baby understands. Repeating strengthens learning.

When you use new words, be sure to connect meanings with them. Point to the objects the words stand for until you are sure the baby understands.

Talk a lot to the baby. The more speech babies hear, the more chance they have to learn.

Babies must learn how to understand what is communicated to them by others through gestures, touch, facial expressions, or words. Babies and young children learn to understand more words than they can say. Thus their comprehension vocabulary is larger than their speech vocabulary.

At first, the words babies hear are meaningless to them. In time, they get some idea of what is being said by watching the face of the speaker. A smile, for example, means approval, and an angry look means disapproval. Understanding the meanings of expressions and gestures begins around the age of 3 months.

By the time most babies are 6 months old, they know their own names. By the time they are 1½ years old they can understand the meaning of such simple questions as "Are you hungry?" or "Are you sleepy?" By the end of babyhood, at 2 years of age, the toddler should understand such simple commands as "Come to dinner" or "Throw me the ball."

If a good groundwork is laid in babyhood, the young child will make rapid strides in understanding what others are trying to say. Some ideas for laying a good base are given in the accompanying chart. They point out that the baby must be taught to understand meanings. Babies will learn some of it by trial and error. But trial-and-error learning is slow and indirect.

Because learning the meaning of words is a long, slow process, most communications to a baby must be done at first through facial expressions, gestures, and touch. Words should accompany these expressions. Then gradually, the baby will come to connect the words with the experiences.

For Discussion

The chart above gives a list of aids to help a baby or toddler understand what others are saying. Read over each aid carefully and explain how it adds to the baby's understanding.

Prespeech Forms of Communication

Because speech is such a complicated skill, babies cannot master more than the basics before babyhood ends. They must use simpler forms of language. These forms come before speech; so they are called *prespeech forms of communication*.

These prespeech forms are only stopgap measures. They let babies communicate until they have developed enough to learn the skills needed for speech itself. When a baby is ready to learn to speak, the use of prespeech forms should gradually be replaced by more mature and more useful forms.

Four prespeech forms are used by all babies. These are crying, gesturing, emotional expression, and babbling.

Crying

Cries of newborn babies are louder and softer at times, but the kind of sound they make is almost the same all through the first month or two of life. Also, a very young baby who is crying moves all parts of the body. As a result, it is impossible to know just why the baby is crying and just what need the baby is trying to communicate. A baby who cries very loudly, though, and who moves very energetically is showing that the need is great.

During the second or third month of life, the sounds of the cries begin to change. Still later, mass activity is largely replaced by specific actions. For example, the hands are put into the mouth and sucked when the baby is hungry, or the legs are pulled up and stiffened when the baby has stomach pains because of colic. It is then easier to understand what the baby is trying to communicate.

A parent who is used to being with a baby soon learns what the cries mean. The following chart gives some of the

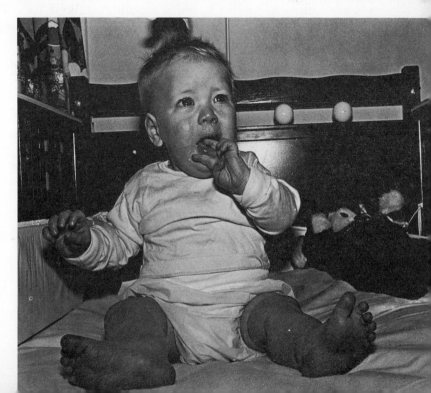

Why do you think this baby is crying? Richard Nowitz

common types of cries made by babies and the usual meanings of these cries.

For Discussion

Why is it important for parents or those who take care of a baby to answer cries even if they know that all the baby wants is attention? Is it as important to answer cries for attention as those for physical needs? If so, why? If not, why not?

Around the middle of the first year of life, when rapid physical growth slows and babies stay awake for a longer time, they begin to be bored when they have nothing to do. To let people know that they want company and attention, they cry. Many parents call this spoiled crying. Until recently, many doctors as well as relatives and friends told parents not to listen to these cries unless they wanted a spoiled brat. In this way, they argued, the baby would soon learn that crying does not pay.

Medical and psychological studies have shown that this advice is bad both physically and psychologically. Until babies can use speech to communicate their needs, they must use prespeech forms, the most useful of which is crying. So those who take care of a baby should answer the cries. They should go to the baby as soon as possible and try to find out, through trial and error if necessary, what the baby's need is. When they discover the need, they should meet it right away.

These studies have also stressed that needs are not only physical ones, such as for food, drink, removal of pain, or removal of discomfort by changing wet or soiled diapers. There are psychological needs as important as the physical ones. When babies are unable to amuse themselves, adults must help them by giving them toys and showing them how to use the toys. When babies are lonely, they should be allowed to be with other people so that they can watch and listen. Often the baby should be picked up, played with, and talked to. This will meet the baby's need for companionship, just as changing diapers will meet the baby's need for comfort.

What Babies' Cries Mean

Piercing screams: physical discomfort or pain

High-pitched, shrill wails, broken by whimpering and groaning: physical discomfort or pain

Piercing screams, abdomen expanded, pulling up and stiffening legs: colic

Short, sharp, piercing cries: physical discomfort or pain

Low-pitched moans: tiredness or general discomfort

Low-pitched moans and feverish look: illness

Low-pitched moans broken by yawns and sighs: sleepiness

Angry howls and sucking movements or biting the hand: hunger

Angry howls broken off and replaced by smile at the sight of a person: loneliness and need for company.

If babies' cries are answered, they cry less. They are also more cheerful and easier to manage. When cries go unanswered, babies learn in time that crying is useless, and they cry little. However, this does not mean that babies are making a good adjustment. Instead, they are learning that when they call for help, people do not listen to them. This makes them withdrawn, uncooperative, and even hostile toward people.

Useful as crying is at first, it should gradually be discouraged. Later on, it will get in the way of the growing child's social adjustments. People expect a baby to cry because they know that babies have no other means of communicating. But they expect children to "act their age" and speak their needs and wants rather than cry.

The shift from crying to speech does not take place overnight. By the time the child is old enough to go to school, crying should largely be replaced by speech. The child will then usually cry only when hurt or when some strong emotion, such as grief or fear, is felt.

Gesturing

Before babies can make a meaningful gesture, such as pointing to an object or holding out their arms to show that they want to be picked up, they must have enough control over their muscles to make these movements.

Gestures communicate in two ways. They may take the place of speech, and they may add to speech. Babies first use gestures instead of speech. After they have learned a few words, they still use gestures to make a sentence by combining gestures with one or more words. For example, a baby who does not know how to say the words "I do not like spinach" spits the spinach out and says "No" or "No spinach."

Later, babies learn (either by trial and error or by copying a person who uses gestures) that combining gestures with words makes the words more meaningful. Even though the babies no longer need gestures to take the place of words, they still use gestures to add to and stress the words' meanings. Adults use gestures for these same reasons.

What Babies' Gestures Mean

Smack lips or sticks tongue out: hungry

Squirms and trembles: cold

Pushes nipple from mouth with tongue: satisfied or not hungry

Turns head from nipple: satisfied or not hungry

Allows food to run out of mouth: satisfied or not hungry

Smiles and holds out arms: wants to be picked up

Squirms, wiggles, and cries during dressing or bathing: resents limits put on activities

Reaches out for object: wants to have it

Pushes object away: does not want it

Points to person or object: wants person to look at it

Pouts: displeased

"I'm hungry!" "Come and get me!" "Don't you know it's lonely here all by myself?" Whatever this baby is trying to communicate, it is important! Alfred Eris/Monkmeyer

For Discussion

How useful are gestures as forms of communication? What gestures do you use often? What gestures do babies of different ages use? Are your gestures more for emphasis than for basic communication? What about babies' gestures?

As in the case of cries, all babies have their own gestures. But the gestures used by different babies are enough alike to make it fairly easy to understand what the gestures mean. The chart on page 107 gives some of the most common gestures and their meanings.

Useful as gestures are for early communication, they are not exact enough to take the place of speech as the child grows older.

Gestures do have value, though. It was once thought that children should be taught never to gesture. This belief is giving way to an understanding that some gestures are part of the culture of many Americans. Types of gesturing differ among various groups.

Gestures are also much more widely accepted today because people are more aware of the importance of non-spoken communication. This so-called body language plays a big part in setting the tone of a social situation. Also, many people interested in children's artistic development encourage much freer use of body movement.

The parents and other adults caring for the baby will naturally be models for the baby to copy. If they use few gestures, the baby will probably not use many either. In this natural way, the baby takes on the accepted customs of a group.

It is important to note, however, that some gestures may be thought of as rude in many groups. For example, pointing at another person is disapproved of in most parts of our society. If parents wish to discourage one or more gestures, those caring for the baby should not use the unwanted gesture or gestures themselves. Also, the baby should have something to take its place, such as easy words. Finally, the baby should be led in a positive way to use words rather than scolded or punished for using the gesture.

Emotional Expressions

Two traits of babies' emotions make them very effective forms of communication. First, babies' emotions are all-or-nothing feelings. When babies are angry, they are angry all over. People who see them have no doubt about their emotional state.

Second, babies do not try to hold back an emotion. Unlike the older child or adult, babies do not try to hide fear, for example, so as not to be called a "fraidy cat" or be judged a coward. Instead, the baby acts completely frightened. This makes it easy for others to know exactly how the baby feels.

Unpleasant emotions, such as fear and anger, are always accompanied by crying in babyhood. This makes it even easier to know what the baby is com-

municating than it would be if one saw the facial and bodily expressions alone.

The pleasant emotions—joy, happiness, affection, and curiosity—are not accompanied by crying, but they are also easy to understand. Babies show them so openly. When they smile, for example, they also coo or squeal.

After babies are 2 or 3 months old, they can figure out the emotional states of others. If a mother is angry, for instance, she shows it in the way she walks and in the sound of her voice. If a father is nervous or worried, he becomes tense. The baby feels this anger or tension in the way the parent holds the baby and takes care of his or her

Babies do not hide their emotions. Instead, the whole body expresses feelings, such as frustration or joy. Left: Lew Merrim/Monkmeyer; right: Erika Stone/Monkmeyer

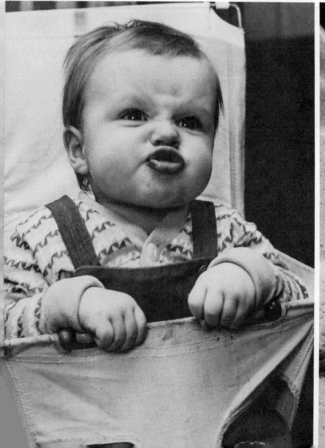

Playing with babies communicates to them feelings of love and acceptance.
Louis Goldman/Rapho/Photo Researchers

physical needs. Angry or happy faces and voices are usually understood in the middle of the first year.

Unlike some other prespeech forms, emotional expressions have a lifelong value. For that reason, babies should be encouraged to use emotional expressions even when they can show their feelings in words.

However, the growing child must learn which ways of showing emotions are acceptable. When the child is angry, for example, she or he must learn to curb the kicking, hitting, screaming, and crying of a babyish temper tantrum and to use instead an angry facial expression. This will make angry feelings clear without causing disapproval.

Babbling

Babbling is called play speech because the baby enjoys making sounds and does so even when no one is around. This may suggest that babbling has no communication value and so should not be thought of as a form of prespeech.

This is not correct. Playing with sounds is a way of learning the skills needed to form words. It is a preliminary to speech. And not all babbling, by any means, is done alone. The baby who is with others babbles as if trying to talk to them.

Babbling, or cooing, begins around the third month and reaches its peak when the baby is 9 months old. After that, babbling sounds are gradually formed into words.

While every baby has a supply of babbling sounds, there are some sounds that almost all babies make. The most common of these are eh-eh-eh, u-u-u, ah-ah-ah, i-i-i, and ow-ow-ow. To encourage the baby to master new sound skills, the adult can offer a model and help the baby copy it. This happens quite naturally when the adult plays little talking games or chatters with the baby.

Babbling does not tell others what the baby wants and needs. But it does help the baby develop the muscular coordination needed for the complicated skills of speech. The more babbling sounds babies can make, the easier it will be for them to learn to say words.

Learning to Speak

Even though not much speech is learned during babyhood, this is the most important time for laying a good base. If this is done, the baby will make rapid progress during the early years of childhood.

Each task in learning to speak is learned in a different way. In spite of their differences, they all need the essentials for learning any skill—readiness to learn, a good model to imitate, a strong desire to learn, help in imitating the model, and supervision.

Pronouncing Words

Pronouncing words is learned by imitation. The more practice the baby has had in making babbling sounds, the easier it will be to imitate words. Even so, learning to pronounce words is always difficult for babies. They may hear the model correctly, but they cannot always control their tongue and lip muscles enough to say the word as they just heard it.

It is a good idea to have the baby master one word before trying to learn another. Sometimes parents try to teach a baby too many words too quickly. If the baby says a word correctly once, he or she may still not have learned it. The baby should be encouraged to say the word correctly many times.

On the other hand, babies within a family or play group are going to hear a great many words every day. It would be silly, unnatural, and probably impossible to keep babies from trying to say words they hear all around them until they have mastered the first word they tried. Babies will naturally try to imitate many words they hear. Adults should not try to stop this. They should help the baby pronounce the words most often used and needed by saying them over and over.

To make learning easier, the first words should be the short, easy words that are made up of the sounds already mastered in babbling. The baby who has babbled the sounds mi-mi-mi, for example, will learn to pronounce "milk" more easily than if the babbling had not included these sounds. Similarly, the baby who has babbled da-da-da will find it easy to say "Daddy."

The process of learning to pronounce words, like most other things the baby learns, is not stern or formal. It is almost like a game, with adult and baby sharing laughter and hugs when the baby says the word correctly.

When one learns any skill, there are sure to be errors at first. These errors should not be overlooked. It should not be taken for granted that the baby will outgrow them or naturally correct them alone. Even more important, errors should never be encouraged because they are "cute." Baby talk is largely words said wrong. Parents who think baby talk is cute and who may even encourage the baby to keep on using baby talk by copying the baby's incorrect pronunciations are not being fair to the baby.

For Discussion

Explain what parrot talk and baby talk have in common and how they differ. How does each affect the baby's social adjustments and the way other people, both adults and children, react to the baby?

This is true for two reasons. First, it makes it harder to learn the correct pronunciations. The mispronounced words must be relearned. Second, baby talk may be cute when babies are young. But by the time they are old enough to play with other children (often by age 2), their playmates will not understand what they are trying to say. Even worse, playmates will make fun of a child who talks "like a baby."

All babies have their own favorite baby-talk words, but there are some words that are more likely to be said wrong than others. These are shown in the following chart. Note that the words

Every new experience gives babies a greater chance to connect words with their meanings. David S. Strickler/Monkmeyer

Common Forms of Baby Talk

Leaving out a letter or letters, as "at" for "that" or "seepy" for "sleepy"

Leaving out a syllable, as "buttfly" for "butterfly" or "matoes" for "tomatoes"

Using one letter instead of another, as "dat" for "that" and "waser" for "water"

Using one word instead of another, as "tick-tock" for "clock" and "choo-choo" for "train"

Saying letters out of order, as "aks" for "ask" and "bicksit" for "biscuit"

that are most likely to be said wrong are the long words and those that have sounds not often present in the baby's babbling.

Building a Vocabulary

All the words a child learns make up the vocabulary. To be useful, this vocabulary should have many parts of speech.

Nouns, especially names for people and things the baby always sees or uses, are the most useful words. As a result, the major part of the baby's vocabulary is made up of nouns. Almost as important as nouns are the action verbs, such as "give," "come," or "carry." Like nouns, these verbs are learned early. However, because gestures can often be used rather than verbs, the baby's vocabulary usually has a smaller number of verbs than of nouns.

The baby finds adjectives useful to talk about likes and dislikes. As a result, adjectives gradually creep into the vocabulary. They are usually limited to such words as "nice," "pretty," "good," and "bad" because these simple adjectives express the baby's feelings fairly well.

Pronouns, adverbs, and prepositions are the least useful part of the baby's vocabulary. So the baby has little reason to learn them. When babyhood ends, few of these parts of speech will be in the child's vocabulary.

Connecting Meanings with Words

No matter how many words the baby can say correctly, these words have no value as communication until the baby has learned to connect meanings with them. They are only parrot talk.

Babies can learn to connect meanings with words by trial and error or by guidance. If they learn by trial and error, they may connect wrong or inexact meanings with words. For example, because people speak of the father as "Da-da" or "Daddy," the baby may connect these words with men in general and call all men "Daddy." With guidance, babies soon learn the difference.

For Discussion

Why is learning to connect meanings with words hard for a baby? Give ideas about how to deal with this difficulty. For example, if you want to teach the meaning of such words as "shoes" or "toy," how would you do so?

113

If given guidance, babies are less likely to make mistakes. When, for example, the word "milk" is used, they can be shown a glass of milk, milk in a cup, and milk in a bottle or carton. In that way, they learn that it is the liquid that is called "milk," not the container.

Putting Together Sentences

The hardest task in learning to speak is putting words into sentences that will carry meaning to the listener. If the baby's vocabulary is composed mainly of nouns and verbs, even if it is large, the baby is not ready to speak in sentences. This, then, becomes a learning task for early childhood.

However, before babyhood ends, most babies are trying to master this task. They do this by putting a word or two together with gestures. The baby who wants a ball will point to one or hold out the hands and say "ball."

In late babyhood, some babies speak in incomplete sentences that have three to five words. The words used are mainly nouns, verbs, and adjectives. It is unusual for a baby to say a complete sentence. This usually does not happen until the child is at least 3 years old.

Highlights of Chapter 7

- [ ] Speech and communication are not the same. Speech is only one form of communication.
- [ ] Learning to speak is hard. Both brain and muscles must develop before it can be mastered.
- [ ] There are two major tasks in learning to communicate: understanding the messages of others and sending messages others can understand.
- [ ] Because learning to speak is too difficult for a young baby, nature provides four stopgap measures—crying, gesturing, emotional expressions, and babbling. Babies use these until they are ready to learn to speak.
- [ ] Each of these four prespeech forms of communication is useful until the baby is able to learn to speak. Then they are given up or their use greatly reduced in importance in favor of speech.
- [ ] There are four major tasks in learning to speak: pronouncing words, building a vocabulary of different parts of speech, connecting meanings with words, and putting words together to make sentences.
- [ ] Learning to pronounce words and to connect meanings with them can be done by trial and error or by guidance. Guidance gets better results.
- [ ] Because babies find nouns and verbs the most useful parts of speech, their first vocabularies are made up mostly of these words.
- [ ] Until babies learn words other than nouns and verbs, their first sentences are made up of words and gestures.

Suggested Activities

1. Watch the gestures made by a toddler and see how many of them you can understand. Refer to the chart on page 107 to help you understand the gestures you see.

2. Listen to the babbling of a baby who is under 1 year of age (the best age is between 6 and 9 months). Try to write down, as exactly as you can, the sounds the baby makes. Later, go over the sounds you have written down to see what simple, short words have these babbling sounds. For example, if the baby babbles the sounds muh-muh-muh, that sound is close to the word "mud." It may help to use a dictionary to get some ideas for words.

3. To understand how babies use babbling to try to communicate with others, talk to one or two people with a baby there. Give the baby a chance to join in by babbling. Note if the baby listens to you silently or tries to copy some of the words you say.

4. Pronounce a two- or three-syllable word in your usual speed of talking, and note how well or badly a toddler says the word. Then say the word again slowly, stressing each syllable. Do you note a difference in the toddler's pronunciation of the word the second time? Explain.

5. Make a list of the words a toddler says over a period of a few hours. Then, taking each word on your list, try to find out if the toddler knows what the word means by having the child point to the object or person the word stands for. How many of the words on your list seem to be parrot talk and how many are real speech?

6. When a baby cries, watch how the parents and other adults react and how the baby's brothers and sisters or other children react. Do adults seem to have an attitude toward a baby's cries different from that of children? Do outsiders seem to have an attitude different from that of family members? Explain.

Chapter 8

Some Common Babyhood Problems

Some goals of this chapter are:
- [ ] To be able to identify what causes problem behavior in babyhood and when it is most likely to develop
- [ ] To know what some of the common behavior problems in babyhood are, what causes them, and what steps can be taken to prevent them
- [ ] To understand why problem behavior should be kept at a low level in babyhood, and how this can be done

Many things are called babyhood problems only because they bother parents and other family members. They upset the parents' patterns of life, slow down activities, and do not match the parents' idea of how a baby should behave. Few parents of first babies, for example, know that their peaceful, helpless newborn may, within a year, become a tyrant who wants to be free from parental care. The baby may even have temper tantrums about it.

At every age, not babyhood alone, there are problems that are part of passing from one stage of development to another. The adult, for example, who must stop working after many years faces problems in adjusting to the new role. So does the baby, who goes from helplessness to gradual independence. Until these adjustment problems are solved, they are emotionally upsetting.

For Discussion

Why are babyhood problems called "problems"? Is this a fair name? If not, what should they be called? Give reasons for the word you would use in place of "problem behavior."

Problem behavior at any age has a cause. If this cause can be spotted and steps can be taken to correct it, the problem behavior will go away. On the other hand, if no try is made to find the cause, and if parents just scold and punish children for such behavior, the problem will get worse. Babies will only become more troublesome.

Common Babyhood Problems

While all babies have their own problems, some problems are so common that few babies escape them. Even if the baby escapes some of the common problems, others are sure to develop.

Some of the common problems have physical causes, such as colic and teething. The baby's doctor will advise parents on how to deal with them. But most of the problems that parents must face are behavioral. They may become worse because of the baby's physical state. Babies who are teething, for example, will be more negative than they would be if they were feeling better.

Some of the problems of babyhood have to do with the baby's daily routine—eating, bathing, and sleeping. Parents have to deal with these day in and day out. Other problems, such as shyness with strangers, come up only once in a while.

Negativism

Someone who is *negative* usually does the opposite of what others want. This is often called being stubborn, ornery, or contrary.

Everything a baby touches becomes an adventure! Could that be a problem? Erika Stone/ Peter Arnold

Negativism is really resisting authority. The stricter the demands made by those in authority, the more that negative people will resist. The accompanying chart explains some common ways negativism is expressed.

Negativism is a stage babies go through which usually begins around the age of 6 months. It tends to get stronger and happen more often with each passing month, reaching a peak around the age of 2 or 3 years. After this, it begins to happen less often. But when it does happen, it is still strong.

Studies of negativism have shown what causes it. Those who take care of babies do not give the babies the chance to do things for themselves when they have developed enough to do so. When babies act angry and stubborn, they are trying to tell others that they want a chance to do things for themselves.

When, for example, babies refuse to eat because they want to feed themselves, they should not be scolded or have their plates taken away. Instead, the baby should be given a spoon and shown how to use it. The baby will quickly go back to eating.

For Discussion

Why should advice about dealing with babyhood problems be tailored to the baby? How can this be done if parents read baby-care books and articles in magazines and newspapers for answers?

In dealing with negativism, it is not enough just to give babies the independence they demand. They must be taught how to use it. For example, if babies do not know how to use a spoon when they are allowed to use one, they will become frustrated. This will just bring up the negativism again. Instead of being angry at the parents, the baby will be angry at the spoon and throw it.

Thus, in dealing with negativism, the first step is to let babies do what they are ready to do. The second step is to show them how to use their independence.

Spoiling

A spoiled baby is a self-centered baby who wants everything and is not willing to give anything in return. In the early

Common Expressions of Negativism

Open Rebellion Expressed in temper tantrums in which the baby cries, screams, kicks, bites, and slashes. If anyone is within reach, the baby hits, bites, or throws something at the person.

Passive Rebellion Expressed in stubbornness, sullenness, pouting, and, when able to speak, refusing to answer a question. Passive rebellion usually develops after the baby has been punished for open rebellion.

Going Back to Babyish Ways Expressed in thumb-sucking, wanting to be fed, or wetting after the baby has learned bladder control. This form happens more often as babies near early childhood than during the early part of babyhood.

Attention without Spoiling

Answer babies' cries, but once in a while let them wait when something more important comes up (such as food burning on the stove or another child's more pressing need). This way babies learn that they are not all the adult has to care for.

Instead of amusing babies by doing things for them, find things they can enjoy doing themselves.

In a group of people, do not make a baby the center of attention. Instead, encourage the baby to watch and listen to other people and have only a share of the attention.

Instead of encouraging babies to babble to themselves, encourage them to babble as a way of talking with others.

Instead of always helping babies, give them simple tasks to help others when they are able to do so (such as bringing something across the room). Praise the baby for doing things for others. This will give the baby pride in doing things instead of pleasure from being the center of attention.

---

months when babies are helpless, most parents are not worried by this self-centeredness. They understand that young babies cannot do things for themselves, much less for anyone else.

Babies are not spoiled by too much attention, but by the wrong kind of attention. When babies cry to let people know that they are bored and lonely, it does not spoil them to pick them up, play with them, and talk to them. Nor will it spoil them to make them part of the family group.

What will spoil them is attention that makes them think they are the most important members of the family and that everyone must jump when they call. Babies may also be spoiled when adults do things for them and expect them to do nothing for others in return.

The usual victims of spoiling are first-born babies. Almost as common as victims are the so-called "babies of the family." These last born are the center of attention, not only of parents, but also of older brothers and sisters. Parents should know about the possibility of spoiling these two groups of babies. However, *any* baby can be spoiled, no matter what the child's position in the family.

It is possible to give babies the attention they need and want without spoiling them. The accompanying chart offers some suggestions for kinds of attention that will not lead to spoiling but will meet the baby's needs.

For Discussion

Suggest ways to show babies that they are loved and wanted without spoiling them. Then explain why your ideas would not lead to spoiled brats.

Jealousy

Few babies leave babyhood without feeling some jealousy. Jealous children are angry. They think their place in someone's affection has been taken by

of these tasks themselves. This is done to get attention away from the intruder.

The usual reason for a baby's jealousy is a new baby in the family. Having been the center of the parents' attention until the new baby arrived, the older baby dislikes the change and takes steps to stop it. The more the toddler has been the center of attention in the family, the greater the jealousy.

For Discussion

The most common cause of jealousy in babyhood is the arrival of a new baby. How does this affect a child? What can be done to prepare toddlers for the new baby and thus prevent jealousy?

When parents give equal time and attention to their children, they avoid spoiling them and give less cause for jealousy. Sybil Shackman/Monkmeyer

another person, whom they see as an intruder. They show this anger by fighting the intruder in any way they can—by kicking, hitting, biting, and shoving. Later, when they can use words, they call the intruder names to hurt his or her feelings.

Besides anger, a big part of jealousy is fear. The baby is afraid of losing love. To keep this from happening, the child tries to get attention in any way that works. The only ways children know of are crying and going back to babyish behavior. They may want to be fed or dressed when they are able to do most

Jealousy usually cannot be prevented when there is a new baby in the family. But it can be made much less of a problem by meeting the toddler's needs for attention and love. As was pointed out earlier, it is a good idea to let toddlers stay around when the new baby's physical needs are being taken care of and to let them help in a simple way to meet those needs. It is also good to give them some time and attention which they do not have to share with the new baby. These steps may help to remove their fear of losing the parents' love and to make them less angry at the new baby.

Babies who have been spoiled are most likely to be very jealous. Therefore, many parents have two common problems at the same time—spoiling and jealousy. If spoiling does not become a bad problem, in part by using

120

the ideas in the chart on page 119, little jealousy problem will be felt. When the older baby's needs for attention are met, there will be little reason for the toddler to feel unloved and unwanted just because there is a new brother or sister.

Unsocial Behavior

There are some kinds of unsocial behavior in babies that may both bother and embarrass parents. Of these, the most common are shyness in front of strangers and grabbing the toys of other children.

No one wants to see these behaviors. But they are so common that no one could call a baby unsocial for acting in these ways. On the other hand, just because almost all babies show these behaviors does not mean that a baby will outgrow them. Parents must find out what is causing them and try to replace them with more friendly patterns.

For Discussion

> Everyone knows that babies have not learned enough to act in a way that society approves. Why, then, are parents embarrassed when their baby's behavior is unsocial, as when their child fights with other babies or breaks things while trying to explore them?

Shyness, for example, comes from fear of the new and the different. This fear is found, to some degree, in all people, not in babies alone. Studies of babies have shown that shyness usually appears between the ages of 4 and 6 months. It reaches its peak shortly after the baby's first birthday, and then it gradually grows less with each passing month.

This gives a clue as to how to deal with it. The more that babies see and hear new and different people and things, the less likely they are to be afraid. So shy babies should be taken to places where they can see, touch, and hear new people and things. But the new things should not come upon them too fast. By looking at a stranger from

Babies have no way to control their desires. When they see something they want, they'll do what they can to get it! Erika Stone/Peter Arnold

the safety of a parent's arms, the baby will learn that there is no need for fear.

Exploring new and different things is just as common in babies as being afraid of them. Once the fear has passed, the next step is to explore. If things belonging to others can be looked at without damage, babies should sometimes be allowed to explore them, under the parents' supervision. If the objects cannot be explored with safety, they should be taken away and something else given that is safe to handle. For instance, eyeglasses are easily broken. So the wearer should take them off before going close enough for the baby to grab them.

Unsocial behavior with other children usually takes the form of grabbing their toys and fighting. Parents can prevent this by teaching the baby to share. For example, they can offer to trade toys with the baby. When the parents show thanks, the baby is encouraged to share more toys. With patience, the patterns of cooperative play learned with adults can become part of play with other babies and children.

Problems in Routine Physical Care

Many parents feel that the most common and serious problems of babyhood are those that have to do with physical care, especially feeding and sleep problems. This is partly because parents face these problems several times a day. Also, parents worry about how these problems will affect the health and growth of the baby.

Because parents worry, doctors and psychologists have given much study to the causes of, and answers to, these problems. Most agree on what causes the problems. There is less agreement on how to deal with them.

In general, problems that have to do with physical care come from some of the causes already discussed. For instance, babies may resist being waited on when they can do something themselves. Or parents may try to push babies into taking on self-care tasks before they are ready. Or babies may not have been taught how to do a task and are then punished when they do it badly.

Many of the problems come from the parents' tension and worry. Some of the problems might come up anyway, but many are made worse by worry.

Knowing the possible causes of these problems makes it easier for parents to understand a problem facing them. For example, when a baby will not take a morning nap, is it because the child is ready to stay awake longer and to take only an afternoon nap? Or, when babies splash water during a bath, does that mean that they want to help bathe themselves and that they should be taught how to do so?

The following chart lists the most common problems parents face in the physical care of babies. Studies of how parents deal with these problems have shown that many ways make the problem worse. For example, when a baby dawdles over a meal, parents often get worried that the baby is not getting enough food. So they actually shove food into the baby's mouth. This upsets the baby, who refuses to open the mouth for more food. Other parents, in frustration, will pick up the dish and, with an angry word, carry it away. This will also upset the baby.

Common Problems in Physical Care

Eating Problems

Changes in appetite, because of being tired, teething, and other discomforts

Food likes and dislikes, because of starting too suddenly foods that taste and feel new

Dawdling over meals, because of distractions, having had enough food, or problems in self-feeding

Sloppiness in eating, because of lack of mastery of self-feeding skills

Distracted, because of not being able to keep the mind on eating while watching what else is going on

Playing during meal, because of not liking food or because of lack of hunger

Wrong use of eating utensils, because of not having been taught to use them correctly

Sleeping Problems

Wakening, because of colic or gas pains, before the usual wakening time

Crying when put to bed, because of not being sleepy or because of distractions in the environment

Resistance to naps, because of distractions in the house from TV, guests, or older children playing

Trying to get out of the crib, because of wanting to get up before parents are ready to take the baby out of the crib

Bathing Problems

Splashing water by kicking

Playing with water toys instead of trying to learn to bathe self

Refusal to have hair shampooed, because of having had soap in the eyes or mouth

Fear of bath, because of earlier slip or fall in tub

Refusal to be bathed except by the father or mother

If the parent had stopped to see what was causing the dawdling, the problem could have been solved without anyone getting upset. Parents should ask themselves the following questions: Am I expecting the baby to eat more than is needed? Perhaps growth has slowed down or perhaps the baby has not been active today. Is the baby being distracted? Perhaps some sight or sound or activity is taking the baby's mind off eating.

While the answer to every question cannot be found right away, some of the possibilities can be tried out. For example, if the dawdling was due to distractions, the baby can be fed in a quiet place until most of the meal has

Strong concentration is needed when babies learn to feed themselves. Erika Stone/Peter Arnold

been eaten. This is especially important while the baby is learning self-feeding.

If distraction does not seem to be the cause, the parent can test the amount of food the baby needs. The parent can try giving smaller amounts and can see if the baby becomes hungry before the next mealtime. Or maybe dawdling was due to the baby's getting tired because self-feeding is still a hard task. If this is the cause, the baby will be eager to let the parent take over. But if the parent tries to take over and the baby gets angry, this is the parent's cue to look for another cause.

Finding causes of problems and trying out solutions based on possible causes is longer and harder than just going by a rule of thumb. But the results are better. For example, suppose the rule says to remove the plate

whenever the baby starts to dawdle. This may make the baby very angry if the dawdling was not due to having enough food but to some other cause. No matter how hard it is and how much time it takes to discover a cause, the result is worth the effort. If the dawdling problem is corrected instead of being made worse, the bother to the parents and the psychological damage to the baby will be avoided. And meals will be pleasanter for everyone.

Emotional Outbursts

Few babyhood problems make parents as angry, embarrassed, or annoyed as emotional outbursts. It seems to parents that these outbursts always take place when outsiders are present. Mothers and fathers, afraid of being judged as bad parents, do everything they can to curb an outburst. But the more they do, the worse it gets, and the more embarrassed and annoyed the parents become.

Emotional outbursts are unchecked expressions of emotions. Few parents dislike emotional outbursts of happiness. Such behavior is charming or "cute." However, outbursts of anger, jealousy, and fear are annoying and troublesome.

Curiosity and Exploring

Almost as annoying and troublesome as an emotional outburst is the exploring that comes from curiosity. It annoys parents to have the baby get into everything within reach—often breaking things, spilling things on carpets or furniture, and causing extra work. It is also frightening for parents to think of the serious accidents that might have happened had they not come into the room in time.

Parents often try to deal with emotional outbursts and unwanted exploring in babyhood by speaking harshly to babies, slapping or spanking them, or picking them up and putting them in the playpen or crib. They hope in that way to stop the outbursts, curb the exploring, and keep the baby from bothering others. But this may give rise to an emotional outburst worse than the first problem.

Babies are not mature enough to control their curiosity or the expression of an emotion. They act out patterns of response that are natural to them. No baby can stop this pattern once it has been set in motion. If, for example, something makes a baby curious, the pattern of response—exploring—will always follow.

Parents should know that control of curiosity and of emotional outbursts is too much for a baby. So they must attack the problem in a way that suits the developmental level of the baby. Studies have shown that there are two methods that can be counted on to work with just about *any* baby.

First, the surroundings should be controlled so that nothing will happen to set off a destructive emotional outburst. For example, if babies show fear when something or someone new comes up to them suddenly, new experiences should be introduced gradually. Then the baby can become used to them. This will keep the baby from being frightened. It will also help the baby learn that many new experiences are pleasant.

Second, if the unwanted exploring or the emotional outburst started before it could be prevented by the adult, it can be quickly stopped by shifting the baby's attention to something else. Babies have a short attention span. They can be distracted from what they are doing and can be made to notice something else. As the baby starts to grab for a visitor's necklace to explore it, the parent can quickly turn the baby's attention to something on the other side of the room. Then the baby will forget the necklace. This may have to be followed up by giving the baby a toy before the attention goes back to the necklace again.

Accidents

Of all babyhood problems, accidents are the most serious because of possible harm to the baby. Physical damage from an accident may be only slight—a bump or scratch—and may be so short-lived that turning attention to something else will make the baby stop crying and forget about it. But there may also be psychological damage. This may last longer because getting hurt may lead to being fearful.

Few babies pass through babyhood without having some accidents. More happen during the second year of life

than during the first. During much of the first, they are too helpless to get into situations where they could be hurt. By the second year, babies have begun to explore. Not knowing the dangers, they explore everything that makes them curious.

Because of this, parents must protect babies from accidents by baby-proofing their surroundings. Everything that might harm babies is removed from their reach. In addition, babies who are no longer helpless must never be left alone to go where they wish, either inside or outside the home. When they are not carefully protected by a playpen or crib, someone must always watch them and be ready to protect them from a possible accident.

The number and seriousness of accidents have a great deal to do with the stage of the baby's development. When babies can move their bodies only by rolling, their chances of hurting themselves are far less than when they can walk and climb. When the hands can only grasp something that is put in them, babies are less likely to have accidents than later, when they can pull a cap off a bottle or a piece off a toy.

Because the surroundings in which babies grow up are different, the baby-proofing needed will also be different. For example, babies who grow up in an apartment that is all on one level will not have to be protected from falling down stairs. The chart on page 128 gives a list of the most common parts of the baby's environment which should be baby-proofed.

While all babies have accidents, some have more accidents than others. They are called *accident-prone*.

For Discussion

What would have to be done in your home to make it safe for a toddler? Refer to the chart on page 128 for some suggestions on baby-proofing your home.

There is little or no reason to believe that any normal, healthy baby is born accident-prone. There is proof, however, that some things in a person's life make the person more likely to have accidents. These things are listed and explained in the chart on page 129. Note that all of them can be controlled. Parents who know this can take steps to keep accidents from happening.

Why Problem Behavior Should Be Kept at a Low Level

When babies are troublesome, it makes the person who is caring for them nervous and edgy. One parent may blame the other for not keeping the baby under better control. This may lead to a strained husband-wife relationship. Older brothers and sisters become angry when the baby upsets their play or takes too much of the parents' time and attention. This often bothers the parents, who feel that the older children are not being fair or understanding. Thus, a vicious cycle is set in motion. The result is a highly charged emotional climate in the home. In such an atmosphere, small problems often develop into larger ones and become more and more difficult to solve.

When problem behavior is kept at a low level, problems are kept from arising, whenever possible. They are also corrected when they do come up, as soon as possible. This will have a positive effect not only on the baby but also on the entire family. The emotional climate of the home will be more relaxed and pleasant for everyone.

Families that often share pleasant moments are usually able to deal with problem behavior as it arises without being overwhelmed.
Michal Heron/McGraw-Hill

Baby-Proofing Measures to Prevent Accidents

Inside the Home

Appliances Keep them all out of the baby's reach and never turn them on unless someone is in the room to watch the baby.

Bathtub Put a towel or nonskid mat in the bottom of the tub when the baby is bathed.

Crib Keep the sides of the crib pulled up at all times. Use a sleeping bag for a young baby and a sleep strap for an older baby. Use no pillow. If toys are tied to the bars, use short ribbons to make sure the baby cannot be strangled.

Electrical Outlets If not being used, cover the outlets with tape or safety caps.

Floors Avoid polishing wood and linoleum floors. Use no scatter rugs unless nonskid mats are under them.

Heaters Radiators should be protected with radiator covers. Portable electric heaters should be used only when someone is in the room to watch the baby.

High Chair Make sure that the chair cannot tip over. Strap the baby in it to keep the baby from standing up or falling out. A low table and chair for eating are safer.

Kitchen A baby should be in a playpen when in the kitchen. Stoves, cleaning fluids, insect poisons, detergents, opened cans, broken glass, etc., cannot always be removed or covered to protect a baby.

Medicines All medicines—whether prescription or not—and all creams, lotions, hair sprays, dyes, etc., should be on the *top* shelf of a medicine chest or on the *top* shelf of a closet.

Ornaments Small ornaments, such as lighters and matchboxes, should be removed from the room. Large ornaments, such as lamps and bookends, should be put in the centers of tables or on the tops of bookcases.

Paint Painted furniture, walls, and woodwork should all be repainted with lead-free paint if the old paint is not lead-free.

Pets No pet—dog, cat, rabbit, etc.—should be left alone in a room with a baby. The baby should not be allowed to touch a pet without supervision.

Plastic Bags The safest thing to do with plastic bags is to throw them away unless they are in use to cover clothes or to store food in the refrigerator.

Playpen Be sure that toys have no parts that can be removed except those meant for safe play. Tie toys to the bars with short ribbon, if at all.

Stairs Have gates at the top and bottom of the stairs, and be sure that they are fastened at all times.

Tablecloths Tablecloths should not be used unless they are small enough to cover only the center of a table. When they hang over the sides, the baby is likely to pull them. Then everything on the table will fall off.

Toys Toys with parts that can be removed (though not made to be removed)—such as plastic or glass eyes in stuffed animals—and toys that are made of thin plastic that can be bitten should be thrown away.

Training Toilet Fix the training toilet firmly to the toilet seat and strap the baby into it. A low training toilet with a potty under it is safer.

Windows Open windows only at the top. If the house has French or sliding windows, open them only when someone is in the room to watch the baby.

Outside the Home

Animals   A baby should not be allowed to touch a strange animal. If a strange animal comes near a baby, the baby should be picked up and held out of the animal's reach. However, this should be done gently, not in a panicky way, or a long-lasting fear of animals may develop.

Automobile Seat   When taken out in an automobile, the baby should be in a carrying basket on the floor until he or she is able to sit. Then the baby should be strapped in a baby seat near an adult.

Baby Carriers   Outdoors, or in buses and shops, a baby can be carried in a baby basket or a carrier on the parent's shoulders in front or in back.

Carriage   When the baby is taken out in a carriage, the safety strap should always be fastened.

Shopping Cart   If the parent must take the baby to a supermarket, the baby should be put on the seat of the shopping cart and watched at all times.

Yard   If the baby is allowed to play in the yard, there should be a fence around it with a gate that is always closed. Unless there is an adult around, it is safer to put the baby in a playpen in the yard or on a porch.

Why Some Babies Are Accident-Prone

Brightness   Bright babies are usually alert and curious. They develop faster than the average baby. This means their environment needs to be baby-proofed earlier.

Firstborn   The parents of firstborn babies may be less aware of possible dangers than parents who have learned from caring for older children.

Member of Large Family   When the parents have a large family, the baby may get less supervision than is needed.

Young and Inexperienced Caretaker   When the care of a baby is turned over to older brothers or sisters or to a young and inexperienced baby-sitter, the baby may get less supervision than is needed for safety.

Failure to Baby-Proof the Surroundings   If possible dangers are not removed, either because the parents do not know the danger or because they do not like a "bare" house, there are more accidents than when the baby is better protected.

Uncontrolled Curiosity   A baby whose curiosity is allowed to be expressed without some attempt to turn it into harmless paths is likely to have more accidents than a baby who is busy with safer activities.

Highlights of Chapter 8

☐   For the most part, babyhood problems are the result of the baby's passing from one state of development to another. These problems are behavior patterns that parents and other family members find troublesome.

- [ ] Early babyhood problems are largely physical. Those of late babyhood are mostly behavioral.
- [ ] Negativism is found in almost all babies because most parents do not know how much independence their babies can handle.
- [ ] Spoiling a baby comes not from too much attention but from the wrong type of attention.
- [ ] Unsocial behavior in babyhood, such as shyness, fighting with other babies, or exploring people, is embarrassing and annoying to parents.
- [ ] Every area of everyday physical care of babies may give rise to problems for parents.
- [ ] Emotional outbursts of babies, especially anger and jealousy, are annoying, embarrassing, and troublesome for parents.
- [ ] Baby-proofing the environment is essential if accidents are to be prevented or reduced.
- [ ] Keeping problem behavior at a low level in babyhood makes the emotional climate of the home more relaxed and pleasanter for all family members.

Suggested Activities

1. Talk to several parents who have two or more children. Ask them if they feel that their later-born children caused them fewer problems than their firstborn children. If they say that they had fewer problems with their later-born children, ask if they feel this was because they had learned how to deal better with babyhood problems. If they say they had more problems with the later-born babies, ask what they thought was the reason for this.

2. Make a list of common physical problems and a list of common behavioral problems in babyhood. To whom should parents turn for advice in meeting the problems on your list? Explain your reasons for choosing these sources of advice.

3. Watch the way a baby you think is spoiled is treated. Compare the treatment an unspoiled baby is given.

4. Study carefully how babies and toddlers react to feeding and dressing situations. If the children cause problems for their parents, what do you think is the cause of these problems? How could the problems have been prevented or reduced?

5. Visit a toy store and examine the toys for babies less than 1 year old and for babies from 1 to 2 years old. Look over these toys carefully to see if they are safe for the babies of the ages for which they are meant. Rank the toys that you examine, starting with those you feel are safest and ending with those you find most dangerous.

Chapter 9

Caretakers of Babies and Children

Some goals of this chapter are:
- [ ] To realize that baby-sitting is an ideal way to learn about children while deciding about caring for them as a job
- [ ] To describe the important jobs of baby-sitters and to know about common emergencies a baby-sitter may meet and how they can be handled
- [ ] To understand how experience gained while baby-sitting can add to a person's self-confidence

Caretakers are people other than parents who do things that are essential to a baby's or a child's well-being.

Even before they are born, babies have caretakers. People in the health field do a great deal to make sure that babies are growing normally. They also run classes to teach new parents how to care for the baby.

For the first two to four days after birth, the nurses in the hospital take care of almost all the baby's needs. The mother takes over when the infant is brought to her at feeding times.

What Caretakers Do

They adjust the environment to meet the child's developmental needs.

They make sure the child is safe.

They give the baby love and a feeling of being safe. These are basic to good physical and mental health.

They lay the groundwork of behavior, attitudes, and feelings on which the patterns of later development will be built.

They encourage the development of the child's physical and mental abilities.

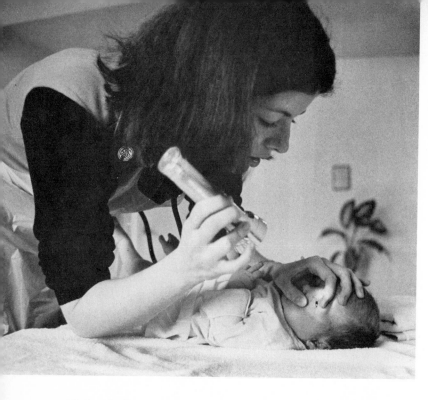

Many communities have visiting nurses who make routine house calls to examine babies.
Richard Watherwax

If the baby is born at home, a public-health nurse often helps the doctor or midwife during the delivery. The nurse remains until it is clear that all is well. Often, nurses are hired to help at home with the new baby for the first week or two after birth.

Doctors like to see the babies regularly. They want to let the parents know that all is well. Nurses, teachers, and aides in day-care centers take care of babies and children for most of the day when parents have to be elsewhere.

There are many more child-care jobs than people think. Some of the better-known ones are on the next page. The greater the responsibility, the more education and training a person will need to do the job well. How much responsibility a caretaker will have varies. It depends on such things as the amount of time the person spends with the child and when, the age of the child, and

what the person does for the child. A baby-sitter who arrives after the baby has been fed and put to bed, for example, will be chiefly responsible for the baby's safety. But a nurse who spends more time with the baby has greater responsibilities of feeding, bathing, dressing, and playing with the baby.

For Discussion

Choose two or three jobs from the list on page 133. Explain why those jobs from the first group do not call for special training, while those from the second and third groups do. How might the jobs in the first group be carried out better by people who have taken a course in child growth and development than by those who had never had such training?

132

Some Careers and Jobs in Caring for Children

No special training in child care is needed, but experience is helpful:
  Baby-sitter
  Mother's helper
  Playground assistant
  Clerk in children's store
  Camp counselor

A high school education plus special training afterward are needed to get a license:
  Practical pediatric nurse
  Day-care-center aide

Assistant teacher in nursery school and kindergarten
Assistant nurse in hospital nursery
Playground supervisor

College and professional degrees are needed:
  Supervisor of day-care center
  Teacher for preschools
  Registered pediatric nurse
  Pediatrician
  Child psychologist

You may be wondering how people get interested in taking care of children. How do they know that they will be happy doing it? You may be surprised to find out that many—from pediatricians to aides in a day-care center—made these discoveries as teenagers by baby-sitting for brothers and sisters or neighborhood children.

Being a Baby-Sitter

A baby-sitter is a must for today's parents. Sometimes emergencies come up and they have to be away from home. At other times parents just want to be free to do the things they enjoyed before the baby's arrival. Baby-sitting not only gives you the chance to earn some extra money but also gives you some ideas of what children are like and how you like being with them. You gain many things from baby-sitting, as shown in the chart below.

Except in an emergency, most parents do not leave a baby with a baby-sitter before the baby is about 2 months old. Even then, they feel safer

What You Learn from Baby-Sitting

You learn to take on responsibilities, to be independent, and to make decisions.
You learn to work with others.
You learn how to meet emergencies.
You learn to adjust to new people, new places, and new situations.
You gain a broader view of life by seeing how other people live.
You learn what it means to work.

You learn about children as they really are.
You learn to make good use of the time spent by yourself.
You learn something about being a manager.
You learn the satisfaction of giving help where it is needed and of being valued, loved, and respected for it.

with an experienced adult than with a high school student. After the baby is 5 or 6 months old, however, they feel better about leaving the baby with a teenager they trust.

When parents are happy with a baby-sitter, they will call the same one every time they need a sitter. It will be easiest to be a good baby-sitter if you know the children, their schedule, and what the parents expect of you. Then parents will feel sure that all will go well while they are away.

When baby-sitting, there are certain things that you should know. The most important are given in the accompany-ing chart. It is wise to arrive at least half an hour before the parents plan to leave. This will give you time to take over some of the care of the baby under the parent's supervision. Older children will not feel deserted when the parents leave if the children are happily busy.

For Discussion

Though baby-sitters are a must in American family life today, the idea of hiring sitters is fairly new. What has made this true and why?

It is comforting to parents to know that their children like and are happy with the baby-sitter. Nancy Hays/Monkmeyer

Important Information a Baby-Sitter Needs

When Taking Care of Children of Any Age

Where the parents can be reached and when they plan to return home.

The phone numbers of the doctor, fire station, police, hospital, and a neighbor or relative who should be called in an emergency.

Where all first-aid supplies are kept—bandages, cotton, and so on.

Where blankets are kept and how to change the room temperature if needed.

Where food is kept and what food is meant for the baby.

Whether or not the doorbell should be answered. Rules about this will depend on the area. They should be clearly understood before the parents leave. In any case, all doors and windows on the first floor should be kept locked.

When Taking Care of Babies

If and when they are to be fed, where the bottles are kept, what needs to be done to prepare a bottle for the baby, and if food other than milk is to be given.

How to lift and hold them in the way they are used to.

When and how they are to be diapered.

What should be done to prepare them for bed and what nightclothes to use.

When they are to be put to bed and what sleep position should be used.

When Taking Care of Young Children

If they are to be given supper, what will it be and when will it be given.

Whether they should be fed or encouraged to feed themselves.

How much playtime they should be given between the evening meal and bedtime.

The time when they should go to bed and important details about their bedtime and sleeping habits.

What the usual pattern is in preparing for bed—bath, cleaning the teeth, going to the toilet, taking favorite toys to bed, a short bedtime story, and so on.

What nightclothes to use and how to air the room.

Important Jobs of the Baby-Sitter

Baby-sitters are usually only short-term caretakers for children. So their two most important jobs are keeping the children safe and keeping them happy while the parents are away. Doing these two things will call for different methods for children of various ages.

The accompanying chart gives some ideas for keeping children safe and happy.

Some of the other functions of a caretaker (see page 131) can also be done while carrying out these two major jobs. To be happy, for example, the baby must feel loved and safe. Playing with

Suggestions for Meeting the Important Functions of a Baby-Sitter

Keeping Children Safe

Never leave babies alone except in the crib with the sides up.

Before giving children a toy, look it over carefully to make sure it will not be harmful to them.

When putting a baby on the toilet seat, strap the baby in and remain in the room.

Babies who are old enough to walk must be watched at all times unless in a playpen or a crib with the sides up.

If babies are put in a high chair, be sure the strap is fastened and remain in the room.

When preparing food, put babies in a playpen away from the stove.

Be sure closets and other rooms are closed off so young children cannot wander into them. If there are stairs in the house, be sure they, too, are closed off.

When carrying babies up or down stairs, hold them in one arm and hold onto the railing with the other hand.

Keeping Children Happy

Try to do things as the parents do them to keep from upsetting the children.

At the first sign of crying, try to catch their attention with something amusing.

Holding, rocking, talking, and singing to young children are good ways to make them happy.

Play simple games with them.

Read or tell stories to them.

Give the children the feeling that you are interested in doing things with them.

Keep the children so busy that they have no time to miss their parents.

---

babies is one of the important ways of keeping them happy. Play can also be used to encourage children to learn something new, like a game or song that their parents have not yet taught them.

Problems while Baby-Sitting

Emergencies, small ones or serious ones, may come up at one time or another whenever one is taking care of a baby. So it is important to be prepared to deal with them.

One problem is very likely to face a baby-sitter. Children get upset if things are done in a way that is new to them. Babies will fuss and cry when this happens. For example, they may refuse to drink their bottle if it is warmer or colder than usual. When toddlers are treated very differently from what they are used to, they may become so angry that they have a temper outburst. Or they may become stubborn and sulky. If they can tell you what they want and if you can change to their pattern, the problem will quickly pass.

This behavior is very common. However, if parents explain how to handle everyday tasks, the problems will usually not occur. Simply saying, "Tommy likes to drink out of the green cup," will do much to prevent them.

By teaching the child a new game, the baby-sitter encourages the development of physical and mental abilities.
Mimi Forsyth/Monkmeyer

For Discussion

When baby-sitting, how often should you check on the baby in the crib to make sure that all is well? Is it safe to think that all is well if the baby does not cry? Why?

Another problem you should be prepared to face is crying. Crying may start when the parents say good-bye or when they have dressed to leave. Usually this type of crying lasts for only a short time. But while it lasts it is upsetting. It could make you feel uncertain about handling the situation alone.

A baby may start to cry after being put to bed and sleeping for an hour or more. Parents are used to the baby's crying. They are usually able to stop it quickly. They know what to look for. But you will have to hunt for the cause. Look to see if the diapers are wet or soiled. Offer a bottle or a drink. Burp the baby in case there are gas pains. Rock and hug the baby.

Toddlers may begin to cry when it is time to go to bed or when they suddenly realize that their parents are not going to tuck them in. When toddlers start to cry, they may tire themselves out so much that they will have trouble falling asleep. Toddlers who have temper tantrums cannot easily be stopped by just turning their attention to something else. Instead, the situation must be handled gently. Letting them stay up a little longer as a special treat usually works. You can then play a quiet game or read to them. Usually, it is only a short time before they are ready for sleep.

It is not unusual for children to waken and start to cry. This may be because of some noise such as television or a ringing telephone. It may be because of some discomfort, such as wet diapers, a stomach pain, or a stuffy nose.

Unless you have experience, it may take a long trial-and-error process to discover the causes of the crying. It will take more time to find out what will stop it.

For Discussion

How might you plan to keep children you baby-sit for busy? Babies, toddlers, and young children should be discussed.

Experienced baby-sitters may be given greater responsibilities in caring for children. Sybil Shackman/Monkmeyer

A major problem is the child who gets sick or has an accident. This is a serious problem. But it is much less likely to happen than the two problems already described. If there are any signs of illness, parents may cancel their plans and stay at home. However, illnesses do come on rapidly in children. A baby who seemed well when put to bed may, a few hours later, have a bad attack of colic, a fever, or a stomach upset with vomiting.

Even with the most careful supervision, accidents sometimes happen. Children may fall. When exploring a toy, a baby may pull off a part of the toy, put the part in the mouth, and start to choke on it.

No matter how minor the illness or the accident, it will frighten the child and lead to crying. You should remain calm and try to find the cause of the trouble. Becoming frightened yourself will only worsen the situation and make the child hysterical.

Some ways to meet emergencies from illness or accidents are given in the accompanying chart. These will help give you some confidence in dealing with emergencies.

Do not make the mistake of thinking that a call to the children's parents, the doctor, or a neighbor for help will make it look as if you cannot handle the situation alone. From the parents' point of view, it is better that the sitter meets an emergency by calling for skilled help. This makes the parents more willing to turn over the care of their baby to that sitter again. From your own point of view, it is better to play safe than to run the risk of having something serious happen to the baby.

Children like baby-sitters who keep them interested and busy.
David S. Strickler/Monkmeyer

What To Do in Case of Illness or Accident

In Case of Illness

If the baby becomes hot and starts to fret, call the parents. They may suggest what to do or come home.

Never give the child medicine unless the parents or doctor directs you to do so.

If the baby keeps on crying after everything has been tried, get in touch with the parents, the doctor, or a neighbor.

In Case of Accidents

If the child has an accident, use first aid and then call the parents or doctor.

If the child is bleeding badly or vomiting, call the doctor at once.

If the doctor suggests taking the child to the emergency room of a hospital, ask which hospital. Then call the police to send an emergency car to get you and the baby to the hospital.

While waiting for the emergency car, call the parents and tell them where you are taking the baby.

If there are older children in the house, call your parents or a neighbor. Ask them to come at once to take care of the older children.

General On-the-Job Guides

Most parents will tell you what you need to know about the child, the house, and what you should do. Baby-sitting should not be thought of as a time to have fun or a social visit. As a baby-sitter you are working and being paid for it. Even when children are sleeping, you are responsible for their well-being. Discuss pay and your responsibilities before you accept a baby-sitting job. Also, know how you will be getting home when the parents return.

Usually, parents like you to feel at home while taking care of their children. However, they also hope that you will not take advantage of this freedom. The following chart gives some dos and don'ts you should remember while baby-sitting.

The more baby-sitting you do, the easier it will become. Experience will make you more sure of yourself. It will also give you a better understanding of children and what it is like to work with them.

Things to Remember When Baby-Sitting

Dos

Be careful of everything in the home. Handle any dishes and glassware you use with care. Have respect for things that others own. Clean up any messes you or the children make.

Find out ahead of time if you can use the television, stereo, or radio. To be sure you know how to run it, ask the parents. If they would rather you did not touch their set, respect their wishes.

Ask if it is all right for you to make a phone call if you need to. Do not make long calls to friends. That ties up the line and keeps you from your job.

Find out if the parents are against your having a friend come over. Some people do not mind; others do.

Don'ts

Don't leave children alone, even for a minute. *Never* leave the house without taking them. If the phone rings, be sure they are safe while you answer it, or take them with you.

Don't go to sleep. Part of being ready for the job is being rested. When you go to sleep, you are just not on the job.

Don't bring a date while you are baby-sitting. Remember this is a job, not a time for social visits.

Don't snoop around the house. Opening doors or closets, looking into drawers of chests and desks, and reading other people's mail are snooping.

Don't talk about the child, the family, or the home with outsiders.

Don't baby-sit when you have a cold or feel that you might be coming down with something.

Don't baby-sit for a child who has a cold or is ill, except in an emergency to help out the family.

Don't hit the children even if you know that the parents discipline them this way. Have patience with the children and keep them busy. This will help keep unpleasant situations from happening.

Highlights of Chapter 9

☐ Caretakers of children do things for them that are essential to their physical and psychological well-being.

☐ There are many jobs in the child-care field. The amount of training needed for a job has a great deal to do with the responsibilities that go along with it.

☐ Baby-sitting is a good way to get an idea of what children are like and to find out if you like working with them.

☐ Baby-sitters have two main jobs—keeping children safe and keeping them happy.

☐ Handling problem situations while baby-sitting will become easier as the sitter gains experience.

☐ Though illnesses and accidents are much more serious than other problems that may come up while baby-sitting, they do not happen as often.

☐ Facts about the child, the house, and what you are supposed to do while baby-sitting should be known before the parents leave you in charge.

☐ Experience gained from baby-sitting can be useful in building your self-confidence.

Suggested Activities

1. Find child-care jobs other than those listed on page 133. What training is needed for each? What are the responsibilities? Report to the class.

2. Question the parents in your neighborhood to find out how many of them employ baby-sitters. Ask how often they use a sitter and if they use the same one time after time. Ask what traits they look for in a sitter. Compare the answers, and share the results with the class.

3. Make up a package of things to do when you baby-sit. Have some ideas that will interest babies, toddlers, and young children.

4. Go to the library and find books on first aid. Learn how to handle emergencies. Find out if a first-aid course is offered in your neighborhood. What would be some reasons for taking such a course?

5. Plan a bulletin board showing how different parts of baby-sitting can develop into full-time jobs.

Unit Three | THE EARLY CHILDHOOD YEARS

The early childhood years go from the child's second birthday to the beginning of first grade in school. They are years of slow growth and rapid development. As a result, when children enter this stage they are not the way they will be when early childhood ends and they enter school. During these years, children are just beginning to learn how to use their rapidly developing mental abilities. They are first learning how to fit their behavior to the patterns accepted by school and society.

Chapter 10, "The Foundation Age Should Be Happy," is about how learning during childhood adds to the child's happiness. Of special interest are the three A's of happiness. These are useful for every age all through life.

Chapter 11, "Facts about Physical Growth," stresses the physical factors that add to the child's well-being and personal and social adjustments.

Chapter 12, "Learning Skills," discusses how skills are learned based on the groundwork laid in babyhood. The self-help skills, the social-help skills, and the play skills are introduced with facts on how and why these kinds of skills are important to young children.

Chapter 13, "Learning to Talk," explains how speech skills are mastered so that children can communicate without having to depend on the prespeech forms of language that were so useful during babyhood.

Chapter 14, "Intellectual Development," introduces factors that affect children's intellectual abilities. It describes those abilities that are most important at this stage.

Chapter 15, "The Child's Emotions," discusses how children's emotions differ from those of adults and why early childhood is the time for children to learn to control the expression of their emotions.

Chapter 16, "Personality Building," looks into the ways adults can help children develop positive self-concepts and traits. These are the factors that make up an individual's personality pattern.

Chapter 10

The Foundation Age Should Be Happy

Some goals of this chapter are:
- [ ] To understand why the early childhood years are thought of as the "foundation years," why foundations are important, and how children learn foundations
- [ ] To understand the connection between happiness and the building of foundations of behavior and attitudes
- [ ] To understand the three A's of happiness and why they are important

Since the time of Confucius, back in the sixth century B.C., childhood has been known as the "foundation age of life." This idea has been expressed in sayings like, "As the twig is bent, so the tree will grow."

Today, there is much to show that childhood is, indeed, the foundation period of life. The basic attitudes and behavior patterns—the way the child feels and acts—are developed in the first five or six years. They largely determine what kind of person the child will be as an adult.

Building Foundations for Life
Two separate but related processes build the foundations for the child's physical development, behavior, and at-

Children need a certain amount of freedom to explore, discover, and learn.
Christopher W. Marrow/Stock, Boston

titudes. These are maturation and learning. *Maturation* is the natural development of the child's inherited traits, both physical and mental. It is an ongoing process that begins before birth.

When maturation reaches a certain point, learning can begin. For example, when the muscles of the legs and the back have matured enough, the baby can begin to learn to walk. Other kinds of maturation and learning will be going on at different rates and times.

Children who are exposed to learning situations early are better able to take advantage of the teachable moment. Henry Monroe

Learning means gaining knowledge, skills, and experience. To learn, the child has to work at doing things over and over again. It will not happen by itself. Nor will maturation do the job alone. Maturation and learning go hand in hand.

However, children must reach a certain level of maturity before they can learn the skills of any given behavior. The state of readiness to learn a certain thing is sometimes called the *teachable moment.*

The teachable moment does not happen at the same time for all patterns of behavior, for all attitudes and feelings, or for all children. For example, babies learn hand skills before they learn leg skills. And certain mental abilities develop sooner than others. For example, imagination develops before reasoning.

When Are Children Ready to Learn?

Children grow and develop at different rates. Because of this, they reach the teachable moment for any given kind of learning at different times. One 3-year-old, for example, may be ready to learn a certain skill, while another 3-year-old may not yet be physically or psychologically ready. A third 3-year-old may have been ready to learn that skill for so long that he or she is beginning to lose interest in it.

There are three simple rules that help to decide if a child is ready to learn a certain thing. They are given in the accompanying chart.

It is important to understand that *all three* of these rules must be used; one or two are not enough. The fact that a child grabs for the soap and washcloth in the bath does not always mean that

First, children must show an interest in the thing to be learned. When a toddler tries to put toothpaste on the brush or tries to climb onto the seat of a tricycle, there is reason to believe that the toddler *may* be ready to learn the skills for these activities.

Second, the interest must last, not just fade when the chance to carry out the activity is given. The interest must go on and become even stronger than many other interests.

Third, the performance of the task must improve with practice. Children may be interested in something that they see. But if they do not get better at a fairly steady rate, they are not really ready to learn. In fact, they will most likely lose interest anyway.

---

the child is ready for self-bathing. The child may just be playing. But when a toddler takes the washcloth at every bath time and tries to use it to scrub, it may well be time to help the child learn to wash.

Types of Learning

Learning may be either self-initiated or outer-directed. In *self-initiated* learning, children decide what to learn and how to learn it. There is little or no guidance from others. In *outer-directed* learning, the learning is directed and controlled by others. It is usually called teaching or child training. "Child training" is more often used because "teaching" sounds like school learning. Short descriptions of the different forms of learning are in the chart on page 148.

Studies of learning show that the best way to learn is the democratic child-training method. The poorest is trial

Enthusiastic teaching and affection will promote learning by imitation. Erika Stone/ Monkmeyer

and error, a form of self-initiated learning. Other methods fall between these two.

The forms of self-initiated learning—trial and error, imitation, and identification—are all free from the "bossiness" a child may not like. But they do not have the guidance that is so important to good learning.

However, the differences between the methods of learning are not always clear-cut. For example, imitation is listed in the chart as a self-initiated form of learning. But imitation may also be used in child training. So it is sometimes an outer-directed form. This is because children often learn best by imitation. It is much easier and more effective to show a child how to do something and let the child copy it than it is to try to explain it.

One might think, from what has been said so far, that children's learning is always carefully planned and formal. Nothing could be farther from the truth. Huge amounts of children's learning take place when neither adults nor children are thinking about it. Children watch what goes on around them and are always learning from the behavior of others.

This is especially true about the development of attitudes and feelings. Children's attitudes are largely shaped

---

Methods of Learning

Self-Initiated Learning

Trial-and-Error Learning   The child tries out one way of doing something and repeats it if it works. If it does not work, the child tries another way and still another. Finally, the child will hit upon a good method.

Learning by Imitation   The child copies the behavior of another person.

Learning by Identification   As in imitation, the child copies the behavior of another person. Learning by indentification is different because the person the child copies is someone the child loves and admires, not just anyone.

Outer-Directed Learning (Child Training)

Authoritarian   Children are forced to learn what a person in authority wants them to learn. They are not told why they should learn. They are not often praised when they do learn.

Democratic   The person helping the children learn explains why and how they are expected to learn. The children's interests and needs play a part in the planning of learning activities. Children are rewarded when they do well.

They are punished only when they fail because they refuse to do what is expected of them. They are offered a chance to explain their side of the story before punishment is planned.

Permissive   This is much like trial-and-error learning because children are allowed to learn as they please. Rewards and punishments are not often given. There is little guidance.

Learning is a continuous process whereby parents use everyday activities to lay foundations for feelings. Michal Heron/Monkmeyer

by those around them. Adults may tell children they should be kind and friendly. But if those around them are usually cross and unfriendly, the children will learn cross, unfriendly attitudes—not the attitudes adults *tell* them they should have.

Children do not learn attitudes and feelings by being told about them. They learn about anger, guilt, and punishment when they see an older brother spill milk and watch the way both he and the parent react to the accident. They learn about good manners when they see how their mother or father greets visitors or answers the telephone. They learn about honesty when they watch parents' behavior in stores. They learn about kindness when someone comforts them when they are sad or hurt.

Adults may not think that they are teaching children at these times. But some of the most important things a child can learn are learned that way. How, then, can parents and other adults guide a child's learning and not leave it to chance or trial and error if so much learning takes place when no one is paying attention? The most important thing is for adults who are with children to look to their own behavior. They are always an example. Parents and other child caretakers need to know that a child is likely to copy everything they do—their speech, their attitude toward other people, the way they react under pressure, their food likes, and everything else. Knowing this, adults may try harder to have the attitudes and behavior they would like their children to have.

149

Guidance in Building Foundations

Guidance—the kind that is found in democratic child training—is the best way to help children learn. Guidance is especially needed in the early stages of learning something, when the ground-work is being laid. When children are first learning to swim, for example, they need help all the time to make sure that they move correctly. Otherwise they may slip into bad habits, using a poor form that will keep them from swimming well.

Once a good base has been laid, the adult does not need to guide the activity quite so closely. Much of what the child does has become a habit. However, some guidance is still needed even in the later stages of learning. This is because the child may still make mistakes. If the mistakes are repeated instead of corrected, they could become unwanted habits.

Guidance is most needed for the development of attitudes and feelings. There are two reasons for this. First, attitudes and feelings are far less noticeable than many behavior patterns. Thus, unwanted attitudes can become deeply rooted before parents know of them. Second, attitudes and feelings, once set, are most difficult to change because they are based on emotions.

Suppose a child is developing a poor attitude toward playing with other children. If the parents think that the child is just tired or likes to watch special shows on TV, they may be overlooking more important reasons for the child's behavior. The child may have had bad experiences with other children or may not enjoy their games. The parents need to try to discover why the child does not play with other children. They then need to make sure the child gets some positive, happy experiences of playing with others. This will make the child's attitude more open to social play.

The example adults set is important here, as always. Are the adults themselves friendly toward other children? Do they welcome other children to play in their home and yard? Do they have adult friends and pleasant times of their own?

For Discussion

Why is it harder to change unwanted attitudes or feelings than unwanted behavior? What ideas can you give that could be used to help a child change an unwanted attitude? For example, what would you do if a child did not like some of the games the other children in the neighborhood enjoyed?

Some people think that nature will see to it that children adjust well to life. However, nature just provides the chance for a wide variety of behavior patterns. The behavior patterns that will be established depend on learning based on the guidance and examples the child has.

Without guidance, children would have to depend on trial-and-error learning. This is just not good enough to prepare them for today's complex world. Since young children are not able to guide their own learning, parents have the major responsibility for guiding and training their children.

Teaching a child new skills is as rewarding for the parent as for the child. This is an ideal time to correct errors and encourage healthy habits. Richard Nowitz

When the neighborhood and the school begin to be part of the child's world, there will be other guides, such as teachers and day-care-center workers. There will be other examples for the child to imitate, including playmates. At this stage, a child may develop a strong emotional attachment to someone outside the home.

The models and guidance of outsiders may strengthen the groundwork laid in the home. Or they may go against it and weaken it.

Foundations: Good or Bad?
Childhood foundations play a great part in the way a person later adjusts to life. If the foundations are good, they lead to good personal and social adjustments and to a greater chance for happiness. If they are bad, they leave the person poorly adjusted to the world and with less chance for happiness.

Anything that is learned—even the foundations of behavior—can, sup-

posedly, be unlearned. But this is not at all easy. The longer a child does something one way, the harder it will be to learn to do it differently. The longer children see poor or negative attitudes around them, the harder it will be to build healthy positive attitudes of their own.

Foundations and Happiness Are Connected
Childhood can and should be a happy time. One of the most important things parents can do for their children is help them find happiness.

Guidance is essential for laying the foundations of happiness just as it is in laying other foundations. Children do not know what will or will not lead to happiness. Parents and other adults must make choices that will make it possible for children to grow up happily.

People have their own ideas about happiness. It has many different meanings. For some, happiness means riches. For others, to be happy is to be without cares. It means freedom from responsibilities.

Happiness is personal. What makes one person happy does not make everyone happy. True happiness is a positive feeling that perhaps only you can explain for yourself. It is a feeling of satisfaction within yourself. The feeling often shows in the way you look, the way you do things, and the way you treat other people.

For Thought

Make a list of the most important things you can remember learning when you were quite young. Ask your parents to help you fill in the gaps. Looking back on them, do you now believe these things were foundations? If so, foundations of what—behavior, attitudes, or personality?

For Discussion

Explain why a childhood without cares may not be a happy one. Are people with responsibilities likely to be happier than those who have none? Give reasons for your answer.

What Makes Children Happy?

Since happiness is different for each person, there is no one thing that will make children happy. There are, however, certain things that add to true happiness. They may be called the three A's of happiness. They are achievement, acceptance, and affection.

Each of the three A's of happiness adds to the others. One A alone does not mean certain happiness; all three must be present. Besides being pleasant, happiness can have many good side effects. They are shown in the accompanying chart.

Showing interest and approval of a child's efforts will give the child a feeling of accomplishment. Sepp Seitz/Woodfin Camp & Associates

The Three A's of Happiness

Achievement   Children feel good about themselves when they have done well in what they set out to do. To do something worthwhile and do it well—even if it seems like a small thing to others—is an important part of self-respect, and therefore of happiness, at any age.

Acceptance   When others accept children as they are, the children feel good about themselves. Being accepted as part of a group, however small, makes people feel secure. A person's achievements may add to acceptance by others. Acceptance may also grow into affection.

Affection   At any age, being liked by others helps people like themselves. Children know that others like them by the way others treat them. When children return the affection that others show, the feeling is strengthened on both sides. Being loved and giving love are essential to happiness.

Foundations for Happiness

Happiness is affected by both inside and outside states. In childhood, the person has little or no control over the outside state of his or her life. Whether children have enough food, shelter, and clothing; whether they feel safe and loved; whether they have chances for fun, for learning, and for new experiences—all these things are decided by those who take care of them. Yet they are essential to the child's happiness.

The first need in building foundations for happiness is that adult caretakers provide the basic physical and emotional needs of children. It might seem that this should go without saying. But the great number of children whose basic needs are not met proves that this fact needs to be stressed. There is not much point in telling children they will be happier when they change some of their attitudes if, in the meantime, they are being beaten or underfed at home.

What Happiness Can Do for a Child

Happiness can improve every child's looks.

Happiness can make children eager and interested. Unhappiness tends to make them uninterested in anything.

Happiness and good health go hand in hand. Being unhappy upsets the normal workings of the body.

Happy children want to do what they are able to do. Unhappy children do not care.

Happiness improves children's relationships with friends and family.

Happiness can help children turn outward and think of others. Unhappy children tend to think only of themselves.

Happiness can help children develop a sense of humor, which is important for good personal and social adjustments.

If the parents—for whatever reasons—cannot meet the child's needs, it is essential that someone else do so.

Once the outside needs for happiness are met—that is, a reasonable standard of comfort, health, security, and kindness—then it is helpful to guide children in understanding how they may add to their own happiness. They can do this by developing certain attitudes and habits.

One of the most important kinds of guidance children can receive is learning how to set goals for themselves that are not too high or too low. Some parents set impossible aims for children. They expect them to reach goals—for example, in schoolwork—that are much too high for the child's age and ability. This happens most often when parents want very much for their child to do better than other children.

Experiencing Unhappiness

No one can go through life without experiencing some unhappiness. Unhappiness comes to the most protected people. It even happens to the youngest children. Their parents can protect them from its worst effects and help build up their *unhappiness tolerance*. That is the ability to stand unhappiness without being overcome by it. The chart below gives some hints for doing so. It would be a mistake to think, as some people do, that examples of unhappiness are needed in order to make children strong enough to face the real thing. Life will present them with enough real unhappiness.

It is wise, however, not to protect children too much from unhappy things that happen near them. For example, if there is a death in the neighborhood, it should not be hidden from the children. It is better that they learn gradually, and at a distance, that death is not terrifying. Then if they should have to face the death of a close relative, it may not be so much of a shock.

Some Children Are Happier than Others

Children's happiness varies. It depends on the time of life and on the individual. A number of factors are responsible.

Children whose parents and other family members love them are happier than those who feel unloved and unwanted. For example, if older brothers

---

Hints for Developing a Child's Unhappiness Tolerance

Be sure that a child's unhappy times do not outweigh the happy ones in either how often they happen or how strong they are.

Let children talk freely about unhappy experiences they have had or have heard about. Answer honestly any questions they may ask about divorce or other painful subjects, using terms they understand.

Try to follow up a bad experience with one that gives a child happiness as soon as possible.

When children fail in one task, quickly have them do another which they can do well.

and sisters always feel that the younger ones are pests, it will be hard for the little ones to feel loved and happy.

Children who behave well are often happier than those who do not. This can be explained from two directions. On the one hand, children who are good are not scolded very much. They do not often have to be told to stop doing something they want to do. They have less reason to feel unloved and unwanted. These children are happy because they are good.

On the other hand, children who are happy enjoy what they are doing and the people they are with. They usually do not get into trouble by trying to do something that is not allowed or by arguing with others. They do not misbehave because there is no reason to. By this reasoning, these children are good because they are happy.

There is some truth in both these explanations. The important thing the second explanation may offer, however, is some understanding of children who are not happy or well-behaved. Adults often tell such children that, if only they would behave well, they would be happy. However, when understanding adults really try to create conditions in which these children can be happy, their behavior often improves a great deal.

Children have different abilities and interests but share the common desires for achievement, acceptance, and affection. George Roos/Peter Arnold

Often children are unhappy because they have nothing to do—they lack the pride of achievement. Try these ideas and see if they make the children happier:

For Babies

Provide toys for them to explore and handle.

Play simple games like peekaboo.

Say simple words and let them babble their answers.

When they can pull themselves to a standing position, hold their hands and let them take a few steps.

For Young Children

Give them a toy for creative play and show them how to use it.

Praise their achievements, even if they seem small.

Give them responsibilities that they can do, such as putting shoes away or emptying a wastebasket.

Let them help with simple household tasks, such as making a bed or dusting furniture.

Teach them play skills. Then play with them and let them win sometimes if you can do it without their noticing it.

Encourage them to feed, bathe, and dress themselves, no matter how slowly or how awkwardly they do so.

Will Childhood Happiness Guarantee Lifelong Happiness?

There is an age-old belief that childhood happiness will guarantee lifelong happiness. This belief is partly true.

A happy childhood gives children feelings of being loved, of being safe, and of self-confidence. These carry over into later life, increasing the chances of lifelong happiness. However, children need to learn to satisfy the three A's of happiness on their own. Parents can guide and help in the beginning, and they can provide the outward states that make happiness possible. But the children's lives will change as they grow older. They must be able to adjust to new situations.

Studies have shown that happy adults usually remember a happy childhood. There is no proof, however, that childhood unhappiness will result in lifelong unhappiness. Unhappy children often become happy teenagers and adults. For some, early unhappiness has given them a strong desire for happiness, and they have made an extra effort to achieve it.

Highlights of Chapter 10

☐ The early years of life are the foundation years. Behavior patterns and attitudes are formed during this time.

☐ Foundations are formed by both maturation and learning.

☐ Children will not learn until they are ready to learn. This state of readiness is known as the teachable moment.

☐ Learning is of two kinds: self-initiated, in which children decide what and how they will learn; and outer-directed (usually called child training), in which learning is directed and controlled by others.

☐ There are three kinds of child training: authoritarian, democratic, and permissive. Of them, the democratic one produces the best results.

☐ The examples set by the people children see daily play a great role in what children learn, most of all in their attitudes and feelings.

☐ Guidance is most important in the early stages of learning.

☐ To make childhood happy, adults must meet the outside needs for happiness and direct the learning of the inner foundations for happiness.

☐ The three A's of happiness—achievement, acceptance, and affection—are all essential to happiness at every age.

☐ Childhood happiness helps make lifelong happiness more likely.

Suggested Activities

1. Think of some strong like or dislike that you have. Try to remember some childhood experience you had that was the reason for the like or dislike. If you cannot trace its beginning, ask your parents to help you. Report to the class. Note that likes and dislikes are there even when the reasons for them are forgotten.

2. To realize the good and bad parts of different kinds of child training, talk about the good and bad effects each is likely to have on a child.

3. Studies show that the important foundations for attitudes and behavior have been laid by the time the child enters first grade. Of what importance is this fact to a first-grade teacher? How does it change what the teacher can expect the child to learn?

4. Make a list of the things you think add most to a child's happiness. Think about each of these factors and discuss how they can affect people of every age.

5. Plan a bulletin board to show how the three A's of happiness are important to you as teenagers.

Chapter 11

Facts about Physical Growth

Some goals of this chapter are:
- [ ] To understand why the very rapid physical growth of babies slows down in early childhood
- [ ] To know the important changes in body proportions in young children and how these changes affect the child's appearance and behavior
- [ ] To understand how illnesses and physical defects affect the child's physical and psychological adjustments
- [ ] To be able to identify some appearance and behavior factors that are used to judge if a child is thriving

A child's physical growth during the early childhood years is different from growth during babyhood. Unless parents and others who act as caretakers for a young child are aware of certain facts about growth, they may worry about whether there is something wrong with the child.

The first fact is that growth slows down after the baby's first birthday. It goes on at that slower rate all through childhood. Young children still grow faster than older children, but their growth is slower than that of babies.

The second fact is that there is more growth internally than externally. The heart, the lungs, and the digestive system now take their turn in rapid growth.

Height and weight increase at a slower rate.

The third fact is that physical *development* is greater than physical *growth*. As a result, children's bodies change greatly in proportions. When children reach their sixth birthday, they do not look like the same people they were as babies.

Height and Weight

When early childhood begins, children are about half as tall as they will be when they reach adulthood. However, their weight is only about one-fifth of adult weight. If people kept on growing at the rate they grew during the first

In just a short span of time, a child goes from a toddler to a tyke who shows wider interests and abilities. Mimi Forsyth/Monkmeyer; Jim Cron/Monkmeyer; Michael Kagan/Monkmeyer

year of life, they would be about 20 feet (6 meters) tall as adults. The weight would have to be measured in tons (tonnes).

During the early childhood years, children grow 3 to 5 inches (8 to 13 centimeters) a year and gain 3 to 5 pounds (1 to 2 kilograms). The accompanying chart gives the ages at which most babies and young children reach certain heights and weights. Note that between the ages of 2 and 6, the child grows between 11 and 17 inches (28 and 43 centimeters) in height. This rate of growth is much slower than the gains of the first two years of life.

Gains in weight are likewise slower in early childhood than in babyhood. By their sixth birthday, children who had tripled their weight in their first year are only six times as heavy as they were at birth! In spite of this gain of several pounds (kilograms), young children look thinner than they did in baby-

Pattern of Height and Weight Increases	
Height	**Weight**
At birth: 20 ins (51 cm)	At birth: 7 lb (3 kg)
At 2 years: 32 to 34 in (81 to 86 cm)	At 4 months: 14 lb (6 kg)
At 6 years: 43 to 45 in (109 to 114 cm)	At 1 year: 21 lb (10 kg)
	At 6 years: 42 lb (19 kg)

159

hood. In fact, many young children look scrawny (skinny and bony) by the time they are old enough to go to school.

There are two reasons why children become scrawny as they grow older. First, the rate of increase in height is noticeably greater than the increase in weight. Three inches (8 centimeters) added to a body that is already 32 to 34 inches (81 to 86 centimeters) tall shows up more clearly than 3 pounds (1 kilogram) added to a body that weighs 24 to 26 pounds (11 or 12 kilograms). The small weight gain is spread over the whole body, which is 3 or more inches (8 centimeters) taller. This means that the weight gain is spread so thin that it can barely be noticed.

Second, the weight gain in early childhood comes more from growth in bones and muscles than from fat tissues. In babyhood, on the other hand, weight gains come more from fat tissues.

Individual Differences in Growth

Even though all children follow the same basic pattern of growth, there are differences at every age. These differences are greater in weight than in height. For example, it is unusual for a child to be more than 2 inches (5 centimeters) taller or shorter than the average height for children of the same age. But differences of 5 to 10 pounds (2 to 5 kilograms) are quite common. Children are more likely to weigh more than the average for their ages than to weigh less than the average.

The reason for this difference is that weight is affected more by environment than is height. Sometimes parents' worries about slow growth lead to forced feeding. This will have little effect on the child's height, but a marked effect on weight. The reason for this is that height is controlled more by heredity than by environment.

Factors Responsible for Differences in Growth

Heredity   Short parents are more likely to have short children; tall parents are more likely to have tall children; and so on.

Poor Nutrition   Though few American children are starving, the growth of many children is stunted by a lack of the right kinds of food, especially proteins.

Emotional Stress   Children brought up in homes where there is a great deal of emotional stress may not grow as fully as they should.

Sex   Boys tend to be taller and heavier than girls, on the average. But there are many exceptions.

Body Build   Children with stout body builds weigh more than children who have slender bodies, even if they are the same height.

Intelligence   In many cases, bright children are larger than dull children and reach puberty slightly earlier. Again, there are many exceptions.

Health   Poor health or illness slows down growth, but this usually does not last. When the child's health improves, there is usually a period of catch-up growth.

Teething   As the last of the baby teeth cut through the gums during the third year, children are less hungry and growth slows down. This does not last. Children usually make up the lost growth after teething is over.

There are many factors that cause differences in body growth during the years of early childhood. The most important of these are given in the accompanying chart.

Today, there are, unfortunately, too many young children who are overweight. Some are even *obese*, or very overweight. They may be 20 percent, or more, heavier than the average for their ages. In the past, trouble with the glands was believed to be the cause of obesity. As a result, it was thought that the person could do nothing about being overweight unless the glandular trouble could be controlled by medicine.

It is now known that only a few people are obese because of glandular problems. Most are overweight because of overeating—especially overeating of starches and sweets, which are usually desserts and snacks.

For Discussion

Many doctors and others are very worried about overweight adults. Why do you think many parents try to get their children to eat more than the children want or need?

Parents' Concerns about Growth

If parents do not know the normal pattern of growth during early childhood, they might worry about the way their children are growing. Their worries are mostly of two kinds: worry because children are not growing as fast as they used to, and worry about variations in body sizes.

Parents watch their babies grow like little weeds during the first year. Then they see little or no increase in height or weight for perhaps a month or two at a time. This worries them. So does seeing chubby babies becoming thin, even skinny, children.

In their search for what is wrong, they very often think that the child is not eating enough. So they are likely to start trying to fatten the child. Many eating problems of children begin this way.

Another kind of problem may arise because of a child's size. Size has an effect on what the parents think the child can and should do. When children are larger than age-mates, adults often expect more from them than the children may be capable of doing. When they do not live up to what is expected, grown-ups may find fault with them for not "acting their age." This is not fair to these children. They may be acting their *chronological* ages (that is, the number of years they have lived) but not their *physical* ages, as judged by body size.

Children who are smaller than age-mates are often treated like younger children. They may not get the rights, responsibilities, and chances to learn that other children their age get.

To young children, differences in size do not matter unless playmates, parents, or other adults say something about it. When adults say that big children look so healthy, a tall child will be pleased. However, she or he will feel differently if a playmate says "you're too big to play" or nicknames the child Stilts. Long-lasting damage to children's self-respect can be caused by unpleasant remarks about their body size.

Differences in heredity and environment make each child a unique individual.
Ginger Chih/Peter Arnold

For Discussion

Suppose young children are self-conscious about being fatter, thinner, taller, or shorter than their playmates. How would you try to help them overcome it? How could the self-consciousness have been prevented in the first place?

Body Proportions

During early childhood, all parts of the child's body grow, but at different rates. As a result, the body still does not have the proportions of adults' bodies. But neither does it have the proportions of babies' bodies.

In the head, the forehead area develops faster than the lower parts of the face. The reason for this is the very rapid growth of the brain. As the child's

face grows longer, it loses its babyish look. However, the nose and mouth remain small compared with the size of the head. And the eyes and ears may still seem too large. When permanent teeth replace baby teeth, they give some shape to the jaw.

The trunk grows longer and broader in the early years of childhood. It seems even longer than it is because the young child develops a neck. At the same time, the sloping shoulders that seemed to blend into the baby's short, thick neck become broader and more clearly shaped. The lower part of the trunk also changes, and a waistline begins to appear.

The young child's arms grow much longer between babyhood and age 6. Because the muscles grow at a very slow rate, the arms are thin and straight.

This gives the young child an all-arms look. While the palms of the hands grow larger, the young child's fingers remain short and stubby. This makes the hands appear much too small for the arms.

The legs, which were proportionally too small in babyhood, grow during the years of early childhood. But they grow at a slower rate than the arms. Compared to a baby's legs, they look longer than they really are because they straighten out, especially at the knees. They are also thin and without well-developed muscles. The feet grow broader and longer, though the toes are proportionally too short for the rest of the foot. The young child's foot has no arch. So it looks larger than it really is.

Changes in body proportions and the fact that a child's body is not shaped like an adult's affect both children's behavior and appearance. This, in turn, affects people's reactions to them.

The way people react has a strong effect on the way children feel about themselves. If, for example, adults scold or punish children for being clumsy, the children may lose confidence in themselves. But if adults praise children for things they do well, the children will develop good feelings about themselves.

The most serious effect of changed body proportions comes when parents think their child is homely. This is caused by things such as long, skinny arms, missing front teeth, and large permanent teeth in a small face. Many people think these short-lived traits are cute. Others take them for granted. If parents become nervous about their children's looks, their children may also begin to worry. This will damage their self-respect. Some parents try to cover up what they think of as their child's homely stage by putting too much stress on clothes and grooming. This can make the child angry and put a strain on parent-child relationships.

Bones, Fat, and Muscles

In the early part of childhood, the bones are still soft enough to mend quickly if they are broken. But they can easily be misshapen. For example, young children should not sit in chairs made for adults. They may get into the habit of slouching or half lying in the chair. This may result in a slight curvature of the spine.

Adipose, or fatty, tissue develops faster than muscle tissue during early childhood. Children who eat too much carbohydrate and too little protein will develop too many fat cells. This may make them tend to be overweight for the rest of their lives. Even when the muscles develop, such children will still look chubby because they have more fat than muscle.

The child with broad, thick muscles tends to be physically stronger than the child with slender muscles. How much energy the child has will depend partly on how much muscle there is compared with fatty tissue. The more muscle tissue, the more energetic the child will be.

Teeth

Most of the twenty first, or "baby," teeth have cut through the gums shortly after babyhood ends. In the meantime,

The loss of baby teeth is an important landmark in a child's growth and development. Kenneth Karp

the permanent teeth are already developing rapidly in the gums. The baby teeth that were the first to cut through the gums will be the first to loosen and fall out—sometime between the ages of 5 and 7.

By the time they are ready to enter first grade, most children have one or two permanent teeth and a hole where a permanent tooth will soon appear. This process of losing baby teeth and replacing them with permanent teeth goes on until the child is 12 or 13 years old.

Many parents put far too little stress on the care of baby teeth. They may have children clean their teeth often enough but not take the children for dental checkups. And once children have learned to use a toothbrush, parents often fail to see that the children give their teeth a good cleaning.

It is true that decay of baby teeth is not quite as serious as decay of permanent teeth. Sooner or later children lose baby teeth, while permanent teeth must last for the rest of their lives. However, decay of baby teeth can spread to the permanent teeth forming behind them.

There are two serious effects of removing baby teeth before the natural pattern. These are explained in the accompanying chart. These apply to teeth removed by a dentist because they are decayed as much as to loose teeth removed by the child before they fall out on their own. Today, when a baby tooth must be removed early, many dentists put a wedge in the empty space. This keeps the remaining teeth from moving. A shift could affect the permanent teeth and the shape of the jaw.

Effects of Removing Baby Teeth Too Early

Effect on Permanent Teeth The teeth next to the empty space may shift slightly while waiting for the permanent tooth to come in. When this happens, there is not enough room for the permanent tooth to come in straight. It then comes in crooked, often overlapping the tooth beside it.

Effect on Speech A gap between the teeth makes it hard for the child to say certain sounds, such as r, d, and s, the right way. Most children lisp or soften sounds while they are changing from baby to permanent teeth. If the baby teeth are pulled too soon, the lisping is more likely to last longer and perhaps turn into a habit.

Children's Illnesses

Even for healthy children, illness is more common in the preschool years than it will be when the child grows older. It is even more common, though far less serious, than it is in babyhood. This is because the baby is less exposed to illness than is the young child.

Illness in childhood need not be serious if children are in good physical condition. Also, parents should quickly attend to any sign of illness.

The accompanying chart shows some illnesses of early childhood. They are in order from most common to least common. Note how much more common are simple colds, respiratory illnesses, and digestive upsets than are the contagious children's diseases. In a family where there are no older children, young children are less likely to get a disease like chicken pox or measles than they are when they go to school. If they have been immunized against such diseases, they will either not get them or will have only a very mild case.

Few young children escape illness. However, some seem to have more than their fair share. These children are *illness-prone.*

There are many reasons why children are illness-prone. Some children are just not as healthy as others. This may be because of inherited conditions, allergies, or poor nutrition and care.

Effects of Illness in Early Childhood

The psychological effects of illness in early childhood are often greater than the physical ones. However, both are serious. Everyone should try to keep childhood illnesses at a low level.

The chart on page 167 gives some of the most common and serious effects, both physical and psychological. The psychological effects play a part in both personal and social adjustments. For that reason they are more far-reaching than the physical results. They are also harder to correct after the child's health returns to normal.

Children sometimes become spoiled while ill. They will expect to be the center of attention when they are well enough to return to their play world.

Illnesses of Early Childhood

Colds, accompanied by stuffed noses and earaches

Upper respiratory illnesses, such as sore throats, coughs, and wheezing

Gastrointestinal illnesses, in the form of stomach aches, vomiting, constipation, and diarrhea

Contagious children's diseases, such as chicken pox, measles, German measles, and mumps

Diseased tonsils

Enlarged or infected adenoids

Allergic reactions, as shown in asthmatic breathing, skin rashes, and hives

Heart diseases

Tuberculosis

Rheumatic fever

Cancer, most of all leukemia

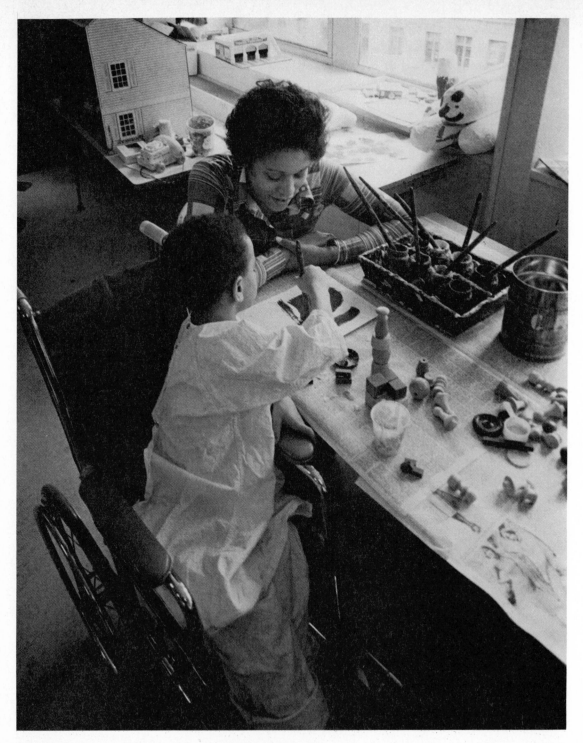

Hospitalization for a child is an unpleasant experience. Love and attention from parents can provide comfort when it is most needed.
Christopher Marrow/Stock, Boston

Effects of Illness on Young Children

Physical Effects

The times of eating, sleeping, and toileting are often changed.

Physical growth may stop for a while.

Children may lose weight.

Lack of activity causes the muscles to weaken and lose coordination.

Psychological Effects

Only quiet play may be allowed during illness. This leads to boredom and fussiness.

The environment is often limited to one room or bed, also causing boredom.

Lack of hunger builds up resistance to eating. This may lead to eating problems after health returns.

Other children are usually not allowed to play with a sick child. This causes boredom.

Children soon learn that they can get more attention than if they were well.

If parents are less likely to scold or punish a sick child, the child may learn that it pays to behave badly.

Boredom and not feeling well may change the child's disposition to that of an unpleasant, fault-finding person.

This may make other children not want to play with them because they seem bossy. Their playmates may also have learned new play skills and games while they were ill.

Hospitalization of Children

Young children may need to go to the hospital if the doctor feels that special care is needed. To most children, it is frightening to go to the hospital. This is partly because they are afraid of being away from their parents and the surroundings of the home.

Fear, especially when accompanied by hard crying, can interfere with the child's treatment. So parents are often allowed or asked to stay in the hospital with the child. They can also help with the child's care, keeping the child from feeling alone in an unknown place.

Imaginary Illness

Some young children who have more than their share of illnesses are not really ill. They just imagine that they are. Such children have learned that they can get more attention when they are ill. They also get out of doing things they do not want to do.

Imaginary illness is far less common in younger children than in older ones. But it is common enough to be a problem. Children who imagine that they are sick really believe it.

In early childhood the child's imagination is usually very keen. If imaginary illnesses start then, they can become a serious problem as the child grows older. Some of the school fears of children may show up as serious emotional upsets accompanied by vomiting and other physical signs of illness.

These may have begun as imaginary illnesses in early childhood.

For Discussion

Give several examples of kinds of situations a young child might try to get out of by not feeling well. Explain how you would deal with these situations to keep the child from becoming an imaginary invalid.

Physical Defects

In babyhood physical defects may not have been too noticeable or may have seemed too unimportant to do anything about. These may become more serious and more of a handicap as the child grows older. The child may also develop some new defects because of an illness or an accident.

For Discussion

How would you try to help a child with a physical defect deal with the problems it causes? Describe a case, such as a child who gets attacks of asthma from active play or a child who must wear eyeglasses even when playing.

Children, for example, who seemed to have good sight and hearing when they were babies, may have problems when they are older. As eyeballs grow, defects may show up. Or some hearing may be lost from an ear infection not treated soon enough.

Physical defects that interfere with a child's activities are most troublesome. Such defects, as noted in Chapter 4, may keep the child from getting the exercise needed for normal growth. They may also make the child dependent on

A healthy child is one who is active and enjoys good relationships with playmates. David S. Strickler/Monkmeyer

others for help at the age when children most want to be independent.

The psychological effects of physical defects come mostly from the way other people react. If others ignore it, so will children, unless it keeps them from doing what they want to do. Children with physical defects should be taught at an early age how to deal with their handicaps. They should be given every chance to learn to do things for themselves. Then they, too, can lead independent, useful lives.

Is the Child Thriving?

Parents who are scale watchers when their children are babies often become other-child watchers when their children begin to play. They compare their child's height and weight with that of playmates.

If a child is taller and more filled out, such parents think their child is healthier. If the child is shorter and thinner, they become worried and wonder what is the matter.

To get a true picture of whether a child is thriving, growth, appearance, and behavior must all be judged. The chart on page 63 gives the standards of thriving in babyhood. It can also be used to judge if a young child is thriving. It is helpful to know the danger signs of poor health in early childhood. These are given in the chart below.

Poor health at any age should not be overlooked or expected to correct itself. Poor health usually grows worse rather than better if no steps are taken to correct it. Very often an illness may go away without medical advice only to come back at a later date because the cause was not corrected.

Danger Signs of Poor Health in Early Childhood

Appearance

Skin with poor coloring, rashes, and sores

Eyes that seem dull and watery

Dull, thin hair

Teeth that are yellowish and have decayed spots

Gums that are pale in color

Poor posture

Legs that tend to bow

Extreme thinness

Extreme fatness or flabbiness

Behavior

Poor appetite

Always tired, lacking pep and energy

Sleep that is restless and broken by nightmares

Always complaining

Argues with everyone

Lack of interest in anything

Lack of attention to what others say and do

Tendency to whimper and cry

Many strong temper tantrums

Highlights of Chapter 11

☐ Growth slows down in early childhood. It is more internal than external, and physical development is greater than physical growth.

☐ Growth in height and in weight during early childhood follow a basic pattern, but there are differences in these patterns due to heredity and to environment.

☐ Parents' concern about the young child's physical growth may lead to the child's problem behavior.

☐ Because of different rates of growth, body proportions in early childhood differ from those in babyhood.

☐ Children's body proportions may affect the child's appearance and behavior.

☐ Developing bones, muscles, and fat during early childhood affect the child's behavior and appearance.

☐ The change from baby to permanent teeth affects the young child's appearance and speech.

☐ Children's illnesses and common physical defects may have strong effects on the child's personal and social adjustments.

☐ To decide if a young child is thriving physically, one should judge growth, appearance, and behavior.

Suggested Activities

1. Watch several young children as they pick up and carry different objects such as plates, cookie jars, and boxes. Does the size of the object give you an idea why young children may drop and break things?

2. Compare the faces of young children of both sexes with those of adults. Which of the features seem proportionally too big and which too small for the child's face?

3. Watch several young children in the toothless stage, between baby and permanent teeth. Note if the children have one or more permanent teeth. How do the permanent teeth compare in size, shape, and coloring with the baby teeth?

4. Discuss reasons for and against parents remaining in the hospital with a sick child.

5. How might parents show that they are worried when the normal pattern of growth begins to slow down at the end of babyhood. What effect might it have on the child?

Chapter 12
Learning Skills

Some goals of this chapter are:

☐ To know the essentials for learning skills

☐ To know the four major groups of skills to be learned in early childhood and the roles these skills play in the child's life

☐ To know the common causes of awkwardness in early childhood and realize that most children go through a stage of being clumsy

Early childhood has been called the golden age for learning skills. It is the ideal time to learn to do as many things as possible. Some reasons why this is so are listed in the accompanying chart.

Even though early childhood is the ideal age to learn skills, not *all* skills can or should be learned at this time. Early childhood is too short for children to learn all the skills they will need for the rest of their lives. Also, children are not developed enough to master any but the simplest skills, which are the basics for the finer skills.

Essentials for Learning Skills

Do you remember the nine essentials for learning skills in babyhood? They are listed and explained in the chart on page 90. These nine essentials are just as true for children as for babies. At every age, motivation, or the desire to learn, is always essential. Also important are readiness to learn, chances to learn, encouragement to learn, and supervision to make sure that practice will lead to correct learning.

Some of the other essentials for learning skills, such as imitating a good

---

Why Early Childhood Is the Ideal Age for Learning Skills

The young child's body is flexible. So physical skills can be learned easily.

Learning skills is fun for children. They usually enjoy doing things over and over, which is needed for this learning.

Because many young children have no fear and love adventure, they are not afraid of getting hurt in new situations or activities.

Young children have mastered few skills to interfere with learning new ones.

Children have a strong desire to learn skills that make them feel grown-up and independent.

Why Skills Are Helpful to Young Children

Skills make children independent of adult aid and give them a feeling of being grown-up.

Skills make it possible for children to amuse themselves instead of depending on others.

Skills are important to the child's social development. The child who does not have the skills other children have will not be able to take part fully in the play group.

Having skills makes it possible for children to do things that they find fun, interesting, or important. This gives children feelings of self-importance and self-confidence, which help develop a healthy personality.

---

model and practicing with guidance, are even more important during early childhood than they are in babyhood. Young children do much more learning by copying models than babies do. Therefore, a good model to imitate is more important for a young child. However, even a good model is not enough unless the child is shown how to imitate this model correctly.

The importance of a good model, especially when combined with guidance, can be seen in play skills. Most young children learn their play skills by copying other children without guidance. As a result, they often develop skills in the wrong way. Later, they may not play games and sports as well as they might have played them.

Practicing newly learned skills is also more important for young children than for babies. Each year skills become more complicated and need more practice to master. Because these skills are complicated, supervision must be carried on longer.

Young children have a little more control over learning than babies do. They can pay attention to what they are doing for a longer time. Also, young children are not quite so easily distracted by what goes on around them. But children can still be distracted. Learning will take place more quickly and with fewer errors if distractions are kept to a low level.

Cautions about Teaching Skills to Children

There are two common mistakes many parents and some teachers make in teaching skills to young children. The first is trying to teach the finer and more complicated skills before children are ready to learn them. Parents often do not realize how much time and practice are needed to lay the foundation skills. These are needed before a child can learn the more complicated ones.

Jumping into a complicated task too soon will bore young children. They may become unhappy and feel defeated when they are not able to do well. Also, children's desire to learn will fade and they will try less and less.

The second mistake many parents and some teachers make is trying to teach too many skills at the same time. This mixes children up. In the end, all the skills are learned poorly.

For Discussion

Suppose some parents will not allow their children to learn some of the skills their playmates are learning, such as swimming, roller-skating, or bicycle riding. They are afraid that the children will be hurt. Are they being unfair to their children, or are they taking good care of them? Give reasons for your answer.

When a skill is being learned, teams of muscles are being trained to work in a certain way. If another skill needs the same team of muscles to work in another way, the patterns will be upset. Suppose young children are learning to throw balls. They should put all their practice into ball-throwing motions until the skills are well mastered. While they are learning this, they should not be encouraged to practice other kinds of throwing, such as horseshoe or ringtoss. These call for different motions.

Most parents know that they should teach skills to their children. But many are not sure which skills they should teach and when to teach them. In every cultural group there are skills a child is expected to learn at certain times. These are the skills that are basic to more complex skills children will need as they grow older. The ages at which children are ready to learn skills will vary. Therefore, it is harder to know when to teach a skill than to know what skills should be taught.

Because all children are different, parents need to decide when their own child is ready to learn. They can do this by using the rules given in the chart on

Children cannot be expected to master skills in childhood, but foundations for skills can be laid then. Richard Nowitz

page 147. When all the standards of readiness are present, the teachable moment has arrived. Until then, trying to teach skills to a child will probably have poor results and lead to a poor attitude toward future learning.

Important Skills in Early Childhood

Among the important skills of early childhood are those that will make it possible for children to do what others their age do. This is essential if they are to take part fully in a play group. Other important skills are those that make it possible for young children to have as

173

much independence as their age-mates have. Children do not want to be called a baby because they cannot do what others their age can do.

Some of the skills learned in early childhood were partly learned in babyhood. Self-feeding is one example. Others are new skills built on simpler ones, such as skipping, which is based on walking. Some skills are completely new, though they make use of some muscle coordinations learned earlier. Forming numbers and letters with a pencil, for example, is a new skill that uses the same muscles needed for scribbling with a crayon.

The skills of early childhood are often called *hand skills* and *leg skills*. Skills are also grouped by the roles they play in the young child's life. There are four major groups. These groups, and the most important skills within each that young children usually learn, are given in the chart on the facing page.

Self-help skills are those that make it possible for children to do things for themselves. In this way they become independent of others. *Social-help* skills, on the other hand, make it possible for children to help other people. Self-help skills satisfy children's desire for independence; social-help skills

Children who have the same skills as their playmates feel confident to join in the fun and games. David S. Strickler/Monkmeyer

Some Important Skills of Early Childhood

Self-Help Skills

Self-Bathing Two-year-olds can wash the front of the body. By 6, they can wash the back and neck. At 6, they try to shampoo their hair.

Self-Dressing At 2, children can put on simple clothes such as T-shirts. At 3, they can put on clothes with zippers and buttons. At 6, they can dress themselves completely, even tying bows on shoes.

Self-Feeding At 2 years, children begin to use forks. At 3, they can cut soft food with a knife. At 6, they can cut most meats with a knife.

Self-Grooming Between 2 and 3 years, children can brush their hair without messing it up. At 5, they are good at brushing it. By 4 years, they can do a good job of brushing their teeth.

Stair Climbing At 2, children can walk up and down the stairs by holding on. By 3 years, they can do so without holding on.

Toileting By 2 and 2½ years, children can go to the toilet alone for bowel movements and for urination. A year later they can go to the toilet alone during the night.

Social-Help Skills

In the Home Children can help parents by shelling peas or beans, putting out bread for sandwiches, setting the table, emptying wastebaskets, putting away their clothes and toys, helping to make beds, and dusting furniture.

In Nursery School or Kindergarten Children can help the teacher by putting away toys, washing tabletops after using crayons or clay, emptying wastebaskets.

In the Play Group Children help age-mates build houses with blocks or build whatever the play group wants to make.

Play Skills

Hand Skills Between 3 and 4 years, children begin cutting, pasting, scribbling, painting with fingers, and throwing and catching balls. Between 4 and 6 years, children begin modeling clay, putting together simple puzzles, drawing, painting with a brush, hammering nails into wood, and knitting with a spool or large needles.

Leg Skills Between 2 and 3, children can walk sideways and backward. At 3 years, they can skip and hop. By 6, they can balance on a narrow board, walk in time to music, dance, roller-skate, and ice-skate. Between 3 and 4, children can ride a tricycle; by 6, a bicycle. At 2, children can learn swimming movements; at 3 or 4, they can do simple swimming strokes; at 6, they can dive.

Work Skills

Copying At 3 years, children can copy vertical lines and triangles. At 5 years, they can copy squares and at 6, diamonds.

Writing At 3 to 4 years, children print a few large letters. By 5 years, they print their first names and numbers 1 to 5. At 6 years, they can print the whole alphabet and numbers 1 to 20.

Some newly learned skills are fun to practice. David S. Strickler/Monkmeyer

add to satisfying their desire for acceptance and affection. These are very important to happiness.

Some children cooperate and try to do things to help others, whether they be adults or playmates. Others try only to be independent. The first kind are far more likely to win acceptance and affection. Trying only to be independent may make children appear selfish and self-centered. This will not make them well liked.

The term "play" refers to doing some thing for the pleasure it gives without thinking of the end result. Children play because it is fun to play and for no other reason. When an activity is no longer fun, children drop it and turn to activities they enjoy. *Play skills* make it possible for children to do things they enjoy.

On the other hand, *work* is an activity that is carried out for the end result it will bring. This activity may be pleasurable or not. What is important is the reward the person receives from the activity. That reward may be wages for a worker or a good grade in school for the student.

Work skills and social-help skills may seem to be the same. In both cases, the end result is an important reason for learning the skills. However, the skills are used for different reasons. Social-help skills are used to help others, even though the reward, acceptance and affection, may have caused children to give help. Work skills are used to help themselves, not others.

There are two important points to notice about the skills shown in the chart on page 175. First, the range of skills is very wide, and the skills are useful to the child. The list shows that a young child is not helpless and does not have to be waited on by adults.

The second point is that the number of skills and the degree of mastery of the skills depend on the needs children have. For example, work is not needed in a young child's world. Even in preschool, play will be the main activity. Most of the play will help children learn to get along with other children.

A child who can accomplish self-help skills will gain feelings of independence. Irene Bayer/Monkmeyer

For Thought

From your own childhood and from watching young children, name some social-help skills, other than those listed on page 175, that young children can learn. How does helping others add to a child's acceptance? Think about how parents react when a child helps with household chores.

Awkwardness

When young children are judged by adult standards, they are all clumsy. They are so uncoordinated that they stumble over furniture, trip when going upstairs, fall down steps, and bump into people. In general, young children seem to be poorly put together. As they learn to coordinate their movements, they gradually become graceful.

Some children, even when judged by standards for their age-mates, are more awkward than others. This may affect all kinds of body movements, or it may be limited to certain areas or to certain skills in those areas.

Causes of Awkwardness

Many parents blame the child's body size for awkwardness. They say that a large child cannot be expected to be as graceful as a small child. Others blame the child's sex. They think that girls are by nature more graceful than boys.

Studies of clumsiness among young children have shown that these reasons are not correct. Some big children are well coordinated, and some small ones are awkward. Clumsy and coordinated children are found among both sexes.

The cooperative effort applied to one task is often carried over to other social-help situations. This is true for skills as well.
David S. Strickler/Monkmeyer

For Discussion

Many parents of young children believe that their children will outgrow awkwardness. So, they do nothing to help the children overcome it, and may even criticize them. Do you think the parents are right? Why or why not? What ideas would you give the parents that might help their children overcome awkwardness?

If parents accept awkwardness as something that cannot be helped, the children may develop habits of doing things in uncoordinated, clumsy ways.

Once such habits are set, they are hard to change. To correct awkwardness, you have to know what causes it. There are many possible causes. The most important of them are given in the chart on page 180.

Note that many of the causes of awkwardness can be traced to poor learning. These factors can be controlled. Parents can help children control body movements so that they will not do things in a clumsy way.

Handicaps of Awkwardness

Awkwardness is physically hard on young children. It may lead to accidents. Accidents may cause physical defects. These will affect children not only during childhood but also as they grow older. Even more important, accidents may keep children in the house or even in bed for a time. This will keep them from getting the exercise they need for normal growth.

Psychologically, awkwardness is hard on children only when it has a bad effect on what other people think of them. This will affect the way children think of themselves. Young children probably will not be self-conscious about their awkwardness. But as they grow older, it may embarrass them, especially if it keeps them from taking part in the games and sports their friends play. They will miss out not only on the fun their friends have but also on a chance to learn to be social.

How to Correct Awkwardness

Awkwardness is a drawback in childhood as well as all through life. Every effort should be made to overcome it as soon as possible.

Before trying to correct awkwardness, the cause must be found. Is it due to the level of the child's physical development, or is it due to poorly learned skills? For example, the children's hands may still be too small and too weak to hold onto many things. If so, adults should give children things they *can* hold and show them how to hold the things. Then, when the hands are large enough and strong enough to hold heavier and larger objects, the children will know how to do so without dropping them.

Poorly learned skills are always part of the reason for awkwardness, no matter what the other causes are. But this is one cause that can and should be controlled. Well-taught and well-learned foundation skills can pave the way for better body control as the child grows older.

When children master a skill, they become less awkward doing it. George Roos/ Peter Arnold

Common Causes of Awkwardness in Early Childhood

Top-Heaviness Until the body grows longer, with greater growth in the trunk and legs than in the head, it is hard for children to be anything but awkward. Top-heaviness has little or no effect on hand skills.

Small Hands As long as the hands remain small and the muscles in the hands and arms are weak, children are likely to drop things when they try to hold them. This makes them appear clumsy.

Overweight Children who are overweight tend to be more awkward than their age-mates whose weight is normal or below normal. Overweight children are more top-heavy.

Intelligence Bright children are often less awkward than others. This is partly because they are more careful and partly because there is a close relationship between the child's mental development and the nerves and muscles used in movement.

Emotional Upsets Children are more likely to be awkward when they are upset. The more often the emotional upsets occur—such as experiences in an unhappy home—the more often the awkwardness appears.

Lack of Need for Developing Skills Children who are usually waited on by others will not develop the skills that more independent children do and will seem to be more awkward.

Lack of Chance for Practice For example, children who live in a warm climate where there is no ice rink will be more awkward on ice skates than children who can practice all winter.

Learning Skills Too Quickly The more children are pushed into learning complicated skills before they have mastered the simpler ones, the more awkward they will be.

Poor Learning Methods If children learn on their own, the skills will not be as good as those of age-mates who had some guidance.

Highlights of Chapter 12

- ☐ Childhood is the golden age for learning skills.
- ☐ Learning skills is important to young children. It makes them able to be independent, to amuse themselves, to play with their age-mates, and to develop healthy personality patterns.
- ☐ There are nine essentials for learning skills, all of which are important if the skills are to be well learned.
- ☐ There are two common mistakes made when teaching skills to young children. First, complicated skills should not be taught before children are ready to learn them. Second, several skills should not be taught at the same time.

- ☐ The important skills of early childhood are divided into four groups: self-help skills, social-help skills, play skills, and work skills.
- ☐ When judged by adult standards, all young children are somewhat awkward. Some children are more awkward than others.
- ☐ Poor learning is the one cause of awkwardness that can be controlled.

Suggested Activities

1. The chart on page 172 gives a list of the ways in which skills are helpful to young children. Discuss their importance, explaining why they are important not only during the preschool years but also as children grow older.

2. Watch a group of young children at play. Rate each child in terms of how well that child has mastered the play skills of the group—playing ball, skating, bicycle riding, and so on. Do you find any relationship between your rating of the children's play skills and how well these children are accepted in the play group?

3. The chart on page 175 lists some of the important skills a young child should learn. Tell at what age you think each of the social-help skills and the play skills should be learned. Think in terms of the skill's usefulness to the child and whether the child is developed enough to learn it.

4. Add some more work skills to the chart on page 175. Explain when and why children should be given a chance to learn them. Then discuss their value from a child's point of view. For example, can young children learn to pull weeds in a garden or do errands for pay? Are these skills important enough to young children's personal and social adjustments for the time and effort needed to learn them?

5. Pick out from a play group one or two children who are clumsier than the others. Watch them closely to see what seems to be the cause of their awkwardness. From what you have seen, list the ways they might be able to overcome their awkwardness.

Chapter 13

Learning to Talk

Some goals of this chapter are:

☐ To know why learning to talk is not only the hardest of all skills for children to master but also the most important

☐ To be able to point out ways parents and other adults can help children improve their speech habits

☐ To realize the importance of encouraging children to talk with others, say things pleasantly, and learn what subjects need not be shared with everyone

Of all the skills young children must learn, the hardest is speech. Speaking calls for control of the finer muscles of the lips, tongue, and vocal mechanisms. Meanings also have to be connected with words. Speech is thus a motor-mental skill, not just a motor skill like the other skills children must learn.

Many babies can say some words by their first birthdays. However, this is often not real speech but parrot speech. Only when they pronounce a word fairly well *and* know what it means have they really started to speak.

As the ability to speak develops, the need for prespeech forms of communication gradually decreases. By the end of babyhood, babbling and crying lose their value as the child learns words to express needs and wants. But, gesturing still serves two important functions for young children. First, it takes the place of some words until children have a vocabulary big enough to get along without it. Second, gesturing helps children stress words. For example, the child may push the bowl away and say "no more cereal."

In the same way, facial expressions of anger, fear, or joy are used until the vocabulary is big enough for children to express feelings. Once speech is learned, facial expressions are not essential to communicate. But they are a natural addition to the emotional tone of speech all through life.

Why Speech Is Important to Young Children

Early childhood is the golden age for learning to talk, just as it is for learning

Until their speech skills are well developed, many children will often stop what they're doing to say what is on their minds. Ginger Chih

other skills. And for many of the same reasons.

Because this is the ideal age for learning, almost all cultures expect young children to learn to talk. It is also expected that they will learn to become a part of the social group. To do so, they must be able to communicate with others.

The ability to talk, important as it is, is not enough. In order to communicate, children must also be able to understand what others say to them. Without this understanding, or *comprehension*, there can be no exchange of thoughts.

The chart on page 104 gives some ideas as to how parents can help babies to improve their comprehension. These ideas also hold true for young children. There are other helps for young children that cannot be used with babies. See the chart on page 184.

Young children's comprehension will improve naturally through experience. Improvement can be speeded up by guidance and supervision. The best way to make sure that children's comprehension is correct is to ask them to tell, either in words or by gestures, what a word means to them. For example, suppose they cannot explain what the word "large" means. They can point to something large and something small so that the adult can be sure that they know the difference.

To make sure that children understand what they are told to do, ask them

Encourage children to be *attentive* (to pay close attention) by talking to them in short sentences and for a short time. When their attention begins to wander, bring it back by asking them questions or by stressing what you say with gestures and facial expressions.

Whenever a new word is used, explain what the word means. If possible, point to an object it stands for.

Ask children questions about what you are saying to make sure that they understand.

Until the child's vocabulary is fairly large, add to what you say by using gestures and facial expressions. They give more meaning to the words you use.

Make use of every possible chance to teach children new words and their meanings.

to tell what they think the directions mean. Many times children seem to misbehave, but they have really just not understood what they were told to do or not to do. A child, for example, may be told not to go out on the street to play. By asking the child to tell what this rule means, the parent may discover that the child does not understand the word "street." The child may think it means only the street in front of the house, not streets in general.

Improvements in Speaking

There are four major tasks in learning to speak. They are pronouncing words, learning new words, connecting meanings with words, and putting words together into sentences. All four improve during the early years of childhood. The amount of improvement depends on desire to learn, chances to learn, and guidance. All young children speak better when early childhood ends than they did at the start.

Words have special meanings when they are shared in a secret. HEW

Each major task in learning to speak always needs guidance. The forms this guidance may take are discussed below.

Pronouncing Words

With a good model to imitate and with guidance in copying it, children will improve their pronunciation with each passing month. Much of the toddler's baby talk will disappear if poorly said words are corrected before they settle into deeply rooted habits.

There are certain things that can be done. First, teach children to pronounce the shorter, simpler words before the longer ones. Children can, for example, learn to pronounce "butterfly" correctly more easily if they learn to say "but" first, then "butter" and "fly," and finally "butterfly."

Second, have children say the same words over and over again. This can best be done by talking with children about things that will call for the use of the newly learned word. Then they will have a chance to repeat it.

Third, have children speak slowly and clearly. Many children get excited when they tell others something that is important to them. They talk too fast to say each word the right way. This makes their words come out as a jumble of sounds that no one can understand.

Fourth, correct any wrong pronunciation as soon as it happens instead of hoping that it will correct itself in time. Besides keeping the child from developing the habit of saying the word incorrectly, the child gets a correct mental image of the sound of the word.

Some children develop problems of pronunciation which distort their speech. The most common errors are described in the chart below.

Common Errors of Pronunciation in Early Childhood

Baby Talk The common forms of baby talk often carry over into the early part of childhood. Because they have developed into habits, it will take time to correct them.

Lisping Lisping is the softening of harsh sounds and the use of other sounds instead. It often comes from a space between the upper front teeth or a missing tooth in this area. A lisper says "wed" for "red," "twee" for "tree," and "thwing" for "swing."

Slurring Slurred speech is not clear. It comes from not using the lips, tongue, and jaw. The child does not open the mouth to let the sounds come out. This may come from being shy, but it more often comes from being excited. In trying to tell something quickly, the child rushes on with a story. This causes a jumble of sounds.

Stuttering In stuttering, a letter, a syllable, or even a whole word is repeated. It comes from severe emotional tension. Stuttering is most likely to begin between 2 and 3 years of age. The next most likely age is at 6, when the child starts first grade in school.

Stammering Stammering is a locking of speech because the vocal muscles tighten. It too is caused by severe emotional tension. When the muscles relax, the words pour out in unclear sounds. Stammering and stuttering often go hand in hand.

If a child develops these problems, it is wise to speak to a doctor. However, parents who know the causes will have some idea of how they can help the child before the problems become serious.

When children begin to lisp, parents can speak the mispronounced words slowly and clearly. If the problem is due to spacing of teeth, a dentist should be seen.

Behind most slurring, stuttering, and stammering is emotional tension. Parents can have some control over this. They can try to see to it that the child's life is kept at a slower pace, that the home is a calm and pleasant place, and that the child feels loved. The child should not have more than the normal number of bad emotional experiences, such as fear, jealousy, and frustration. Also, the child should learn how to deal with emotions.

One step parents can take is to tell children that no one can understand what they are saying when they speak so fast. Ask them to repeat more slowly. Most children want to communicate enough that they are willing to try to slow down. If parents' efforts do not bring good results, no time should be lost in going to a doctor for advice.

Learning New Words

Young children build up vocabularies rapidly. Vocabularies usually become larger each year. How much larger depends on the chances children have to learn new words and new meanings for old words and their desire to do so. Children who play often with other children, for example, are more likely to increase their vocabularies than are those who mostly play alone at home. So are children who listen to the radio and watch television. Children also pick up new words when their parents read to them and when parents let them take part in family conversations.

Children learn words as they need them. If children are not expected to say "thank you" when someone does something for them or gives them a present, they will have no need to learn these words. If they never handle money, they will have no need to learn the names of coins. The more experiences children have and the more adults talk with them about these experiences, the more their vocabularies will grow.

Understanding Word Meanings

If children are shown or told what a word means, they will usually connect the word with its meaning. Sometimes a word is made up of two or more words they knew. However, the new word has nothing to do with the meanings of the old ones. Then children may get mixed up. For example, a child may know what "butter" means and also what "fly" means. So the child may think that a butterfly is a fly made out of butter. Unless asked what a butterfly is, the child may keep on connecting the wrong meaning with it.

Another common error comes from words that sound alike but have different meanings. "For," "four," and "fore" sound alike. So the child thinks they mean the same thing and is mixed up when they are used to mean different things. But children quickly get the idea that two or more words can sound alike, once it is explained. They often enjoy playing rhyming or nonsense games with such words. These games help them learn and can be played at any time and in any place.

There are two ways to help keep children from associating wrong meanings with words. First, when children learn a new word, show them what the word means, if possible. For example, show them a banana when they are learning to say the word. Or bend over to explain the word "bend."

Second, make sure that children have the right meaning for a word. Ask them to point out or in some way show what the word means to them.

For Action

Help young children build a vocabulary by teaching them words that are related, either in meaning or in sound. This can be treated as a game. For related words, you might use "big" and "large." Words that sound somewhat alike might be "ham" and "hammer." When you teach the child words that, in part, sound alike, stress that their meanings are very different. Be sure the child understands the difference.

Vocabularies increase when children hear new words and are shown what they mean. Nancy Hays/Monkmeyer

Building Sentences

No young child is mentally ready to learn grammar. But, a child can learn to put together words correctly in sentences.

Children's first sentences are made up of one or two words—a noun or verb or a noun and verb together. Gestures are used to add to the meaning. By the child's second birthday, sentences are usually three to five words long. These sentences are made up of nouns, verbs, and sometimes adjectives and pronouns. Adverbs and prepositions are usually not used. In time, all parts of speech will creep into sentences. The 3-year-old often uses complete sentences.

These early sentences are very often long and poorly put together. Several thoughts may be put into one sentence by using "and." The most common grammar mistakes are using singular verbs with plural nouns or the reverse, using pronouns the wrong way, and using past and present tenses in the same sentences.

Like any habit, the longer grammar mistakes are made, the harder they will be to correct. Therefore, careful attention should be given to the way a child builds a sentence.

Young children should not be expected to understand the rules of grammar. They learn to speak correctly by imitating good models. They use these good models as standards for their own speech.

Some television shows for preschool children carefully screen the language used. This gets children used to hearing correct models. It trains their ears to use these models as standards. Children who watch those shows make fewer mistakes in grammar than they would otherwise. However, this is by no means true of all TV shows. Children can pick up poor language habits from many shows and especially from commercials. This is one of many reasons why parents should supervise what children watch on TV.

It is best to wait until a child finishes a sentence before correcting a mistake. Then the correction should be short and pleasant. Never be angry or impatient. The child may become frustrated and annoyed and may develop a stubborn attitude. Such an attitude will get in the way of learning.

When correcting a child's speech, the adult does not need to give a long explanation. Simply repeat the word or phrase the right way. Have the child say it correctly and then just go on with whatever he or she was saying. Children become used to this and are not upset by it. Yet their mistakes are being corrected all the time.

Young children cannot be expected to speak as well as they will when they grow older. They simply have not lived long enough to master such a difficult skill. However, they should gradually improve in pronunciation, sentence form, and other elements of speech. If they do, parents can be satisfied that a good foundation has been laid.

For Discussion

Which of the four major tasks in learning to speak do you think is hardest for young children to master? Which do you think is easiest? Give reasons for the way you judge the difficulty of each task.

Groupings of Young Children's Speech

Egocentric Speech

Children's speech is said to be egocentric when it centers on themselves or things that have to do with themselves. Among these are their activities, toys, clothing, and family members. Only if other people, animals, or things have something to do with the child and the child's activities are they part of egocentric speech.

Socialized Speech

When children talk about people, animals, and things that have nothing to do with themselves, their speech is social. They often talk about many of the same subjects—toys, clothes, homes, and activities—as they do in egocentric speech. The difference is that in socialized speech these subjects have to do with other people. Many of the early forms of socialized speech are questions. This is the beginning of conversation because it leads to an exchange of ideas.

What Young Children Talk About

The things that young children talk about can be divided into two major groups—*egocentric* (self-centered) and *socialized* speech. Each group is explained in the accompanying chart.

Without knowing it, many parents encourage young children in egocentric speech. They ask children questions that have to do only with the children, their feelings and their wants.

Instead of encouraging egocentric speech, parents should encourage socialized speech. This can be done by asking the child questions about playmates, school, a pet, or shows they saw on television. The more parents talk about subjects other than the child, the more quickly the child will learn to talk about other subjects, too.

Most subjects in the young child's speech are about everyday things. However, not all subjects are socially acceptable. No young child will realize this unless told. For example, at home you may talk frankly about going to the bathroom. It is then natural for the child to think that it is all right to talk about such matters at any other time and place.

No young child can be expected to keep from talking about things that embarrass adults. However, parents can help young children learn that certain things should not be talked about outside the family. This, of course, does not mean that the child will remember not to talk about them.

For Discussion

Egocentric speech can and will develop into a habit if encouraged or allowed to go on. Will this block good personal and social adjustments as children grow older? Explain.

Dramatic play not only excites a child's imagination, but also provides a great way to improve speech skills. Frank Siteman/Stock, Boston

How Children Say Things Is Important, Too

Even when socialized speech begins to replace egocentric speech, what the child says may not lead to good relationships with other people. In fact, when children talk to and about other people, they often say things that hurt or anger. They may, for example, talk about family members rather than about themselves. But they may not say pleasant things. Some of the common things young children say that hurt others are given in the accompanying chart. If children say nice things to and about other people, it will please them and the children will be more likely to make friends.

Children's words and actions largely mirror those of the people around them. If children say nasty, unfriendly things to others, it is likely that they have heard such things said by the adults and older children in their home or neigh-

---

Unsocial Ways of Talking to Others

Demands   "Give me that ball or I'll kick you."

Commands   "Mary will be the mother because she's a girl, and Johnny will be the baby because he's little."

Threats   "If you use my tricycle, I'll tell Mommy."

Exaggerations   "Why do I have to eat spinach *every* day?"

Boasts   "Our house is bigger than yours."

Name-Calling   "You're a mean stinker."

Tattling   "Mommy, Danny took my tricycle and won't give it back to me."

Teasing   "You look like a silly frog."

Criticism   "You shouldn't draw the man bigger than the house."

Unkind Comments   "If you weren't so fat, you could run faster."

Make sure that the speech children hear daily is correct so that they have a good model to imitate.

Choose books and TV shows with good English so that children will hear correct speech when being read to or when watching TV.

Encourage children to speak in front of adults, who will then know if their speech is correct.

Be pleasant and helpful when correcting speech errors and unsocial ways of saying things.

Encourage cooperative speech by asking children questions and answering their questions.

Use family meals as a time for cooperative talking. See to it that every member has a fair share of the talking time. This will discourage any one family member from taking over the conversation.

Encourage children to listen carefully by talking about subjects they can under-stand, by reading to them, and by letting them listen to certain radio and TV shows.

Talk to children about a wide range of interesting subjects, partly to encourage listening and partly to add to their general knowledge of things to think about and talk about.

Discourage egocentric speech and encourage socialized speech by spending time on other people and things rather than on the child.

Explain to children that if they want to have friends they must speak kindly to and about other people.

Never wait for a child to outgrow poor speech or the saying of unpleasant things. The more the child does these things, the sooner they will develop into habits.

borhood. When children hear mostly kind things and good manners, their speech is likely to reflect this.

Every child, at some time or other, says unpleasant things about other people or speaks in a way that hurts or angers them. Parents should always be on guard for such comments. The child who gets into the habit of saying pleasant things about and to family members will usually carry this habit into the playground and school. It will go a long way toward guaranteeing social acceptance. Parents can do much to help children improve their speech habits. The chart above gives some suggestions for how it can be done.

The Chatterbox and the Nontalker

When children learn to talk they want to talk all the time. Between the second and third years, children enter what is often called the "chatterbox" stage. When no one is around, they even talk to themselves. Children between 3 and 4 years of age speak about 15,000 words a day (not different words, but many of the same words over and over again). At this rate, a child would say about 5 1/2 million words in a year.

This chattering often bothers adults. They tell the children to keep quiet or send children out of the room when they talk too much.

For Action

Bothersome as the young child's talking may be, it is very valuable for learning to talk correctly. Talking gives the child practice in pronouncing words and putting them together in sentences. On the other hand, talking all the time has two important drawbacks. Both of them may partly take away some of the good that comes from practice.

First, when children talk all the time, parents often shut their ears to what children are saying. So they do not hear wrong pronunciations and grammar.

Therefore, children repeat their mistakes, which develop into habits.

Second, chatterbox children get into the habit of taking up so much of a conversation that other people are not given the chance to talk. Family members may ignore this, but playmates will feel differently. They want to have a chance to talk, too. They will not like one child's trying to do all the talking. This will not make the child a very welcome member of the play group.

When one child talks about things that are interesting, then other children listen and learn and want to share their experiences too. Kenneth Karp

Just as bad as talking too much is not talking at all. Children may become nontalkers because they have grown up in homes where they were not allowed to talk freely. Or people may have laughed at their speech or criticized it.

Whatever the cause, nontalkers have a social problem. They may not bother others by too much talking. But they may make others think that they have nothing to offer and are uninteresting. This causes them to be overlooked both on the playground and in school.

Too many parents overlook the need for helping children to learn when to

talk, when not to talk, and how much to talk. If speech is to be used to communicate, children must learn to listen to what others say just as they must learn to talk to others.

During the chatterbox stage, it is important that parents pleasantly guide the amount of talking young children do. This can be done by gently but firmly telling the children that it is someone else's turn to talk and their turn to listen. To help children realize that they should be listening, they can be asked questions every once in a while and given a chance to answer.

Parents need to use wise judgment to know when to control a child who is bothering others by talking too much. The child's enthusiasm should not be squelched. Whenever a chatterbox has to be quieted, the parents should do it kindly. They should be sure the child has a chance to talk freely some other time. In the same way, they should gently encourage nontalkers to join the conversation.

For Discussion

What can parents do to encourage nontalkers to speak more than is needed for only simple conversation? What kinds of activities might make such children want to share their experiences with others by talking to them?

Highlights of Chapter 13

☐ Speech is a motor-mental skill. It is the hardest skill young children must learn.

☐ Comprehension is very important for communication. Adults should help improve the young child's understanding of what others say.

☐ With help from parents and teachers, all parts of learning to talk— pronouncing, learning new words, connecting correct meanings with words, and putting words together into sentences—normally improve during the early childhood years.

☐ All speech can be divided, roughly, into two major groups—egocentric speech and socialized speech. In early childhood, egocentric speech is more common.

- ☐ Children should be taught not to speak to others in unpleasant, unsocial ways. Their speech should be pleasant and show good manners. The example of those around them plays a big part in this.
- ☐ Children must learn when and how to talk if they are to make good social adjustments.
- ☐ There are many ways in which parents can help young children improve their speech. This should be done before a child develops poor speaking habits.
- ☐ The chatterbox stage is an important period in speech development. It gives young children needed practice in talking.

Suggested Activities

1. The chart on page 184 gives some ideas for improving a young child's comprehension of what others say. Take each idea, think about it, and then explain how it aids the child's understanding.

2. Choose several children who are in the toothless stage—those who have lost one or two of their upper front baby teeth. Then ask them to say words that begin with harsh sounds, such as "r" (red), "s" (single), or "z" (zero). If they soften these sounds, ask them to repeat the words after you have said them slowly, stressing the harsh sounds. How well can the children say these words if they try hard to do so?

3. Make a list of speaking mistakes you have heard children make. Group these mistakes by wrong pronunciation, wrong use of a noun or a verb, or awkward sentence form. What type of error is most common and what is least common? What problems may develop if parents think such mistakes are too cute to correct?

4. The chart on page 190 gives a list of unsocial ways of talking that many young children use. Explain how each might affect other people and why this might affect a young child's acceptance among playmates.

5. Listen to a group of young children playing together. Write down any unpleasant speech patterns you hear, such as criticisms, demands, and unkind comments. Also take down the pleasant remarks they make to and about each other. Discuss how the tone set by the speech patterns affects their play.

Chapter 14

Intellectual Development

Some goals of this chapter are:
- ☐ To realize that intellectual abilities are the result of heredity and environment
- ☐ To realize that among intellectual abilities are memory, imagination, creativity, association of meanings, and reasoning

Children differ in intellectual abilities. Some are bright, some are slow learners, and some are "average." For hundreds of years, there has been a hot debate about intellectual differences. Are they caused by heredity or environment? Today it is generally accepted that these differences are caused by *both*. It is possible to affect, to some degree, the child's intellectual development through the environment.

Two environmental factors have the greatest affect on the child's intellectual development. These are *nutrition* and *stimulation*. Both play their most important roles during the babyhood and early childhood years. This is when the brain is growing and developing most rapidly.

Poor nutrition, also known as *malnutrition*, is caused by not getting the proper nutrients needed for normal growth and development. During the

months before birth and through the early childhood years, malnutrition interferes with the development of the brain. This, in turn, affects the child's ability to learn. If malnutrition is not corrected at this time, the brain growth and development will be stunted forever. As a result, children will never be as bright as nature had meant them to be.

A dull environment also stunts intellectual abilities. Later stimulation, when the child goes to school, may partly make up for the early lack of it. But studies show that this is not enough to develop the abilities the child was born with.

Intellectual Abilities

As the brain grows larger, the ability to use it increases. The brain develops internally as it grows in size. Not all intellectual abilities develop at the same

195

time because the different parts of the brain develop at different times. Memory, for example, develops sooner than imagination, which develops sooner than the ability to reason.

Memory

Being able to remember is one of the first intellectual abilities to develop. Even before babies are 6 months old, they show that they remember people. They act pleased when people they know do things for them and afraid when strangers do so. They also show fear of strange places, sounds, sights, and animals. These all show that babies have memory.

Memory is the basis for imagining, creating, associating meanings, and reasoning. Parents can do much to help children improve their memories. Some ideas as to how this can be done are given in the accompanying chart.

If children learn how to use their memories when they are preschoolers,

Parents who are aware of their child's nutritional needs should be able to plan meals that are healthful, as well as appealing and tasty.
Ginger Chih

Aids to Better Memory in Early Childhood

Encourage careful listening and watching. If children are to remember things, they must have clear sight and sound pictures of these things.

Make the sights and sounds to be remembered meaningful to the child. The more meanings you can connect with it, the easier it will be for the child to remember it.

Repeat often to prevent forgetting.

Play memory games with children. Show them several objects and then remove one to see if they can remember which is gone.

Read the same stories to children several times. Then ask the children to tell you as much of the story as they can.

Teach children nursery rhymes, days of the week, numbers, the alphabet, and so on. Go over them until the children can say them by themselves. This should be treated as something fun to do, not as a formal lesson.

Help children learn things as a meaningful whole—a whole sentence or a whole verse of a poem—instead of learning it in small parts. That keeps children from understanding its meaning.

they will be prepared for much of the work of the early school grades. Equally important, they will have laid the foundation of how to memorize. That skill will be a very valuable aid to them all through life.

Imagination

Imagining is a form of mental play. Ideas are put together about people and things in forms different from those found in real life. This is not done with some practical purpose. It is done for the enjoyment it gives. Until children can speak, it is impossible to know what they imagine. They are unable to share these imaginings with others.

Studies show that imagination begins to be vivid around the age of 2 years. It becomes more and more vivid with each passing year. By the time children are 5 years old, they can usually tell the difference between imagined experiences and real ones. They still go on imagining because of the enjoyment they get from it.

Imagination is based on memories of what children have seen, heard, or otherwise known in daily life. Material that is read to them and that they see in movies or television shows, in comics, in daily life, or in pictures in books are all used to create new imagined experiences. The more striking these sources of imagining are, the more clearly the child remembers them. These will play the more important roles in imagined experiences.

Some toys lend themselves to imaginative play better than others do.
Freda Leinwand/Monkmeyer

Adults have no problem telling what is real from what is imagined. So they may not realize that the child can not always tell the difference. Parents know that the things they read in storybooks or see in storybook pictures or in make-believe films are purely imagined. These are not mixed up with the real world. So they may be upset when young children get so frightened by such stories that they refuse to go near people or things that remind them of the story or film. Parents also may be worried when children wake up at night, crying after a nightmare.

For example, imagine a movie where the trees act like people. They use their branches as arms to reach down and pick up children who walk through the woods. Adults may think this is charming make-believe. But some children become afraid of going near a tree. They think the tree's branches may reach down and pick them up.

Imagination in early childhood may take many different forms. The most common are given in the accompanying chart. Some of these are harmless. They present no cause for alarm. Others are harmful because they lead to mistaken ideas about the real world. Also, because of the instant satisfaction they give, they may develop into habits. These habits will interfere with good personal and social adjustments later on. Children will give up some of this behavior as they grow older. By then they have learned that it is purely imagined, and they have new sources of satisfaction to replace it.

Common Forms of Imaginary Experience in Early Childhood

Daydreaming   Daydreaming, or *fantasy*, takes place while awake. It is based on things children learn from what is read to them, what they see on the screen or in pictures, and what they see in daily life.

Imaginary Friends   Children play with an imaginary friend as they would like to play with real children. The imaginary friend has all the traits the child wants a real playmate to have.

White Lies   White lies—or tall tales—are reports of imaginary experiences the child believes. The child does not mean to fool anyone, as in the case of lying.

Imaginary Illness   In imaginary illness, children imagine that they are suffering from some ache or pain. This imagining is so real that they believe that the ache or pain is there. They do not mean to fool others.

Animism   Animism is imagining that nonliving objects—toys, furniture, or other things—have the traits of living creatures; for example, toys have feelings and can speak. The child may believe that a chair feels the weight of the person sitting on it.

Exaggeration   When children exaggerate what they say about themselves and other people or things, they often believe what they say. The more children think about these matters, the more they exaggerate.

Dreams   Dreams differ from daydreams because they take place during sleep. Some dreams may be so frightening that they waken the child. Such dreams are called *nightmares*.

Creative abilities are most often developed during unrestricted play.
Sam Sweezy/Stock, Boston

However, imagination is a potential source of trouble, just as it is a potential source of value. So parents should watch carefully and gently guide the direction the child's imagination takes. There are four ways parents can help young children develop their abilities to imagine.

First, parents can help children carefully think about experiences to see if they are real or imaginary.

Second, parents can keep children from hearing and seeing things that will serve as the basis of harmful or upsetting imaginings.

Third, parents should gently discourage an imaginary experience that will be harmful to children, even though it may give the children satisfaction for the time being.

Fourth, parents can give children good sources of material for imagination. They can read children stories in which the make-believe parts are enjoyable and positive. They should see to it that, along with the make-believe, children also hear stories that deal with real life.

For Discussion

How should parents deal with a young child's white lies or imaginary illness? Is there any proof that the child is lying, in the strict sense of the word? If not, should parents accuse their children of lying? How should they treat the matter to keep white lies and imaginary illness from becoming habits?

Conditions Affecting the Development of Creativity

Child-Training Methods Strict, authoritarian discipline stifles creativity. Democratic discipline and permissive discipline encourage it.

Adventurousness Children who are encouraged to be adventurous tend to be more creative than those who are always warned to be careful.

Decision Making Chances to take part in family decisions and to decide about their own affairs encourage children to be creative. Having choices made for them makes children less likely to be creative.

Pressures for Conformity The less children are pressed to conform to what the group and family expect, the more

chance they have to be creative in whatever they do.

Play Equipment When play equipment is too detailed, it cannot be used in many different ways. This discourages creativity.

Criticism Constructive criticism offers ideas for improving. This encourages creativity. Destructive criticism stresses only what is wrong and discourages creativity.

Ridicule or Praise Ridicule and unkind comments about what the child has done discourage creativity. Praise for what has been done, even when accompanied by constructive criticism, encourages it.

Creativity

Creativity is a controlled, or harnessed, form of imagination. It is used not only for the instant pleasure it gives but also for some end result. This end result usually takes a form that can be seen by others. It may be the creation of a painting, a dress, a new piece of music, or a new food dish.

No matter what a person does in life, creativity is a plus. Through creativity, the person can add to human progress. Those who are creative usually are better at whatever they do than are those who lack creativity.

Many believe that some people are born creative and some are not. There is nothing to prove this belief. However, the brighter person has greater possibilities for creativity.

Early childhood is the age when the possibilities for creativity are develop-

ing most rapidly. It is essential that stimulation and guidance be given at this time. The accompanying chart lists some of the most important ways to encourage or discourage the development of creativity.

There are many times in children's lives when parents can encourage them to be creative. None offers so many chances as during play. Children who learn to play creatively develop the habit of doing things in a new way. They can then use this habit in other things they do. And since the results of creativity are satisfying, children are generally eager to want to do everything in a new way.

Drawing, painting, coloring, modeling clay, and other forms of play offer young children wonderful chances to be creative. Children should not be given a model to copy. That is a sure way to stifle creativity. Instead, parents should show them how to use the materials and then let them make whatever they like. Only if a child asks, "What shall I make?" should parents help. And then help should be only in the form of ideas.

Creativity gives more enjoyment to children if the end result is fairly satisfactory. So guiding them every once in a while by giving ideas for improvements is helpful.

Another creative kind of play is acting out scenes from stories children have heard or seen. If parents will provide old clothes and furniture, the children will do the rest.

When children are asked to tell a story or to add to a story being told by someone else, they have a good chance to use their imaginations. They can create plots and people that will interest their listeners. They should be encouraged to use their own ideas, however simple or confused, rather than to tell stories they have heard somewhere else.

Dancing to music is less likely to be affected by something already learned than is storytelling. Few young children have taken dance lessons. When they dance, they dance in their own way. This offers them a chance to express their creativity without the blocks that come from having learned to do something the "right" way.

Association of Meanings

The association of meanings is known as *concept development*. A concept is a group of meanings connected with certain people, animals, or things. It is developed through learning. In time, a label, in the form of a word, becomes a part of this group of meanings. And the child's emotional reaction—a like or dislike—is added.

The association of meanings does not come about quickly. It is a lifelong, complicated process. It uses memory,

Real life experiences help children to grasp the basis of concept development. Sylvia Johnson/Woodfin Camp & Associates

imagination, and reasoning to tie together meanings. These meanings are gained at different times and in different situations. For that reason, concepts are never finished. They are always changing as new experiences give rise to new meanings.

The aids used to pick up meanings are explained in the chart on page 202. They show that it is possible to pick up wrong meanings unless careful guidance is given. Suppose, for example, a young child is trying to learn the meaning of "clouds" and asks, "What are clouds made of?" If someone answers that they are made of whipped cream, the child will associate a faulty meaning with clouds. The adult knows that the answer is totally silly. The idea may never enter his or her mind that the child—who does not have the experience on which to base judgments—may take the answer quite seriously.

Children do not have much experience or knowledge of word meanings, and they cannot reason the way an adult does. As a result, many young children associate wrong or partly wrong meanings with certain kinds of objects or situations. For example, the child who has had a frightening experience with a big dog may believe that all big dogs are to be feared.

Wrong concepts, or *misconceptions*, are very common among young children. Parents should always be on guard to spot and correct them before they become firmly set in the child's mind.

Association of meanings is a very complex mental process. Children cannot be expected to have fully developed concepts when early childhood comes to an end. Nor can it be expected that all concepts will be correct. Going to school will help children learn new meanings and correct concepts.

Aids in Learning Meanings

Exploring   By looking, listening, smelling, tasting, and feeling things, babies learn much about meanings. Young children also use this aid. It gives them meanings they otherwise could not get.

Handling   By touching things, the child learns about weight, smoothness, softness, and warmth. A child who is forced to keep "hands off " things loses one of the most valuable sources of meanings.

Asking Questions   By the time children can put words together into sentences, they use questions to discover meanings they have been unable to get by exploring or handling. If adults refuse to answer children's questions or give them wrong answers, the adults hurt the children's efforts to learn new meanings.

Mass Media   Children gain many meanings by looking at pictures in books and comics and on the movie or television screen. Many of these sources sometimes make mistakes or give one-sided views. The child may build up concepts with partly or totally wrong meanings.

Reading   Children get meanings from reading, whether material is read to them or they try to read by themselves. Most reading material for young children is illustrated with pictures. This helps them pick up new meanings.

For Discussion

Explain why a misconception is very hard to change. Use examples, such as the old-fashioned belief that men are brighter than women. Why would the emotional coloring of this misconception make some people hold on to it in spite of scientific proof that men are not brighter than women?

Reasoning and Making Decisions

The ability to reason is one of the slowest and last of the mental abilities to develop. During childhood, reasoning is mostly making decisions between two or more choices. To make a decision, children must be able to remember facts and their meanings and judge which choice is best. Making a decision takes practice. If young children have had most of their decisions made for them, making a decision is a very hard task.

Even though young children are not able to make major, complicated decisions, most are able to make simple ones at an early age. Children should be allowed and encouraged to do so. Children can, for example, choose which one of two or three pieces of clothing they would like to wear; which toys they would like to play with; whether they want corn, peas, or beans for dinner; whether they want to hear a story or look at a book.

The ability to make decisions is essential to doing well and being happy in life. The earlier children learn to make proper decisions, the better prepared they will be to deal with situations in which they do not have someone to make decisions for them. Psychological studies have given ideas about aids in learning how to make decisions. The most important of these aids are listed in the accompanying chart.

To make sure that the child knows the value of making a decision, the parent

Aids in Learning to Make Decisions

Number of Choices   Until the child has gained skill in making decisions, only two choices should be given. More choices make the decision hard to reach and slow down the learning process.

Pros and Cons of Each Choice   Each choice should be studied for things in favor and things against it. Children should be asked questions that will encourage them to draw on what they know.

Advice from Others   Few children know enough about any but the simplest problem to make a good decision without getting some advice. This does not mean the decision should be turned over to others. Rather, it means getting other points of view on the problem.

Reaching a Decision   After getting the facts and advice, the two choices must be weighed. The child should see which has more in its favor. On this basis, a final decision can be made.

Testing a Decision   Every decision should be tested after a period of time to see if it was a good one and, if not, why not. This may show, by looking back, where the decision making may have been faulty. It also encourages the child to be more skillful the next time.

can later ask if the child is happy with the choice. Parents should not make the child feel tense or upset if a poor decision was made. They should know that young children change their minds often. The chance to make a poor choice without suffering serious results is one of the main reasons for having children make some of their own deci-sions at an early age.

The pattern of decision making has to be learned by many experiences in which the child makes a decision super-vised by an adult. This pattern will then become the way the child solves problems. However, decision making is still a tough intellectual task. No

child can be expected to be skilled in this ability during early childhood.

When training should begin in deci-sion making will vary with children. A good rule of thumb is that children who can speak well enough to ask questions, can put together meaningful sentences, and can understand what others say to them are ready for help in learning to make decisions.

This is the teachable moment. If teaching is not begun when children are ready, they are likely to begin mak-ing decisions in a trial-and-error way that leads to *snap judgments*. These are decisions made quickly, without think-ing enough about all parts of the matter.

If children are allowed to make snap judgments, they may get into the habit of doing so.

Snap judgments are hardly ever as satisfactory as carefully thought-out decisions. Even before early childhood has ended, children may feel unsure about decision making if many of their decisions turn out to be poor ones. When this happens, children will become the easy prey of adults or age-mates who want to make decisions for them.

It is also common for children who have not learned decision-making skills to become *vacillators*. They swing from one choice to another and never make a final decision. For example, they want to do this today and that tomorrow. When tomorrow comes, they are still unsure and think perhaps they want to do what they first thought of doing. While swinging back and forth, they do nothing and feel guilty about it. In their uncertainty, they often turn to someone else and let the other person make the decision.

Parents cannot guide the decision making for every choice the children will make in daily life. However, they should spend some time on this training. If a decision is important to children, it is worth taking enough time to explore the problem before a final decision is made.

Intellectual Differences

We have seen how differences in body size, skills, and the ability to speak affect the young child's personal and social adjustments. So, too, do intellectual differences.

There is no need for intellectual differences to cause unsocial behavior unless adults allow it to happen. They should not place great stress on the differences. Parents and other adults can do a great deal to create an environment of helpfulness and respect among their children.

For example, adults do not need to fuss over the very bright child. They should not make the child feel different and better than others. They can praise the work of all children and show the same interest and pleasure in them all, even though they are different. Adults can encourage children to respect each other. They can put a stop to both boasting and unkind words about what other children can do.

Above all, adults should never, never criticize children for not doing as well as another child. They should not hold up a bright child's work and say to others, "Why don't you do as well?" This hurts the bright child by making the others dislike her or him. It hurts the others by making them feel they are not as good. Adults must help all children develop self-respect, along with respect for others, no matter what their intellectual abilities.

For Discussion

Letting others help a young child make a decision can be both helpful and harmful to the child's process of learning to make decisions. Why? List some ways it is helpful and some ways it is harmful. How can these harmful effects be controlled so that they will add to the good ones?

Highlights of Chapter 14

- [ ] Intellectual development depends on the growth and development of the brain and on the stimulation of developing intellectual abilities.
- [ ] Memory is the basis for other important intellectual abilities: imagination, creativity, reasoning, and association of meanings.
- [ ] Imagination in early childhood takes many forms. The most common are daydreaming, imaginary friends, white lies, imaginary illness, animism, exaggeration, and dreaming.
- [ ] Creativity is a controlled form of imagination. It can best be stimulated in early childhood through different forms of play.
- [ ] Concept development means learning to associate meanings with people, objects, and situations.
- [ ] Learning to make decisions wisely calls for guidance from adults.
- [ ] When children do not learn how to make decisions, they may make snap judgments, become vacillators, or rely on others to make their decisions for them.
- [ ] Differences in intellectual abilities appear in babies and become greater as children grow older.

Suggested Activities

1. Help a young child learn a nursery rhyme or a short poem. Treat the remembering as a game by singing or using records. Use the chart on page 196 for some aids.
2. Help children develop their imaginations by beginning a story and letting them finish it. Or let them begin a story for you to finish.
3. Watch as many children's TV shows as possible for a week. List the shows you see. Explain how each show adds to the development of children's intellectual abilities.
4. Go to the children's area of the library. Ask to see books that are for children under 6 years old. Judge the books on how they add to the development of children's intellectual abilities. How do the TV shows and books for children compare with each other?
5. What role does decision making play in your everyday activities? Make a list of the decisions you make for a day, starting with your choice of clothes. Refer to the chart on page 203. How often do you use the aids listed?

Chapter 15

The Child's Emotions

Some goals of this chapter are:
- ☐ To know about children's emotions and how they differ from those of adults
- ☐ To know what usually causes heightened emotionality in children, how it affects children, and how it can best be dealt with or prevented
- ☐ To understand that parents can teach their children to control their emotions and why it is important for them to do so

There is no question that early childhood is an emotional age. Emotional outbursts are stronger and take place more often at this age than at any other time of life. The reason is that young children have not yet learned to behave as society expects. As their social environment broadens and they meet people outside the home, they learn that they must control strong expressions of emotions such as kicking, biting, and hitting when angry; running away and hiding when frightened; or jumping up and down and screaming loudly when happy. Emotions, though, are an essential part of children's lives, as shown in the accompanying chart on the next page.

Every child is born with the potential for emotional expression. This can be seen even in newborn babies. At birth, for example, every infant is able to have a generalized pleasant emotional response. This is shown by the baby's relaxing the body and making simple cooing and gurgling sounds. The newborn is also able to have a generalized unpleasant emotional response—tensing the body, waving the arms, and kicking the legs while crying.

How Emotions Develop
From the simple emotional states present at birth, new and more complex emotions develop. This development

What Emotions Do to and for Children

Emotions Add Pleasure to the Child's Life All emotions are stimulating and exciting. They add pleasure to everyday experiences. Pleasure can come even from unpleasant emotions, such as fear, anger, and jealousy, if these are not too strong. The pleasure comes mostly from their aftereffects—the feelings of relaxation and well-being.

Emotions Can Upset Skills When emotions become too strong, children become awkward or stutter, stammer, and slur when they speak.

Emotions Can Interfere with Intellectual Activities Strong emotions make it hard to learn to reason and remember. Mild emotions stimulate intellectual activities.

Emotions Serve as Forms of Communication Without using words, children can let others know how they feel by the facial expressions and the bodily changes that accompany all emotions, weak or strong.

Emotions Leave Their Marks on the Child's Expression Pleasant emotions make children look happy. Unpleasant emotions distort their faces, making them look the way they feel.

Emotions Have a Socializing Effect Other children want to be with those who seem happy and who show pleasant emotions. People avoid those who show unpleasant emotions. Children learn that they must control their emotions if they want to have friends.

Emotions Color the Child's Outlook on Life When pleasant emotions are present, the child's outlook on life is good. When the emotional state is unpleasant, the child's outlook is bad and the child is unhappy.

Emotions Affect the Psychological State of the Home When a child has pleasant emotions, the home is happy and relaxed. Temper outbursts, fears, and jealousies upset all family members and make the home unpleasant.

---

comes partly from maturing but mostly through learning. By the end of the first year, the baby feels fear, anger, jealousy, envy, curiosity, joy, and affection. These emotions are fairly well developed. They are much like those of older children and adults.

Learning is very important in the child's emotional development. It affects the causes of emotions as well as the kinds of behavior that result. The chart on page 210 describes how this is so. Parents should try to guide the development of their children's emotions. They should control the environment and give their children positive learning experiences. Then pleasant emotions will show up more than unpleasant ones. They should also see to it that any poor emotional patterns that develop be changed before they become firmly set.

In the case of fear, parents can control what children see on television or in books and comics. Then the children will not have material on which to base imaginary fear experiences. To keep children from becoming jealous of brothers and sisters, parents can show equal love and attention to all. Each child should know that she or he is special.

Children's Emotions Differ from Adult's Emotions

There are certain differences between children's emotions and those of adults. Knowing what they are is important for two reasons. First, it keeps adults from judging children harshly just because a child's emotional behavior differs from their own. Second, it shows where adult supervision is needed. The child can be guided to learn to control emotional behavior so that, in time, the behavior will meet social standards.

For Thought

The chart on page 208 lists important things emotions can do to and for children. Using this list as a guide, think about what emotions do to and for *you*.

For example, children's emotions are more easily aroused than adults'. Parents can control the environment so there will be fewer times that the child becomes upset. Perhaps the child could be given more chances to be independent. That will take away some of the frustrations that could lead to angry outbursts.

For the most part, children express affection easily, spontaneously, and without embarrassment.
Rick Smollan/Stock, Boston

For Discussion

When young children envy things other children have, how should parents deal with it? Should they give children what others have? Should they call them "poor sports"? Should they make fun of them by saying, "Your face is turning green with envy"? Should they try to explain that they simply cannot spend the money to buy these things? Explain why you think each of these methods is good or bad. Suggest any other ways that you think would be better than those given above.

Role of Learning in Children's Emotions

Learning by Trial and Error Affects mostly the response of the emotion. When children discover that a certain response is satisfying, they keep on using it. For example, exploring things makes them curious. If they find little satisfaction from exploring or if blocks are put in their way to keep them from exploring, they will try out other ways, such as asking questions, until they find one that meets their needs.

Learning by Imitation Affects both the cause of the emotion and the response. If a friend, brother, or sister is afraid of dogs, the child will imitate that person and also be afraid. If others show their fear by running away and hiding, the child will show fear in the same way.

Conditioning Learning by association. The child learns to like people who are kind and to dislike those who are unkind. In time, these conditioned emotions spread to people who seem like those whom the child likes or dislikes. Conditioning mostly affects the causes of the emotion; it has little effect on the emotional reaction.

Training When the emotions develop under supervision, children learn to respond with behavior that is accepted by the group. Children learn when certain emotions are all right and when they are not called for or not needed. For example, children discover with guidance that many of the things they once thought frightening are really no cause for fear.

Anything new and strange will frighten a child slightly. However, curiosity is often stronger than this fear. Henry Monroe

Heightened Emotionality

All children have times when they are more emotional. Some children are, in general, more emotional than others. Normal emotional behavior for them would be heightened emotionality for another child who is usually calmer.

When pleasant emotions are aroused, such as curiosity, joy, and affection, the state of heightened emotionality is called *excitement*. The children may wear themselves and the parents out by their loud laughter, running around, jumping up and down, and hugging everything. While they like to see their children in a good humor, parents know that children will not eat or sleep well unless they calm down. Even worse, as

---

Common Emotions of Childhood

Affection Anything that gives the young child pleasure—a person, a pet, or a toy—becomes the object of the child's affection. This is shown by wanting to be with the loved one all the time, patting, kissing, or fondling it, and saying, "I love you."

Anger Children become angry when they are kept from doing what they want to do, are attacked by another child, have toys grabbed from them, are taken away from doing something important to them, or fail to do something they think they are able to do. Anger may be expressed in temper tantrums. Children may hit, kick, jump up and down, throw themselves on the floor, cry, and scream.

Curiosity Things that are new and different may make children want to explore them. Later, when children can ask questions, they add facts given in answers to what they learned from exploring.

Envy The usual causes of envy in young children are the things other children own or can do. They express their envy by wishing they had these things, by complaining about what they have, or by taking the things they envy.

Fear Anything new, especially when it comes on them suddenly, may frighten young children. Running away and hiding, running to the parent, and crying are the usual fear responses of very young children.

Grief The loss of anything important to children—a family member, a pet, or a loved toy—makes them cry and refuse to do what they usually do. Until grief passes, they are inactive, withdrawn, and likely to cry a lot.

Jealousy Whenever a parent or other adult shows more interest in, and gives more time and attention to, another child, young children may resent it. They show this by attacking the child or by going back to infantlike behavior themselves. They may demand that they be waited on as they were when they were babies.

Joy Anything that makes a young child feel satisfied and important, such as doing something well and winning praise for it, gives rise to an all-over feeling of happiness known as joy. In mild forms, joy is shown by smiling and laughing; in stronger forms, by jumping up and down, shouting with glee, and hugging anything nearby—a person, an animal, a toy, or a piece of furniture.

When children are feeling a strong emotion, they cannot hide it! Kenneth Karp

children become tired, they generally become disagreeable, which is one way to respond.

The emotions that are usually heightened are the unpleasant ones—anger, fear, envy, jealousy, and grief. They upset children physically. Children in such states are hard to live with and hard to handle.

Cause and Effect of Heightened Emotionality

Some children become emotionally upset when they are not feeling well. This may be because of illness, malnutrition, or some disease that never goes away, such as asthma or diabetes. Most heightened emotionality, however, stems from the child's environment. At holiday times, for example, there is more excitement in the home than usual. There may be guests, meals may be off schedule and richer in carbohy-

---

Differences between Children's and Adults' Emotions

Strength   Children's emotions are felt more strongly than are adults'. Children are unable to control their emotions; adults can. When children are angry, they are angry all over. Angry adults are more likely to control their anger so that it is less easily seen.

Length   Even the worst childish temper tantrum lasts less than five minutes. Then it is over. The same is usually true of fears, jealousies, and other emotions. Adult emotions may drag on for hours or days, because adults keep them bottled up inside instead of expressing them, as children do.

How Often   Children feel emotions much more often than adults. Children have not yet learned to ignore or control certain situations that give rise to emotions. Adults have. The child, for example, loses patience and becomes angry when not able to put a puzzle together. The adult who is having a hard time with a task may take a break or rethink the problem before going on.

Ease of Onset   It is much harder for an adult to become emotional than it is for children.

Expressiveness   Children's faces and bodies show to all what their emotional states are. Adults often work hard to hide their true feelings.

Children are more prone to heightened emotionality when they are tired. A little understanding during this time might help keep uncontrolled outbursts from happening. Mimi Forsyth/Monkmeyer

drates than the child is used to, and bedtime may be later than the usual hour. Such things may get young children so excited that they wear themselves out and become disagreeable.

The usual environmental state that gives rise to heightened emotionality in young children is stress in the home. There may be stress because parents or other family members argue. If children are always surrounded by an emotionally charged environment, they will be upset by it.

No matter what their health or homelife is like, all children are upset when a big change takes place in their lives. This is especially true when this change comes suddenly and children have had little or no preparation for it. Suppose the mother goes to the hospital and a stranger comes in as a caretaker; the

family moves; the child is sent to a day-care center, nursery school, or kindergarten; or a stepparent comes into the home. A huge adjustment must be made in the pattern of the child's life. Until this is done, there will be times of heightened emotionality.

With some children, heightened emotionality takes place only once in a while and passes quickly. In other

For Discussion

It has been found that one of the best ways to deal with emotions in a child is to redirect the child's attention when the emotions begin to be too strong or troublesome. Do you feel this works well with all emotions? When would it work best, and when would it not work at all?

213

cases, it keeps coming back, though there are calm times. This second kind of heightened emotionality is most damaging to a child.

The child whose emotions are always heightened becomes tense and nervous. Such a child often develops nervous mannerisms, such as nail-biting, eye-blinking, or speech problems. These may develop into habits and happen even when the child is calm.

Intellectual abilities are also affected by heightened emotionality. Emotions affect the ability to remember, to do any creative work, to learn new meanings, and, above all, to reason. Children then seem unreasonable and unable to understand what is said to them. Not until they calm down can parents "talk sense" to them.

Teaching the Child Emotional Control

Most parents know that children must learn emotional control. This is essential to living in any society. If parents see emotional outbursts taking place more often and becoming stronger, they begin to feel that the children are not likely to outgrow these outbursts.

Unfortunately, far too many parents believe that punishment of some sort—spanking, slapping, sending children out of the room, or keeping them from having something they especially enjoy—is the best way to teach control. Children may be frightened by punishment into controlling their emotions. But this is far from a satisfactory way to handle the problem.

Emotional control must come from within, not from some outside force.

Children must control their own emotions. At what point children are ready to learn to control their emotions depends on their abilities. They need to understand what others say to them, to express themselves clearly, and most important, to reason. Before they are 4 years old, few children have even the foundations for these abilities. Unless parents know this, they will expect children to have emotional control earlier than children are able to.

Before children can learn emotional control, they must want to learn it. They must also be able to express their feelings in another way. And they must gain some satisfaction from this other method.

Learning emotional control is a long and very hard task. No one should expect children to have their emotions totally under control when they are ready to go to school. Studies of temper tantrums have shown that they usually reach their peak between the ages of 4 and 5 years. Then they begin to lessen. This is probably true of all other emotional outbursts as well. Even by the time they reach adolescence, few children have a mature level of emotional control.

For Discussion

Why should young children be encouraged to talk about things that bother or scare them? Why is this better than feeling disapproval or being called names? Explain why the first way to deal with the problem will work better than the second.

Emotional Tolerance

The young child's reasoning ability has to develop enough to make it possible to begin to learn to control emotional outbursts. When it has, the child is ready to begin to learn how to deal with unpleasant emotions without becoming too upset by them. This is known as *emotional tolerance.*

Little by little, parents' control over the environment should be relaxed. Sometimes children should be in situations that can be expected to anger or frighten them or cause jealousy and envy. If possible, children should be told in advance why they cannot have or do something they want. This will keep them from staging a temper tantrum. In time, it will lead to *frustration tolerance*, or the ability to deal with things that keep them from getting what they want.

Children should also be told ahead of time what to expect when they are taken to a doctor or dentist or when they have to be hospitalized. They will be less frightened than if they were not at all prepared. In that way, a basis for *fear tolerance* is being laid. This is the ability to face new situations without being overly frightened. Foundations can also be laid for *jealousy* and *envy tolerance*. Parents can explain why they must give more time to a new baby than to them. Or parents can explain why they cannot spend the money needed to buy some of the things the children's friends have.

Children will, in time, begin to be able to tolerate unpleasant emotions, even anger. Until they do, it is essential that their environment be controlled. This does not mean that children should be protected from all unpleasant emotions. Pleasant emotions should be the main emotions in children's lives. But they should learn, through careful guidance by parents, to deal with the unpleasant ones. These are sure to be felt when the child's world grows beyond the home. Learning this is essential to the building of a well-adjusted personality.

To help children build emotional tolerance, parents can calmly talk to their child and try to explain why things are as they are. Mimi Forsyth/Monkmeyer

Highlights of Chapter 15

☐ In spite of differences in children's emotions, some are common to all children. Among these are affection, anger, curiosity, envy, fear, grief, jealousy, and joy.

☐ Emotions develop by four methods: trial-and-error learning, imitation, conditioning, and training.

☐ Children's emotions differ from adults'. These differences should be kept in mind. Knowing them keeps adults from judging children harshly when children express their emotions in a manner that is normal for their age and level of development.

☐ Heightened emotionality may be physical in origin, but it is more often caused by environmental states.

☐ Heightened emotionality can best be dealt with by control of the environment until children have developed enough to learn to control their own emotions.

☐ For children to learn to control their emotions, three factors must be present: The children must want to do so, they must have a substitute for the emotional outburst, and they must gain satisfaction from the substitute.

☐ To ensure that children will have more pleasant than unpleasant emotions, they must learn *emotional tolerance*, or the ability to deal with unpleasant emotions without becoming too upset by them.

Suggested Activities

1. Prepare a bulletin board for the classroom using photographs or cartoon figures to show some of the facts in the chart on page 208, "What Emotions Do to and for Children."

2. Role play situations in which children learn about emotions through trial and error, imitation, conditioning, and training. Discuss afterward if it is possible or practical for children to learn emotions in only one of these ways. Give examples of how these methods of learning might overlap.

3. Divide into groups, one for each emotion listed on page 211. Within each group, make up a situation in which the emotion gets out of hand. Share each situation with the rest of the class. Discuss what could be done to keep from losing control.

4. There are differences between children's and adults' emotions. Discuss the pros and cons of each difference. How do adults often seem "childish" in the way they express emotions?

5. Find out what parents do to control their children's environments to keep emotional outbursts from happening. What can parents do to help their children learn emotional control?

Chapter 16

Personality Building

Some goals of this chapter are:

☐ To know what the terms "personality" and "personality pattern" mean and know what affects their development

☐ To know what most people think is an attractive personality and explain how it adds to a person's well-being

Personality is a word that is widely used in everyday speech. But its technical meaning is not always understood. When used in discussing human development, it is not some hard-to-describe trait within a person. Instead, it is the quality of the person's behavior as judged by others.

When someone is said to have an *attractive personality*, it means that others like the way the person behaves. As a result, people like that person. If, on the other hand, someone's behavior is bothersome, it is said that the person has a disagreeable, or an unattractive, personality.

The Personality Pattern

The quality of the child's behavior is the result of the child's traits and self-concept. Together they make up the *personality pattern*. The personality pattern can be thought of as a wheel. The spokes are the different traits, and the hub is the concept of self.

Children's self-concepts mirror what they *believe* important people in their lives think of them. If children believe that others think they are important, it is natural that they see themselves as important people.

Personality traits show how a child has adjusted to life. They are patterns of behavior that children have learned while growing up. These traits are greatly affected by the self-concepts children have developed. Some children learn to think of themselves as more important than other people because of special treatment given to them by a parent or a relative. These chil-

217

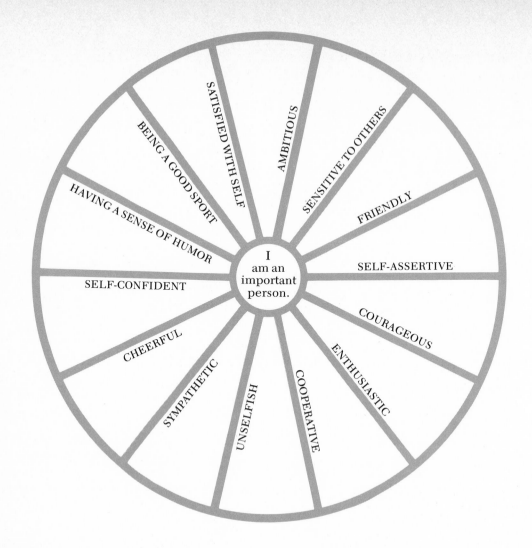

The wheel shows personality traits that contribute to a person's sense of self-importance: SATISFIED WITH SELF, AMBITIOUS, SENSITIVE TO OTHERS, BEING A GOOD SPORT, FRIENDLY, HAVING A SENSE OF HUMOR, SELF-ASSERTIVE, SELF-CONFIDENT, COURAGEOUS, CHEERFUL, ENTHUSIASTIC, SYMPATHETIC, UNSELFISH, COOPERATIVE, surrounding the center: I am an important person.

dren become cocky, bossy, self-centered, and selfish, and they think too much of themselves.

Before children are ready for school, their main personality traits are very much set. Studies have been made of the same people, from early childhood into the adult years. These studies have shown how important the early childhood years are in personality building. Children who are aggressive usually develop into aggressive adults. The way of expressing the aggression just changes as they grow older. Self-confident children who make good personal and social adjustments often become self-confident adults. This is much less likely to happen if, in early childhood, they had little faith in their abilities.

How the Personality Pattern Develops

Learning plays a leading role in the development of personality. Children base what they think of themselves on what they believe others think of them. A few parents may use direct training to help children develop their self-con-

218

cepts. But most of the time, the way children learn to think of themselves happens without anyone's being especially concerned about it.

Parents usually do give thought to helping children develop personality traits that will lead to good social adjustments. They try, for example, to teach children to cooperate, to be good sports, and to be unselfish. Parents know that these are traits others like. They are also essential to doing well in life. Some other positive traits are listed in the chart on the next page.

If personality building is to work, learning a positive self-concept must be stressed as well as learning traits. The self-concept is the core of the personality pattern. It affects not only traits but also the way they are expressed.

For Discussion

The child's self-concept is called by psychologists a mirror image. Explain the meaning of this name by taking a specific case. Use, for example, a child who has a very poor self-image and who feels that everything she or he does is not as good as what brothers or sisters or playmates do.

For example, suppose children have been trained to be unselfish. Since that is a trait people like, it should lead to good personal and social adjustments. But what if these children's self-concepts are very bad? They think everyone is better than they are. They may then express their unselfishness by

Children's earliest experiences with family members become the basis for their personality patterns. David S. Strickler/Monkmeyer

Some Positive Personality Traits

Ambition   Encouraged by helping children set goals. These should be high enough to call for a real effort, but not so high that they cannot be reached.

Assertiveness   Encouraged by giving children a chance to express themselves in family talks and to make simple decisions.

Being a Good Sport   Encouraged by guidance from parents and good examples of how to take losing gracefully and winning humbly.

Calmness   Developed by controlling the environment so that there will not be strong, uncalled-for excitement. Children should also be given good models to imitate.

Cheerfulness   Developed by good health, being surrounded by those whose outlook on life is cheerful, and avoiding unneeded curbs and frustrations.

Cooperativeness   Encouraged by letting children take part in family chores, having family members enjoy doing things together, and letting children know that their help is of value.

Courage   Developed not by criticizing fear but by giving the child plenty of praise and support for even a slight show of courage.

Enthusiasm   Encouraged by good health, being surrounded by enthusiastic people, making plans and looking forward to carrying them out, and stressing pleasant parts of what the child does.

Self-Confidence   Developed best by praising children when they try to do what is expected of them, judging their abilities favorably, and letting children do things for themselves as soon as they can.

Sense of Humor   Encouraged by helping children see the light side of problem situations. This also gives children a good model to imitate.

Sympathy   Developed very slowly. It depends on the development of imagination.   Besides being interested in others, children must learn to imagine themselves in another's place. They have to know how they would feel if something bad or sad happened to them.

Unselfishness   Developed by encouraging children to share and to do kind things for others. Rewarding any unselfish acts with praise also helps.

being too giving. They may give "the shirt off their backs" to anyone who wants or likes it. They do not do this because of a healthy desire to share, but because they think that everyone else is more deserving.

Children with better self-concepts learn to be unselfish in a more honest way. They respect themselves. So they are not likely to let people take advantage of them. Nor will they feel any need to try to "buy" friendship.

To help children develop positive self-concepts, parents should control situations that often lead to negative self-concepts. It is much easier to keep a poor self-concept from developing than to correct one once it has already developed.

Often parents need to take a look at their own personality patterns. They have to think about how these affect their children. The result may be a shift from stressing criticism and punish-

Being accepted by another admiring child will help a child develop a more favorable self-concept. Hella Hammid/ Rapho/Photo Researchers

ment to stressing praise. Criticism for wrongdoing may be replaced with ideas about how children can do things the right way. Being treated in a positive way shows children that parents approve of them. It shows that parents are trying to help them do better. It also gives children the chance to think well of themselves and feel good about who they are.

In building the personality pattern, all parts of the pattern should be given attention. Traits, like self-concepts, are hard to change once they are set. For example, some children have a pattern of wanting things done their way at any cost. They will have a very hard time learning to be cooperative.

For Thought

What could you do to improve your own self-concept? If you think you are not as good-looking as your friends, you would take steps to improve your looks. What can you do to develop positive personality traits?

Environmental Effects on the Personality Pattern

During the early years of life, family members are responsible for the self-concept and personality traits the child develops.

The home environment also plays an important role. The environment may

221

Being part of a family where adults are cooperative and cheerful, a child cannot help but develop similar personality traits. Christy Park/Monkmeyer

be pleasant or unpleasant. It may be calm or full of arguments, marked by small dislikes and jealousies or by cooperativeness.

All family members add to the emotional environment of the home. But it is the parents who have the greatest effect. Suppose, for example, a parent comes home from work tired and edgy. He or she is likely to cloud the whole household with gloom. If this happens often, it will show up in the child's personality. The child may develop a gloomy, unhappy pattern of reacting to people and to different life situations. But the parent with a happy, cheerful outlook adds to a cheerful home. Just as important, the parent presents a good model for the child to imitate.

Other family members—brothers, sisters, grandparents, uncles, aunts, cousins, and even caretakers—also affect the type of personality the young child will develop. How much effect they will have depends upon how much time they spend with the child and how great the child's affection is for them.

For Discussion

> How do you think children who believe that no one likes them are likely to behave toward others—children as well as adults? Is their behavior likely to make people act positively or negatively to them? Base your discussion on things you have personally seen and known of other people.

The ideal home environment for personality building is one in which all members are happy and friendly. Family members should be respected and given rights and responsibilities suited to their ages. Either or both parents should not rule by an iron hand. Nor should older children be allowed to boss younger ones.

Children feel safe in the ideal home. They know that they are loved and welcomed members of the family. When they try to do what is expected of them, they are encouraged and praised. In this way, they gain self-confidence.

An Attractive Personality

An attractive personality is one in which most of the personality traits are those people like. This does not mean that *all* the traits must be socially desirable. It would, in fact, be impossible to find anyone who had only pleasing traits.

Most parents want their children to have attractive personalities. They know that this will be of value to their children all through life. They also feel that when their children have attractive personalities it reflects well on them as parents. When children develop unattractive personalities, parents are upset. They may hope that their children will outgrow the traits that make them unpleasant to be with. Or they may take more positive steps. They may try to develop traits in their children that others like better.

In helping a child to develop an attractive personality, adults should keep two factors in mind. The first is that not all socially desirable traits lead to good adjustments both during childhood and all through life. Fearlessness, for example, may make a child a hero in the eyes of playmates. They may envy her or him and wish they, too, could be that fearless. But as children grow older, fearlessness may become foolhardiness. Instead of being a hero, the child who does things that are dangerous is thought of as a show-off. Envy turns into scorn.

The second factor is that an extreme form of a desirable trait will not always be more desirable. Take ambition as an example. A fair amount of ambition goes far in helping a child reach goals and improve skills. But an extremely ambitious person can become pushy, disagreeable, too self-confident, and uncaring about others. Extreme ambition can also make a person feel driven, restless, and never satisfied.

Positive traits may develop on their own through trial and error or through imitation. But the matter is too important to leave to chance. The chart on page 220 shows some ways to help children develop positive personality traits.

For Discussion

Why are the extremes of desirable personality traits not useful to children? Give some examples using such traits as generosity, cheerfulness, and assertiveness. How can children be kept from developing these traits in such an extreme form that they lose their value as aids to good personal and social adjustments?

Self-Satisfaction

Children who have attractive personalities have an inner sense of well-being. This is expressed in a cheerful, happy outlook on life. They feel satisfied with themselves because they come from homes where others are satisfied with them. Self-satisfied children see themselves as worthy of the love and respect of those who mean most to them. This makes them want to live up to that love and respect. So they try to do their best all the time.

When children grow up in a home where they are always criticized and punished but not often praised, they learn to think of themselves as second-

Children develop self-confidence and satisfaction as they are given chances to express themselves freely. Irene Bayer/Monkmeyer

them. Other children do not want them as playmates. The accompanying chart gives some of the common ways in which young children show dissatisfaction with themselves.

At the other end of the scale is too much self-satisfaction. This is usually called smugness. It leads to bragging and too much self-confidence. Such children have a false sense of their importance. They are likely to take on more than they can handle. This, in turn, leads to failures which they do not believe are their own fault. Instead, smug children blame someone else for their failures. This increases the dislike others have for them.

For Thought

Of the ways young children show dissatisfaction with self that are listed in the chart, how many are also used by adults? If they are not used by adults, why has their use been given up? Do adults, for example, tattle or destroy things others own when they are dissatisfied with themselves?

rate, unworthy people. This makes them dissatisfied with themselves.

Children who are dissatisfied with themselves are unhappy. They behave in such a way that others come to dislike

Common Ways Children Show Dissatisfaction with Self

Complain all the time of how badly they do things, which others often see as a bid for attention and sympathy

Cruel to younger or smaller children and to animals

Complain that they are punished more than others

Blame others when criticized

Make up an excuse when behavior is criticized

Tattle on other children to win adult attention or approval

Overly critical of and self-righteous toward others

Angry about discipline and authority

Clown to get attention

Overreact to real or imagined slights

Destroy toys and things of others

Lie when caught doing something wrong

Highlights of Chapter 16

☐ Personality is the quality of a person's behavior in any situation. It is not just a single trait.

☐ The personality pattern is the self-concept and various traits. The self-concept has an effect on traits.

☐ Learning plays a leading role in the development of both the self-concept and the various traits.

☐ Environmental conditions help determine how the self-concept will develop and what forms the different personality traits will take.

☐ Every child can have an attractive personality if traits are developed that are admired by members of the social group.

☐ Dissatisfaction with self is mainly caused by being often criticized, punished, and left out of the group. It leads to poor adjustments. Reasonable self-satisfaction leads to happiness and a desire to live up to one's best possibilities.

Suggested Activities

1. Watch the facial expressions of people—children, adolescents, adults, and old people—you see on the street, in stores, or in public gatherings. Do their faces give you an idea as to what type of personalities they have? When do you think facial expressions seem to tell most about a person's personality? When do they tell the least? Can you be sure of what you have decided? If not, why not?

2. List the traits in the chart on page 220 in order of their importance to an attractive personality. If there are other traits you feel should be in the chart, put them in your list. Then explain the reasons for your choices.

3. Discuss why the positive traits developed in childhood also add to an attractive personality in adulthood.

4. On the basis of what you have learned in this chapter about how personality develops, what arguments would you give a person who says that children outgrow undesirable personality traits? When *might* a child outgrow undesirable traits?

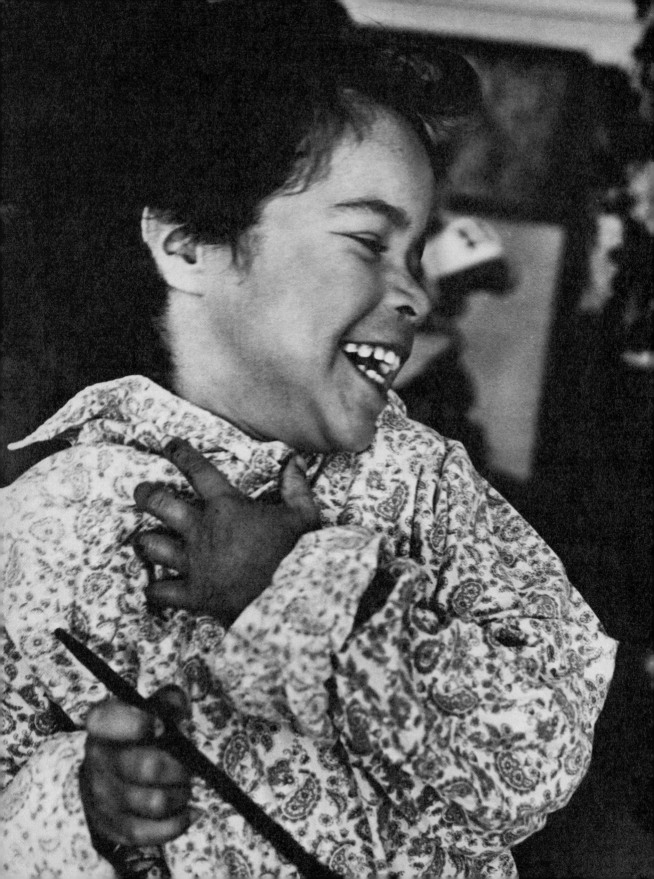

Unit Four

THE CHILD IS AN INDIVIDUAL

With more and more control over the body and ability to communicate with others, young children want to put the dependency of babyhood behind them. Independence is important to young children. This is easily seen in their negativistic responses to those who try to dominate them and in their temper outbursts when they are frustrated in trying to gain independence. Young children want to use their newly developed abilities to establish themselves as people in their own right. The more this desire is blocked, the more children will protest and the stronger will be their demands for independence.

The desire to be an individual does not only show up as demands for independence. It also expresses itself in a desire to be seen as a person, not just a child in a family.

This unit shows some of the ways young children can satisfy their needs for independence and individuality within their limited abilities. This is important if they are to make good personal and social adjustments.

Chapter 17, "A Place of Their Own," explains how important this is to all children. If they can call something "mine," it is a great satisfaction.

Chapter 18, "The Young Child's Clothes," points out that clothes are a sign of growing up. They also help identify children with age-mates.

Chapter 19, "The Child's Companions," explains why companionship is so important to children. Parents and other family members no longer fill this need as they did during babyhood. So children seek companionship with other children.

Chapter 20, "Play and Playthings," describes the common forms of play young children enjoy. Also covered is the role of playthings in making play enjoyable.

Chapter 21, "Sex Roles," discusses the early awareness children have of sex roles, how they learn roles, and how adults can encourage favorable attitudes toward sex roles.

Chapter 22, "The Child in the Family," shows how different the child's place in the family is from that of the baby. The changing relationships between children and other family members are stressed.

Chapter 17

A Place
of Their Own

Some goals of this chapter are:
- ☐ To understand why young children want a place of their own, no matter how small it is
- ☐ To realize that an "ideal" home for young children not only meets their needs, but also the needs of other family members
- ☐ To see the psychological advantages young children gain from being given a chance to take on responsibilities in the home

The home is every child's castle. It is where young children are surrounded by the people who mean most to them. It is where they can feel safe and secure.

Within the home, young children want a place that is theirs and theirs alone. They are still not social enough to want to be a part of the group all the time. Nor has their social development advanced far enough for them to want to share their belongings all the time. They like to feel that their things are their own to do with as they please.

Security from Ownership
No matter how small the family's home may be, young children want a space they can think of as their own. If they cannot have a room to themselves, they

want part of the room they share to be theirs. They want to feel that everything in it is theirs. They also want a place in the bathroom where their towels, washcloths, and toothbrushes will always be found. If they still eat at a small table, that table should have a place set aside in the kitchen or dining room. If they eat at the family table, they want a place there.

Many adults are puzzled about why a place of their own means so much to young children. Some are amused by it. But many see it as a sign of selfishness that should be curbed. These adults fail to see the psychological gains this gives a child. A place of their own makes children feel secure, feel that they are being accepted as individuals. It gives them a sense of pride that comes from ownership.

Value of Permanence

Children can get psychological benefits from a place of their own. But to do so, the place must be fairly permanent.

Nothing will make young children angrier about a new baby than being put out of their room or having some of their space taken away and given to the new baby. This is why it is better to make the shifts weeks ahead of the new baby's arrival. Then children will have time to gain a sense of permanence about their new area. If the crib is to be used for the new baby, the child should be given a big bed in plenty of time to get used to it. This will avoid anger about having the new baby use "my" crib.

When a family moves—for business reasons, for more space, or to be nearer better schools—all family members are upset. But none are more upset than young children. They find themselves in places they do not know. Things are no longer where the children are used to finding them. The permanence that meant so much to their security is gone.

Older children usually look upon a move as an exciting adventure. But the young child's world seems to fall apart. The child goes through a period of depression marked by crying, loss of appetite, sleeplessness, and a lack of interest in the new surroundings.

When moves are essential, many of the harmful effects on young children can be avoided or greatly lessened. This can be done by trying to re-create a feeling of permanence. The new home can be made as nearly like the old one as possible. There are many ways that this can be done. The color of the walls of the new room can be the same as

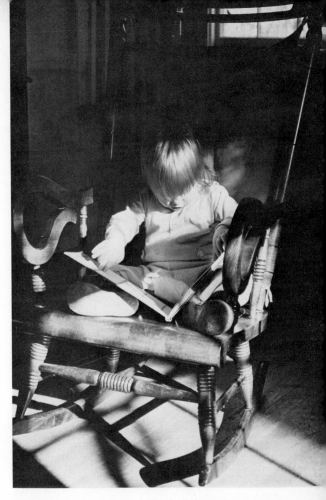

Security is having a favorite spot all to yourself! HEW

that of the old room. Pictures can be placed in the same places on the new walls. The furniture can be placed as nearly as possible where it was in the old room. And the child's place at the family table can be the same. If children have had a certain place in the house or yard for toys, a place like it can be given to them in the new home.

Many parents fail to realize how important a feeling of permanence is to young children. They make the mistake of redoing the child's room when they move into a new home. This makes the child's adjustment to the new home harder than it need be. It takes away the familiar sights that gave a feeling of permanence.

An "Ideal" Home for Young Children

An "ideal" home for young children is one that meets their most important needs. Can any house or apartment meet all the needs of young children as well as other family members? Probably not. However, each one's basic needs can be met fairly well.

There is no one kind of home that will meet the needs of all young children. However, there are certain features of a home that will meet most of the basic needs. These are given in the accompanying chart.

To come close to an ideal home for young children, the home must also meet the basic needs of other family members. When people are unhappy with their home, their attitude affects the emotional environment. In such cases, there will be disturbances and unhappiness, which will affect the entire family.

For Discussion

How can parents, busy with the job of packing and unpacking, ease the problem young children face because of a family move? In what ways can they let children help with the packing and unpacking?

An Ideal Neighborhood

Where the house or apartment is found is also important. The business part of any city is not usually suitable for family living. There is not enough play space. Also, there is too much noise and danger from traffic.

Basic Needs Met by an "Ideal" Home

Close enough to where the parents work to let them spend time with the children and be around for home emergencies

Large enough to let every family member have some space to think of as "mine"

Easy to care for, so that parents can spend more time with children and less on chores

Enough space to allow children to play indoors when the weather is bad

As safe as possible, especially nonskid floors and protected windows and glass doors

Neat appearance, with few and simple decorations

Near enough to shopping to let parents take children

Near other families with young children

Safe outdoor space for play without adult supervision at all times

Play space in family living area where children can be with family members and also do their own activities

Near relatives and friends so that children can see them often and parents can have a feeling of security

Playing with other children, especially in the neighborhood, helps a child to be emotionally healthy. Henry Monroe

An apartment or house in one of the residential areas of any city or suburb is a better place. There should be a park, public library, grade school, and facilities for preschool children. Many neighborhood parks have playground supervisors who will watch children as they play. Public libraries have children's rooms where young children can look at picture books, hear stories told, or watch children's films.

A country home offers children safety and plenty of outdoor space for play. But if the home is far from others, children may be lonely. For young children, a front yard or a backyard is useful. Toys and outdoor play equipment can easily be brought from the house, and parents can keep a watchful eye out while they do home chores.

Having a play space belonging to the home gives young children a feeling of ownership. They do not have this if they share play space with other children in a public park.

As children grow older, they need the companionship of other children. Then a yard has little to offer them, unless the neighborhood children can come there to play. If the yard is not big enough for group play or if parents object to the noise of the rough-and-tumble play of young children, the children will want to play with their playmates elsewhere. They no longer want to play alone.

Housing developments in cities or suburbs offer many of the features that are desirable in a home for young children. They have reasonably large outdoor play areas. And many of the

What features of a home meet the needs of young children, older children, and parents? What kind of home—a house or an apartment—would meet the most important needs of every family member? Where should it be—in a city, a suburb, or the country? Is there any one right answer to these questions? Why or why not? What kind of home might meet the needs of young children but not of their parents and older brothers and sisters? What kind would best meet the needs of parents but not of the children of the family? Give reasons for your answers.

streets are dead-end streets, with little or no traffic. Children can play there with safety.

Even more important, there are other families with young children living there. Children will have no trouble finding age-mates with whom to play. Most important of all, there is often a neighborhood spirit among the parents. Parents take turns watching the children play outdoors. This frees other parents for other activities.

It is wise, when choosing a house or apartment, to think seriously about whether rooms can be changed or added on. Such changes may be needed to meet children's changed needs. If changes in the home can be made, it will take away at least one reason for moving to another home. Since moving always causes tension and may cause feelings of insecurity for young children, anything that can save families a move is useful.

An Ideal Room

Just as there can be no one ideal home, so there is no ideal room for children. Any room, with adjustments made at little expense, can meet the needs of young children. The accompanying chart explains what features of a room are important to young children. These features meet important needs in children's lives at that age.

Whenever possible, children should have a room of their own rather than sharing one with another child. Since children develop at different rates, the interests and activities of a child of one age are different from those of an older or younger child. Sharing a room does not always meet the needs of two or more children.

However, it is often impossible to give a child a single room. When that is the case, it may be better to put the oldest child with the youngest than to put two children of nearly the same age together. The older child usually spends less time in the room than the younger. Also, an older child is often more tolerant toward a younger child. However, these general rules will not apply to all families. Parents need to take the personalities of their own children into account.

When sharing a room, each child should have a part of the room that is his or hers. The children may have to share the same chest of drawers, closet, and shelves. If so, a part of each should be

Features of a Young Child's Room

Size   Even a small room can appear larger if the amount of furniture is kept down and is pushed close to the walls. Space in the middle of the room allows for quiet play when indoors.

Walls   To make the room seem large and cheerful, washable paint or wallpaper in light colors can be used. Children can be given a choice of color. A few children's pictures, chosen by the children, can be placed where they can be seen easily.

Windows   For safety, windows should be opened only at the top unless metal bars are put across the lower part of the window frame. If at all possible, the windows should get the morning sun. Then the sun will not interfere with the afternoon nap and early bed hour at night. If possible, the windows should face a place where there are interesting things for children to look at. To be able to darken the room for naps and early bedtime, the windows can have blinds, shades, or curtains.

Floor   Because all young children are floor-sitters, some kind of rug or carpet, at least in the center of the room, will help keep them from getting chilled.

Lighting   A ceiling light, with cover, will help spread light through the room and help prevent eye strain. If extra lighting is needed, pin-up wall lamps can be easily put up by the parents. Floor and table lamps are too easily knocked over and should not be used.

Closets and Storage Space   To encourage neatness and responsibility, there should be plenty of hooks within easy reach of young children. That will help them learn to hang up and take down their own clothes. An open shelf for toys, within the child's reach, can be put in the back or side of the closet, or in the corner of the room.

Children are usually able to adjust to available play space. In an "ideal" room, a child's play will not interfere with anyone else's activities. Robert Capece

For Discussion

When a young child has to share a room with a brother or sister, what age difference is the best for both children? If there is only one boy and one girl in the family, should they be put in the same room? If so, how long should they share the same room? Give reasons for your answers to both of these questions.

given to each child to use as he or she wishes.

Even when there is space in the house or apartment that can be used as a playroom, most young children like to do some of their playing in their own room. To make this possible, the room should not have too much furniture. What it has should meet children's needs, not only for sleep and dressing, but also for play.

Parents sometimes make the mistake of buying youth-sized furniture to replace the nursery furniture used when the child was a baby. If cost makes no difference, this is all right. But it is far better to get adult-sized furniture. Today it comes in sizes suitable for use in small rooms. A chest of drawers, for example, can be small enough to use in a child's room. Yet it will still be usable as the child grows up.

Many secondhand furniture stores and garage sales have furniture which, with a coat of paint, can be used in a child's room. The cost is far less than that of new furniture. A secondhand coffee table, for example, can serve as a play table in a child's room. A small chair can be bought at a sale or in a department store.

Children's rooms mean very much to them. Parents should, whenever possible, give children the chance to say how they feel about the furnishings. Children could also be asked what color to paint their room. The chance to make such decisions adds to children's pride of ownership. It makes them feel that a room is truly theirs.

For Discussion

How old should children be before they are allowed to decide about the colors and furnishings for their rooms? Should children help pick out furniture, or should the parents make this-decision? Give reasons for your answers.

Unlike most adults, young children are "bed-sitters." They like sitting on beds better than sitting in chairs. This must be taken into account when choosing a bed for a young child. If the bed has a firm mattress and good springs, it can be used as a place to sleep as well as to sit. It can be covered with a spread of strong material and pushed against a wall. By adding a few colorful throw pillows, it will look like a sofa.

The furnishings young children need are suggested in the accompanying chart. The chart is divided into two groups: essential and valuable but not essential. Note how little is in either group. A young child's room needs less than some parents realize. It needs far less than ads would have one believe. Nonessential furniture is an unneeded expense for parents. It also clutters the room for the child.

Furnishings for a Young Child's Room	
Essential	
Bed	Shelves for toys and books
Chest of drawers	Small table and chair for drawing and other play activities
Child-sized chair (rocking or stuffed chair), for relaxing	
Valuable but Not Essential	
Mirror on back of closet door as an aid to good grooming	Adult-sized chair for parents to use when reading to the child
Inexpensive child's record player	

Responsibility for Their Place

Much of the pleasure of a place of a child's own, as well as much of the psychological value, comes from the child's being responsible for it. This means not only a room, but any part of the home where there is a space a child thinks of as his or her own. This may be, for example, a corner in the family living room where the child is allowed to keep some toys.

Of course, young children cannot be expected to be fully responsible for their area. But most young children can take more responsibility than they are given. Too many parents fail to give

Children gain a sense of pride by doing some things for themselves. Erika Stone/Monkmeyer

children the chances to learn to take on responsibilities. Their children miss out on a means of pride and satisfaction.

Seeing how slowly and badly young children do the things these responsibilities call for, parents sometimes take over the tasks. This makes children feel that they are not able to do them.

Because care of their space calls for learning certain tasks, the principles of learning must be used (see pages 147–148). Children must have guidance in carrying out the task, a strong drive to learn it, enough chance for practice, and, most important, they must learn one task at a time.

The following chart gives some of the tasks young children can learn in taking responsibility for their space. These tasks are not given in any order. Each child will want to learn different tasks, depending on his or her interests and abilities. However, most children can carry out these tasks by the time they are ready to go to school. They need only the chance to learn them and guidance in doing so. If children learn all these tasks, they are able to take almost full responsibility for the care of their area. And they can do this at an earlier age than most parents realize.

Sharing Responsibilities

Young children should do more than care for their own space. They should also have some responsibility for the parts of the home they share with other family members. Having such responsibility helps children feel that the home is theirs and that they are a part of the family unit.

Small duties can be given to young children for which they and they alone are responsible. They must be guided in learning how to carry out these responsibilities. They should be expected to do these tasks daily until they can do them well.

Responsibilities Young Children Can Take for the Care of Their Space

Put toys and play gear back on shelves

Put away nightclothes and slippers

Hang coat on hanger and put hanger on hook in closet

Put clean clothes in drawers of bureau

Put dirty clothes in hamper

Pick up paper scraps from floor

Empty wastebasket

Water plants

Hang up towel and washcloth

Put dirty towel and washcloth in hamper

Put toothbrush and toothpaste in their proper places

Put away outdoor play equipment

Dust furniture with dustcloth

Move small pieces of furniture for floor cleaning

Use mop on floor

Run sweeper or vacuum over rug

Rinse out bathtub and basin after use

Help parent make bed

Fold things such as towels and washcloths and put them away

A child can learn to be responsible for important little tasks, such as a nature corner. Mimi Forsyth/Monkmeyer

When children become skilled in the duties given to them, it is wise to change their duties. This keeps children from becoming bored, which leads to a sloppy job. It also gives young children a chance to learn new skills. In this way they will be able to take on new responsibilities.

After young children have a fairly large number of skills needed in the care of the home, it is a good idea to have all members of the family decide what duties each family member is to do for the coming week. Having some say in what they are to do helps keep children from feeling that their home duties are a drudgery. The jobs are not forced on them without any thought as to how the children feel.

If possible, children's responsibilities in the home should be ones that can be carried out along with other family members. The more children are with members of the family, the pleasanter the tasks will be for them. It will also make them want to do the tasks as well as other family members do them. Furthermore, working with other family members will give young children the feeling that they are being treated more like grown-ups than like babies.

Holidays and other special times offer especially good chances for group responsibilities in the home. Even the youngest child in the family can help prepare food, can help make and place decorations, and can help clean up after everything is over.

Psychological Values of Responsibilities

Many parents feel that the help of a young child in everyday responsibilities hinders more than it helps. This is probably true from their point of view. Children cannot dust as well as an adult can. They may drop and break a dish they are drying. And they are very likely to spill milk as they pour it into a glass. Certainly whatever they do will be at a much slower rate than the adult's.

Other parents may see household tasks as such drudgery that they want to spare children as long as possible. As a result, they will not ask children to help.

Such attitudes, well-meaning as they may be, are unfair to young children. They dampen children's desires to learn the skills that will be needed as they grow older. They keep preschoolers from learning skills while they have plenty of free time to practice. They may also encourage an uncooperative attitude. That could affect children's relationships with playmates and their adjustments to school. Far more serious, children who are not allowed to take part in home responsibilities do not get many psychological values such

participation can give. Some of the most important values are listed in the accompanying chart.

Young children who are encouraged to be a part of the family team are far happier than those who are sent off to play with their toys alone. This suggests that they are rejected by those who are important to them. Even worse, it makes them feel they are not able to help others. These unfavorable psychological effects may be the beginning of an antiwork, uncooperative attitude. This can have serious effects on children's personal and social adjustments as they grow older. On the other hand, children who are allowed to help are laying foundations for good personal and social adjustments for the rest of their lives.

For Discussion

Young children tend to hinder busy parents more than help them in carrying out different household tasks. Why should young children be given a chance to carry out the tasks they are developed enough to learn? Why is it unfair to young children not to give them this chance?

Values to Young Children of Sharing Home Responsibilities

Pride from achievement of tasks

Learning that work can be fun, not drudgery

Learning to cooperate with others

Prevention of boredom that often comes from too much play

Feeling of being a full member of the family team

Feeling that help is of enough value to be worth the effort

Feeling of being grown-up enough to do what other family members do

Highlights of Chapter 17

☐ To all young children, the home is their castle. Places of their own in the home are essential to feelings of security and happiness.

☐ To get the psychological benefits from places of their own, there must be some sense of permanence there.

☐ An ideal home for young children is one that meets their needs as well as the needs of other family members.

☐ Ideal rooms for young children meet their need for being alone, for pride of ownership, for space to play, and for quiet to keep them from being too stimulated or from having their schedules broken.

☐ Young children can take on many more responsibilities for the care of their space than many parents realize.

☐ Helping with home responsibilities encourages young children to develop favorable attitudes toward cooperation and a desire to learn social-help skills.

☐ The psychological values to young children of taking on home responsibilities are far greater than the aid they are able to give.

Suggested Activities

1. Make a list of furniture you feel a young child's room needs. Then visit the furniture department of a department store and price the children's furniture on your list. Price the same things in adult sizes. Do you feel the children's furniture is worth the cost, considering the fairly short time it will be used?

2. Visit the children's department of a department store and ask to see pictures, lights, and other decorations for children's rooms. Price them to see how much it would cost to decorate a young child's room. Then try to find magazine pictures that might be used for wall decorations or as decoration on plain lampshades. List ways parents could use homemade items to decorate a young child's room for a small part of the cost of decorations bought in a store.

3. Plan a garden for a young child, in a yard, in a window box, or in indoor plant pots. What would you plant, vegetables or flowers? What types of each? Give reasons for your choices and ideas of ways to help the child feel responsible for it.

4. Draw to scale a room of the size and shape of a child's bedroom. Then make a plan for arranging the room for two children so that each would feel that the room is "mine." Show where furniture might be placed and what areas would be used by each child.

5. Make a list of activities needed to clean and care for a bedroom and a bathroom. Then decide which of these could be carried out by a 4-year-old, a 5-year-old, and a 6-year-old. Which could not be carried out by the children? How do you feel about these activities?

Chapter 18

The Young Child's Clothes

Some goals of this chapter are:
- ☐ To be aware of what young children like in their clothes and why parents should take this into account, along with needs, when choosing clothing for young children
- ☐ To understand what is appropriate clothing for children
- ☐ To understand why grooming and caring for their clothes is important to young children

Clothes have very different meanings and values for adults and for young children. Because of this, there may be clashes between children and parents over clothes.

Parents, for example, often want the children's clothes to improve the children's appearance. Some parents want their children to be neat and well-groomed all the time. They feel this shows that they are good parents. And other parents may want their children's clothes to be as much in fashion as their own.

None of these values are important to young children. Instead, they want their clothes to be comfortable, serviceable, and enough like those of playmates to keep them from feeling different. At the same time, they want

their clothes to be special enough to be admired.

In the past few years, many changes have taken place in the attitudes of our society toward clothes. For one thing, fashion is followed far less closely. There is much more room for individual taste. For another thing, casual clothes, for both children and adults, are now much more widely accepted.

The move toward more casual clothes has been most noticeable among young people. They will be the new parents of the coming years. So it may be expected that parents will care even less about fashion. They will be more interested in the practicality of their children's clothes. This may result in fewer parent–child arguments over clothes.

Interest in Clothing

To babies, clothes are a bother. Clothes get in the way when they want to move their bodies. Getting dressed or undressed is frustrating for babies. They often stiffen their bodies, cry, and kick during the process.

The first interest children show in their clothes is in dressing and undressing themselves. Before babyhood is over, all babies, if given a chance to pull off clothes, can strip themselves naked. They can also put on some of their clothes, even though they may not be on the right parts of the body or in the right position on the body. This interest is not in clothes themselves. It is in the challenge of taking them off or putting them on.

Only when children become aware that clothes can get them attention do clothes become a point of interest. By the time children are 3 or 4 years old, their clothes give them much pleasure and pride. The satisfaction children get from their clothes grows rapidly as their world goes beyond the home and family.

Clothes can give children pleasure and self-confidence. But too much stress on clothes is not healthy. Children should not be encouraged to place too much value on clothes—their own or others'. That may give them a materialistic outlook on life. Other values, such as friendliness, cooperation, and skills, are more important.

Above all, parents should try to teach their children not to judge other children on the basis of their clothes. Few children have much say in what they wear. So it is not fair for other children to reject them because of their clothing.

Children can understand this idea if parents both explain and act on it themselves. At the same time, wise parents will be aware of their children's feelings. Parents will not choose clothes that may become the cause of jokes or may get too much attention.

What Young Children Like

In choosing clothes for children, too many parents are guided by what they like. They ignore what children like. Many adults, for example, like clothes that are in fashion. The clothes may not even be becoming. Young children are

Children feel they have something in common when their clothes are similar. Nancy Hays/ Monkmeyer

What Young Children Like in Clothes

Color   Children like clothes of their favorite colors. They are hardly ever aware of whether or not the color is becoming on them or fits the occasion. They may want to wear clothes of two or more favorite colors at the same time, whether or not they match.

Decorations   Colorful buttons, sewn-on figures, and the like all add interest to clothing. Children are interested in and attracted by these rather than the style of the clothing.

Newness   Because people often say things about new clothes, young children like to wear them. Often they beg to wear new shoes home from the store.

Ease of Self-Dressing   Clothes that are easy to put on and fasten have a strong appeal to young children trying to be independent. However, they are not likely to think of this by themselves when making a choice in a store. They may not be able to judge how easy it is to put on.

Texture   Texture means more to young children than most adults think. They especially like soft materials, such as furs, silks, and velvets.

Similarity to Clothes of Playmates   Young children like clothes similar to those of playmates in color or style. They do not want to feel noticeably different.

different. They do not care about fashion or the way something looks.

All children have individual tastes in clothing. But there are certain things that most children feel are important. These are explained in the accompanying chart. Not all of these interests develop at once in a young child or at the same time in different children. Their development depends on the experiences of the child. For example, a child who does not often play with children outside the family will not care about having clothes like those worn by other children as soon as will a child who plays with neighborhood children.

Appropriate Clothes for Children

When most parents choose their own clothes, they are guided by their needs and interests. A working adult will need totally different clothes from those of one whose life is centered around the home.

Appropriate clothing does not mean clothing that is in fashion or that holds to the styles worn by others of the same age. It means clothes that meet the person's needs and interests. The clothes, then, depend on the person's life-style.

Adults have differing life-styles, and so do young children. However, the life-styles of young children are far less varied than those of adults. But there are enough differences to think about life-style when judging whether clothes are appropriate for a given child. If children are to gain satisfaction, pride, and independence from their clothes, their clothes must be appropriate for them, not for others.

Very young children are not concerned with fashion, but they do enjoy clothes that allow them to play and move without restriction.   Lew Merrim/ Monkmeyer

For Discussion

Should a child be made to wear a hat, rubbers or boots, and a raincoat on rainy or snowy days if the other children in the neighborhood do not usually wear them? If the child resists, saying that the other children make fun, how would you deal with the problem?

The Child's Wardrobe

Young children like to wear their favorite clothes over and over again. Therefore, a large wardrobe is not important to them. Most children's clothing can be washed and needs little or no ironing. So clothes can be washed one day and worn the next. If the wardrobe is small, clothes that wear out or are outgrown can be replaced by new ones of a slightly larger size. Children are delighted by getting a new outfit once in a while, no matter how much they may have liked the old one.

Children do not know the difference between clothes that are costly and clothes that are not. Parents should not take pride in buying expensive clothes for their children. Even if they have the money, it could be spent on other things that are more useful to the child.

Clothes Young Children Need

Playclothes During the hot days of summer, little children wear clothes that leave much of their bodies exposed to the sun. Shorts, pants, or overalls with T-shirts should be well-fitting and comfortable. For outdoor wear in the winter, a snowsuit with a hood is essential in cold places.

Clothing for Extra Protection For cool days, indoors or out, young children will need a sweater. A pullover is best. They can put it on and take it off without help. Coats or jackets are needed in cold weather. Rubbers are needed for outdoor play when the ground is wet and boots when there is snow. A plastic or rubberized raincoat with hood will protect children better than an umbrella, which is awkward to carry.

Sleepwear Pajamas should be made of soft, lightweight materials for summer and heavier materials for winter. When buying sleepwear, parents should choose only those that meet the standards of safety.

Shoes Most doctors recommend that a young child wear an oxford shoe at all times except during summer. Then sneakers or sandals are more comfortable. To avoid blisters, socks should be worn at all times. Children's feet grow rapidly. So they should have only one pair of shoes at a time.

Clothes for Special Occasions Some children need at least one dressy outfit—for holidays, for religious services, or for children's parties. For winter, this might be a dressy suit or dress. However, because of changing values, clean casual clothing is acceptable for just about everything.

Dressing-Up Clothes To make dramatic play more real and more enjoyable, young children need clothes to turn them into the people whose roles they play. Old hats, dresses, ties, or any other adult clothes can be used. Ready-made or homemade costumes are often needed for children's parties or for some holiday, such as Halloween.

When buying clothes for children, there are a few things to keep in mind. It is a good idea to allow for children's growth. Clothes that fit when they are bought are often outgrown before they are worn out. A garment that is a little too large when it is bought can be fixed to fit the child. Tucks can be put in the shoulders and at the waist. Hems can be taken up. Then, as the child grows, the tucks can be taken out and the hems let down.

In putting together wardrobes parents should talk to children about their likes and dislikes. Parents can choose several garments that are suitable. Then the children can pick out the one they like best and would like to have. The chance to make a decision gives children an important sense of satisfaction in their clothes. It also takes away the possibility that they will rebel against wearing something because they do not like it.

The most important clothes in the child's wardrobe should be those for play and for sleep. Children spend so much time doing these things. However, every child needs other clothes as well, as described in the chart.

Hand-Me-Downs

In a family where there are several children, it is likely that the younger children will wear the outgrown clothes of older brothers or sisters. Even if the family has plenty of money, it would be a foolish waste to throw away or give away a child's partly worn clothes when there is a younger one who could use them.

Some parts of a young child's wardrobe are usually outgrown before they are worn out. These are underwear, bathrobes, shoes, rubbers and boots, and dressy clothes. There may also be shorts, shirts, sunsuits, overalls, and pajamas that are too good to throw away.

Shoes are the only part of a young child's wardrobe that should not be handed down. Shoes that fit one child may be too short or too long, too narrow or too wide for another. Even more important, shoes take on the shape of the wearer's feet. This makes them unsuitable and uncomfortable for someone else.

Basic clothes, such as underwear, boots, rubbers, shorts, and T-shirts,

Old clothes often inspire creative, dramatic play!
Erika Stone/Peter Arnold

present few problems when handed down. However, other clothes have individuality. They might cause a problem. The younger child may not like the color or would rather have different trim.

There are some things parents can do to keep a hand-me-down problem from arising or to deal with it should it arise. First, keep a young child's wardrobe as small as possible. There will be few things in good enough shape to hand down.

Second, before outgrown clothes are passed down, they can be changed for the next wearer. New buttons can be put on. Some decoration can be added. Or the clothes can even be dyed the new owner's favorite color.

If young children are given a chance to say what changes they would like, it will make them think of the clothing as "mine," not someone else's. In fact, many children actually like hand-me-downs that have been changed for them. Wearing the clothing of an older child suggests that they are growing up.

Finally, by playing down, in general, the stress on clothes, parents can avoid hand-me-down problems. Children should not feel that their personal worth depends on the clothes they wear. Then they will not be likely to be upset by wearing hand-me-downs.

Clothes and the Young Child's Personality

Young children seem to be careless about their clothes. Therefore, many adults think that clothes are too unimportant to children to have any effect on their personalities.

That is not true. As soon as young children begin to be interested in learn-

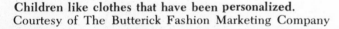

Children like clothes that have been personalized.
Courtesy of The Butterick Fashion Marketing Company

ing to dress themselves, clothes begin to have an effect on their personalities. Young children think of their clothes as a part of themselves. Clothing they like lifts their spirits and adds to their self-confidence. Clothing they dislike or are afraid other children will make fun of may undermine their self-confidence.

In dealing with children's feelings about clothing, parents need to try to keep a sometimes-difficult balance. On the one hand, they should realize that, in our society, clothes *do* play an important role in building children's self-image. Therefore clothes are important for self-confidence. On the other hand, parents need also to realize that clothing is important to children only because others make it so. It is not good for children to try to win respect by means of clothes. Parents have to help their children learn to put more stress on the real values of friendship than on the surface values of clothes and appearance.

For Discussion

What kinds of problems can develop because of hand-me-downs? Do you feel that the ideas given in this chapter are good enough to deal with a problem? What other ideas can you think of that would work better?

Grooming

The basic skills for self-dressing and grooming are learned during babyhood. During the early childhood years, these skills can be fully mastered. To do so, children need encouragement, guid-ance, and a chance to practice. These are essential for mastery. The major skills left for the young child to master are putting on their shoes and socks correctly, tying shoelaces or fastening buckles, handling different types of fasteners, and telling front from back in slip-on clothes like T-shirts and pants with elastic in the waist.

While still in the early stages of learning to dress themselves, young children cannot be expected to do a good job of self-grooming. However, as learning progresses, stress should be placed not only on how to put on clothes and fasten them but also on how to put them on neatly and correctly.

This stress encourages children to learn good self-dressing skills. It also makes them aware of what good grooming means. They learn, for example, that hair should be neat, hands and nails clean, and clothes clean and not too rumpled.

There are two aids to good grooming in early childhood. The first is a mirror. This should be full length. Children should be able to watch themselves dress to see if they are putting their clothes on correctly and neatly. The second is the "inspection test." Before going to a meal or leaving the house, the parent should take a close look at the child's hair, face, clothing, knees, nails, and hands. This will help put the child's attention on these things and create a desire to see that they are neat and clean.

Good grooming in early childhood cannot and should not be expected. Healthy, active children cannot remain neat and clean all day. They should not have to. To do so would mean that they

When children show an interest in caring for their clothing, they become eager to learn how.
James H. Karales/Peter Arnold

could not play as all children like to play. On the other hand, early childhood is none too soon to learn that it is important to be neat and clean at certain times. Among these times are mealtimes, bedtime, and times when children are with adults. Children can also be expected to learn how to be neat and clean without needing adults to tell them when or how.

Care of Clothing
Young children get satisfaction and pride from taking some responsibility for the care of their clothing. Of course, young children cannot be expected to take on the full responsibility. They cannot, for example, mend a tear. But they can, as early childhood draws to a close, learn to sew on a missing button. They cannot and should not operate washing and drying machines. But they can collect their dirty clothes and put them in a laundry hamper. They can

For Discussion

How do you feel about letting children learn to take some responsibility for the care of their clothes? Is it a useful way to encourage young children to be interested in good grooming? Why?

also learn to fold clothes that have been washed and put them in neat piles in a dresser drawer.

How soon young children can take on responsibilities for the care of their clothing depends on how well coordinated they are. Hand and arm movements are most important. The task itself also plays a part. Wiping dust off shoes after play, for example, is easier than polishing the shoes.

Like other skills, those needed for the care of clothing should be learned one at a time. Each should be well mastered before a new skill is learned.

248

Highlights of Chapter 18

☐ Clothes have somewhat different meanings and values for adults and children. These differences must be kept in mind when choosing clothes for young children and when judging the effects clothes have on them.

☐ Young children's earliest interest in clothing is centered on self-dressing. Later it turns into an interest in clothes themselves.

☐ Young children's interests in clothes are centered on color, decoration, newness, ease of self-dressing, texture of materials, and similarity of clothes to those of playmates.

☐ Appropriate clothes for young children are those that meet their needs.

☐ In putting together a wardrobe for a young child, parents should try to keep it small and take into account the child's tastes.

☐ To meet the young child's usual needs, a wardrobe should have clothes for play, for extra protection, for sleep, for special occasions, and for dress-up play.

☐ Hand-me-downs often give young children a feeling of growing up.

☐ Clothes have a great effect on children's personalities. Care needs to be taken to keep too much attention from being placed on clothes. That would encourage shallow values.

☐ During the early childhood years, basic grooming skills can be mastered if children are given encouragement, guidance, and the chance to practice them.

☐ Young children can take on more responsibility for the care of their clothing than most parents realize, and they should be given the chance to learn to do so.

Suggested Activities

1. Do some research on the history of children's clothes. Find out when children's clothes began being styled for them and their needs.

2. Ask several children 4, 5, and 6 years of age what they like most in their clothes. Do you find that children's reactions to their clothes change as they grow older, or do their interests stay just about the same?

3. Plan a bulletin board showing young children's clothing needs. Use the chart on page 244. Gather color pictures from magazines as examples of the groupings listed.

4. Examine the clothes that you and your faimly members have decided to throw away at the end of a season because they are worn or out of style. How many of these clothes could be given to children for dramatic play? How could children use these clothes in their play?

Chapter 19

The Young Child's Companions

Some goals of this chapter are:
- [ ] To be aware of the important effect of companions of different kinds on young children's personal and social adjustments
- [ ] To know the different kinds of companions a young child needs and how they add to a young child's development
- [ ] To know what makes young children popular and unpopular and what parents and other adults can do to improve children's popularity
- [ ] To realize the importance of guiding children to be good leaders and good followers

Interest in companions begins early. Whenever babies are awake they look around for someone to watch. If they find they are alone, they send up a loud wail. Each month, as babies spend more and more time awake, the need for some human companionship becomes stronger. If they see other family members doing things together, they want to join in the fun.

There is also a change in what babies and young children want from their companions. At first, they are happy to be near people just so they can watch and listen. Later they want to do things with them and, still later, to talk with them.

The number of companions young children must have to meet their needs varies with age. When children are young, one or two are usually enough. They will need more and more as their interests widen. When children become interested in playing such games as hide-and-seek, they need more companions than they did when they played with toy cars and trucks.

The kind of companions young children want and need also changes as they grow older. When still fairly helpless babies, anyone of any age or sex can fill their needs. As childhood draws to a close, children near their own age are needed to satisfy play interests.

A child can learn some of the wonders of nature from an older companion. Mike Mazzaschi/Stock, Boston

Young children have many needs besides play needs. So they must have companions other than playmates. *Friends* are companions who play with children and can also talk with them about interests and problems. Friends are usually the same age. Sometimes an older child or an adult becomes the friend of a young child. *Associates* may be adults, such as the neighbor next door, or they may be older children or adolescents who are the children's baby-sitters. These companions give children a feeling of security, just by being there. Children like to listen to and watch them when they are around.

The Importance of Companionship

Children's companions have important effects on their lives. Companions affect children's developing personali-

ties. There are also certain things children can learn from people—both adults and children—that they could learn in no other way. Some ways companions affect the young child's personal and social adjustments are listed in the following chart.

Sometimes children do not get enough human companionship during the early years of life. Sometimes they see only a few adults in the home. Such children tend to develop into shy, self-conscious people. As they grow older, children may try to change these personality patterns. However, the basic patterns of their personalities usually stay the same.

It is important that children have plenty of chances for companionship when the natural desire for it appears. It is equally important that they receive guidance in how to get along with different kinds of people. Then their early

251

They help carry out certain activities that children could not carry out by themselves.

They help take away feelings of loneliness.

From them, children learn how to get along with others.

They give children the satisfaction of knowing that others like them and want to be with them.

They give children the chance to show an interest in people and the things they do.

Through them, children learn what others expect of them and what others will and will not put up with.

They help children meet the standards of speech, behavior, and appearance others expect.

They give children feelings of security and self-confidence from knowing that others want their companionship.

From them, children learn new skills, especially play skills.

They give children a broader outlook on life.

social relationships will be so pleasant that they will want to repeat them.

The Importance of Early Social Experiences

There is a traditional belief that some children are born social and others are born unsocial. Studies have not shown that this is true. Instead, they have shown that early social experiences lay the foundations for children's attitudes toward people and social activities. They are also the basis of children's ways of behaving in social situations.

These early social experiences are shaped by the companions young children have and the things they do together. Children, for example, who always play with aggressive, grabby children are likely to develop the habit of being aggressive and grabby themselves. But if they spend time with kind, thoughtful people in the home, they learn to be kind and thoughtful.

Attitudes toward people and social situations are affected by early social experiences. If babies find the companionship of others enjoyable, they will want to repeat the experience. If, on the other hand, young children have unpleasant experiences when they first seek the companionship of other children, they will generally want to play alone or with adults. No one can blame children for wanting to be alone if the children they have known have bossed them, teased them, or left them out.

For Discussion

Who are the playmates, friends, and associates in your life? Who might they be when you are an adult? Look back at the chart above and discuss what companions do for you.

Kinds of Companions

Babies' first companions are family members. Gradually, the circle of companions widens. The following chart

A good time can be even more fun when it is shared! Michael Hardy/Woodfin Camp & Associates

shows how wide this circle is before early childhood comes to an end.

Companions have different kinds of relationships with the child. Some are only associates, such as adult neighbors whom the child may watch or say a few words to as they work in their yards. Others, like brothers, sisters, cousins, and children from the neighborhood, are playmates. Some playmates become friends as well.

Because the relationships children have with these companions differ, some companions have a greater effect on attitudes and behavior than others.

Parents

More time is spent with the parents than with any other family member. For the most part, early experiences with the parents are pleasant. Babies are likely to receive the parents' undivided attention. Because they are helpless, babies can count on having their every want satisfied. With such treatment, babies find the companionship of parents a pleasure.

Brothers and Sisters

Older brothers and sisters may pamper and pet young children. More likely,

The Young Child's Companions	
Parents	Neighborhood children
Brothers and sisters	Children and teachers in a nursery school or a child-care center
Other relatives—grandparents, uncles and aunts, and cousins	Baby-sitters
Adult neighbors	

however, they will boss the younger ones around and show scorn when their behavior falls below the older ones' standards. They may even make the younger ones feel unwelcome.

If older children are given some responsibility for the care of the younger, it adds to their feelings of importance. This helps bring about favorable attitudes toward younger brothers and sisters. In this way, brothers and sisters learn to find pleasure in one another's company. This solves the problem of companionship for them when there are no outsiders around.

Relatives

The kind of companions relatives make depends on their attitudes toward the child more than on how much time they spend together. When aunts and uncles feel that a child "should be seen but not heard," they will play the role of associates only. On the other hand, grandparents who play the "fun role" with grandchildren enjoy playing with them and often become their friends. They also enjoy communicating with them. They tell children about their own interests and are willing to listen to the child's interests and problems.

The ages of the cousins will largely shape the relationship between them. When a cousin is close to a child in age, the two are likely to be playmates. This is less likely when there is a large age difference. If they see each other often, cousins who get along well as playmates may also become friends.

Neighborhood Children

From the neighborhood, children may choose as companions others whose interests and abilities are similar to their own. The more they play with these children, the more interests and activities they have in common. Then they are more likely to become friends as well.

To young children, the social and economic level of playmates is not important. In the same way, religion, ethnic background, and skin color are not important. They have just as much fun playing with children whose parents are richer or poorer than theirs as with children whose parents' income is similar to their family's.

Substitute Companions

Sometimes young children cannot find enough companionship outside the home when family members are no longer enough to meet their needs. There are two reasons for this. First, there may not be other children of the same age or level of development living in the neighborhood who can be counted on for companionship. Second, even if there are plenty of children, the child may not be welcome in the neighborhood play group. This may be because of unsocial behavior, lack of play skills, or some other reason. Such children are lonely.

Lonely children make up for loneliness in a number of ways. The two most common are creating imaginary companions and playing with pets. Both of these methods help meet children's companionship needs. But both have one major drawback. They do not help children learn to behave in a social way with other people. They may even encourage children to develop patterns of unsocial behavior.

An *imaginary companion* is usually another child. It is often the child's own sex, age, and level of development. Sometimes, though, the imaginary companion is an animal.

Because the imaginary companion is the child's creation, it is always to the child's liking. Often the imaginary companion has traits the child would like to have. Children give their imaginary companions names and play with them so much that real companionship is not needed.

A judgment might lead one to believe that this is an easy and satisfying answer to the lonely child problem. This is not correct. Although it fills the child's need for companionship at that moment, it in no way adds to the child's social development.

Instead, it could have exactly the other effect. Imaginary companions never object. Children can have everything their own way and can even cheat or play out of turn. As a result, children may begin to behave in ways that real children would not stand for.

This does not mean that an imaginary companion dooms a child to a lifetime of unsocial behavior and poor social adjustments. It can, however, make it harder for the child to learn to be social.

Children who, for one reason or another, are lonely often like pets better than other children. The pets fill a gap in the young child's life. They satisfy the need for companionship. Of course, many families have pets when there is no lack of companionship. They just like pets.

Dogs and cats are the best pets as companions for a young child. They are more responsive than most other animals. They will play with a child and let the child play with them.

Like imaginary companions, pets may meet young children's companionship needs at that moment. But they have no real social value unless they react by biting, scratching, barking, or growling

Sisters and brothers who usually get along well also may have conflicts. Mimi Forsyth/ Monkmeyer

When a child understands how to treat a family pet with kindness, there is little need to worry about harm coming to either. Ginger Chih

when they do not like the treatment they are getting. In such cases, they let children know that there are limits beyond which the children cannot go in play. This is a lesson that can be useful if carried over to play companions who are children. However, few parents will put up with possible harm to a small child for the sake of such a lesson.

In many cases, animals that parents feel are suitable as pets for young children are very old or very gentle. They let children have their own way in play. They will even let children pull their ears and tails, sit on their backs, or dress them up in clothes. Such pets actually make it harder for children to learn to be social. Parents who allow children to treat pets badly may be overlooking the beginnings of unsocial traits. Also, children who treat pets roughly may be seriously harmed by other animals. The children may think they can treat strange dogs or cats the same way. Finally, being able to act

roughly without bad results may lead children into thinking they can do the same with playmates.

What Makes Children Popular?

To be popular means to be liked by many people. Just about everyone— adult and child—wants to be liked. It is a normal desire. The word "popular" is *not* used here to mean the kind of short-lived or shallow attention paid to good-looking people. It simply means being liked as a friend or companion. Unpopular people are not well liked. They find it hard to make friends.

Studies of popular and unpopular children have shown what makes some children popular. A careful study of the next chart will show that many of the traits of popular children lead to satisfactory relationships with their playmates. Unpopular children want companionship just as much. But they make playtime unpleasant for others.

Behavior of Popular and Unpopular Children

Popular Children

Are willing to play the way others want to play

Are cooperative and willing to do more than their share

Are generous and willing to share things

Ask to use others' toys and playthings

Talk to playmates

Say pleasant things to playmates

Offer ideas for play activities

Look cheerful and laugh

Are good sports about winning and losing

Act self-confident

Are willing to follow wishes of the majority in the group

Have a sense of humor

Treat playmates thoughtfully

Unpopular Children

Want others to do things for them

Act stingy and selfish

Grab and fight for others' things

Add nothing to the conversation

Call others names and say unpleasant things about them

Wait for others to suggest play activities

Look unhappy

Gloat when they win and cry when they lose

Are ill at ease and lack self-confidence

Act bossy and insist that others do what they want to do

Think all humor is directed against them

Have feelings easily hurt

Improving the Child's Popularity

All young children tend to be unsocial in their first relationships with other children. Because of this, far too many parents believe this is normal and no cause for worry. Worse, they believe that children will outgrow these unsocial patterns.

There is no proof that children outgrow unsocial behavior. But there is plenty of proof that, if such behavior is allowed to go on, it will become a habit. Like all other habits, it will be easiest to correct as soon as the first signs appear.

There is another reason for correcting unsocial behavior as soon as it appears. It keeps children from getting an unfavorable name among playmates. It may be harder for pushy children to change people's ideas about them than it will be to change the way they act.

For Discussion

How do the behavior patterns that add to popularity or unpopularity in early childhood also affect teenagers and adults that you know? Which patterns of behavior are more important to adults and teenagers than some of the others? Explain your choices.

All children can be liked by others. All can enjoy companionship. They simply have to learn to behave in ways that please others and to curb behavior that bothers and angers others. Some guides are briefly discussed below.

Good Manners. When good manners, such as saying "thank you," "please," and "I'm sorry," are stressed at home, they will become a habit. Children will naturally treat others this way.

Respect for Rights and Possessions of Others. Young children must learn to recognize and respect the rights of

Cooperation at playtime is one sign of healthy social development. Nancy Hays/Monkmeyer

others. This can be done by taking turns doing things or talking, by sharing with others, and by asking to use possessions of others instead of just taking them.

Respect for Privacy of Others. The best way to teach children to respect the privacy of others is to respect their privacy. Every day, during the afternoon rest or the quiet period before dinner, children should be given time to themselves. They should be able to close the doors of their rooms and expect others to knock and ask to enter.

Accepting Blame. To help children learn to accept blame for wrongs, they should have a chance to tell their side of the story. If this is done, children are less likely to blame others so as to escape scoldings or punishment.

Limiting Demands for Attention. Many young children, through no fault of their own, think they are much more important than they are. This leads them to demand attention, to take over the conversation, to talk when others are talking, or in other ways to push themselves into the center. It is the responsibility of parents and other adults to curb attention-getting acts. Children must learn to take their turn in talking and in other social situations.

For Discussion

Many parents feel that children will naturally learn good manners. Do you agree with this point of view? Or do you think that parents should teach young children manners as soon as the children are old enough to understand? Give reasons for your answer.

Common Forms of Unsocial Behavior in Childhood

Quarreling   Between the ages of 2 and 6, nearly all young children quarrel when playing together. Their quarreling is usually over some plaything. The form it takes may be a knock-down, drag-out fight. The worst quarrels are usually between children from the same family and between best friends.

Bullying   To make themselves feel they are better, some children will physically hurt others. The bully forces other children to pay attention by tripping, pinching, pulling away chairs as people start to sit down, or slamming doors in their faces.

Teasing   Like bullying, teasing is a way of trying to show that one is better. It means causing mental pain by hurting another person's feelings. The tease usually tries to find out what other children are touchy about, such as being fat, skinny, slow, clumsy, or having some unusual feature. Then the tease points out these facts, time after time, in front of others.

Name-Calling   When children learn that they are likely to be punished if they fight or when they discover that other children will not play with them if they hit, kick, or punch, they begin name-calling. It is a form of fighting.

Tattling   Some children carry tales of a bad sort about another child to an adult. This gives them the satisfaction of being the center of attention. Tattling helps make up for some of the anger they feel toward those about whom they tattled. To be sure that they get the attention and sympathy they need, tattlers are likely to exaggerate what they say.

Curbing Unsocial Behavior

It is just as important to curb unsocial behavior as it is to help children learn patterns of behavior that will make others like them. There are many forms of unsocial behavior that are found among young children. Those described in the accompanying chart are the most common.

Unsocial behavior may have long-lasting harmful effects. Because of this, adults should not wait for children to learn from experience that it must be curbed if the children want to be popular. Instead, adults should take action at once. One useful method is to explain to children why their unsocial behavior will make others dislike them. The children should be told that they will not be allowed to play with other children for a day or two if they do it again. One or two experiences of being alone are usually enough to help children realize that they should try to curb their unsocial behavior.

For Discussion

Why do many parents allow or even encourage young children to tattle on their brothers and sisters? Why do some parents seem to listen readily and believe everything the tattler says without bothering to check? Do you think this is fair to the tattler? To the children who are being tattled about? Give reasons for your answers.

Unsocial behavior during playground activities may be a warning of problems in a child's social development. Sepp Seitz/Woodfin Camp & Associates

Foundations for Leading and Following

Almost all children, as they grow older, would like to be leaders. Our society stresses the value of leadership. Children learn quite early that the leader is popular and can count on having playmates and friends. They also soon discover that being a leader gives them a feeling of importance.

Foundations for leadership should be laid with supervision. Adults have the experience to know what makes for good and poor leadership. Without this guidance, young children may lay foundations that work only while they are still young. For example, young children may at first accept a bossy group leader. They are used to taking orders from their parents. But, as they grow older and begin to think more for themselves, they rebel against both parents and bossy child leaders.

Being a Leader

There is an old belief that leaders are born, not made. Studies of leaders have shown that this simply is not true. The foundation for leadership qualities may be hereditary. But whether or not these qualities will be developed into real leadership will depend mostly on learning. This means that any child who is born with the possibilities for leadership can become a leader. Most children do have them.

However, if the possible leader is to become a real leader, certain traits should be developed. Studies of leaders have shown that, at all ages, they possess certain qualities. The qualities commonly found in all leaders are listed in the accompanying chart. Remember that these are *average* or *typical* findings only. In any given case, a person who does not have a number of these qualities may still become a leader.

A careful study of these qualities will show that, with few exceptions, they are the result of learning. With guidance, all children can have them.

Early social experiences will affect children's ability for leadership. For example, children who are spoiled by adults want everyone to humor them. That is the way they have been treated at home. They have little chance of becoming leaders unless they change their social behavior.

Other children have been expected to do as others wish in the home and have had plenty of chance to play with other children. They learn to get along well with others and to think about the rights and wishes of others. In this way, such children are developing some of the traits every leader must have.

Ability to get along well with others is, alone, not enough. Leaders must also have initiative and some assertiveness. This will enable them to do more than suggest what the group might do. They can also show the others how to carry out their ideas.

In order to be leaders, people need to learn certain skills. The foundations of these skills are laid in childhood. Children should be allowed to make some decisions for themselves. They should also be encouraged to plan their own activities in their playtime, to take on simple responsibilities in the home, and to assert themselves when it comes to their wishes.

Training for leadership can be very helpful. But parents and teachers should be careful that they do not push children into trying to be leaders to satisfy the adults' own wishes. There are always fewer leadership roles than there are people who want them. The

---

Qualities of a Child Leader

Has intelligence slightly above that of the group as a whole

May be slightly larger in build than other group members

Is attractive and well groomed

Is cheerful and happy

Is willing to do more than her or his share to make an activity go well

Is willing to give up personal interests for those of the group

Is cooperative in any group activity

Takes initiative in undertaking any task

Has slightly better play skills than those of group members

Uses imagination in planning group activities and games

Is interested in others and what they are doing

Is sympathetic toward anyone who is in trouble

Has respect for the rights, wishes, and privacy of others

Is a good sport when doing well or badly

Says pleasant things to and about others

Understands others and is tactful

Understands what group members like and suggests activities they enjoy

Is fun to be with and do things with

Is self-confident but not overly so

Has a sense of humor

competition that results can be damaging to children. Helping children's leadership abilities blossom is one thing. Making children nervous and competitive about becoming leaders is quite another. It should be carefully avoided.

For Discussion

A child who wants to be a leader but is not chosen for a leadership role is, of course, upset and is often angry. Anger is especially felt toward the child who is chosen to be the leader. How would you try to get the child to see that he or she was being a poor sport? What else could you and the child do to deal with the problem?

Being a Follower

All children cannot be leaders all of the time. And every leader will, at times, be a follower. If young children are to have a chance for the companionship they crave, they must learn to be good followers. To be a good leader, one must first be a good follower. Laying good foundations for being a follower can be done when young children first begin to play with other children.

Little or no guidance in learning to be a follower often results in the child's becoming an unhappy follower. When, on the other hand, supervision and help are given, children learn to get satisfaction from being followers. They also increase their ability to get along with playmates. By so doing, they increase their chances of being leaders later.

A child who is comfortable as a leader or as a follower is likely to be a popular playmate. Richard Nowitz

Children must learn to be good sports. This means that they must learn not to make critical, unpleasant remarks about the leader. They should not refuse to do their share on the grounds that the leader can do it. And they should not be against every idea the leader has, especially if most of the other children like the leader's ideas.

Parents can encourage children to develop attitudes and behavior patterns that will make them good followers as well as possible leaders. They can encourage them to be cooperative, to do their share or even more in any group activity, and to offer ideas for activities. But children should be pleasant and willing to follow the ideas others suggest if that is what the group would like to do.

Today many people who work with groups—adults or children—are finding that the most helpful approach of all is to stop stressing the difference between leaders and followers. Instead, cooperative relationships within the group as a whole are stressed. In democratic groups, people change roles. They go from leaders to followers and back again easily and often. Parents can help keep their children from worrying about whether they are leaders or followers and teach them to be good group members.

Highlights of Chapter 19

- ☐ Interest in companions begins early in babyhood and increases rapidly in early childhood. With this increase comes a change in what young children want in their companions.

- ☐ A companion adds in important ways to young children's personal and social adjustments. What is added depends on whether the companion is an associate, a playmate, or a friend.

- ☐ Early social experiences, in the home and outside, help determine whether the child will develop into a social or an unsocial person.

- ☐ There are many kinds of companions for young children. Each kind plays a different role and has a different effect.

- ☐ The two most common forms of substitute companions for young children are imaginary companions and pets. Both give pleasure to young children but do not teach them how to make good social adjustments.

- ☐ Overcoming young children's unpopularity means teaching them to behave in a way that will make their association with others pleasant. They have to learn not to do things that will upset and anger others.

- ☐ All young children, through guidance and direction by adults, can learn patterns of behavior that will prepare them for future leadership roles.

- ☐ Because everyone sometimes plays the role of follower, it is essential that all young children learn to be good followers.

Suggested Activities

1. Watch several children when they quarrel with their playmates. Notice what led to the quarrel, how the children treated each other when they were quarreling, what ended the quarrel, and how the children reacted to those with whom they had just quarreled.

2. Make a list of the names children call their playmates when they are angry and the negative things they say to and about them. Note how the children who have been called names react.

3. Watch several children when they are playing with pets. How do the pets react to the way the children are playing with them? Do pets react in a way that would help make a child social? If not, what does the child do that would anger other people if they were treated like the pet?

4. In a group of young children at play, try to figure out which child is the leader. Make a list of the child's noticeable qualities. How does your list compare with the chart on page 261?

Chapter 20

Play and Playthings

Some goals of this chapter are:
- ☐ To be aware of the many benefits of play and understand why play activities should be varied and balanced
- ☐ To know some common mistakes adults should try to avoid when choosing play equipment for children
- ☐ To realize the importance of having play equipment that will stimulate all areas of a young child's physical, intellectual, and social development

Play is any activity done for the enjoyment it gives. *Work*, on the other hand, is an activity done mostly for the end result. Play is also different from *drudgery*, which is an activity that gives one little enjoyment. Drudgery is imposed upon one by an outside person or situation. It is not of one's choosing.

The child's attitude toward the activity makes it play, work, or drudgery. For example, young children may enjoy dusting and sweeping together with a parent who is cleaning a room. That, then, will be play. When children clean their rooms because of the pride they get from caring for their space and from parents' praise, it is work. On the other hand, it may be a chore given to them which they do not like. That will be drudgery.

Enjoyment of the activity is the essential element of all play. Children play only as long as the activity amuses them. When they become bored, they drop what they are doing. They turn their attention to something else which, for the moment, they find more enjoyable. Half-finished activities are common to the play of all young children. This shows that the end result is not nearly as important as the enjoyment that accompanies the activity.

Play is exhilarating! Isabel Gordon/Monkmeyer

For Discussion

Choose five daily activities. What is your attitude toward each? Classify them as play, work, or drudgery and give reasons why you classified them as you did.

Values of Play

Play is not a waste of time. Nor is it just a way to keep young children busy or out of mischief while parents take care of their own responsibilities. Instead, play is essential to the development of a normal, well-adjusted personality. It gives the child a chance to develop physically, emotionally, mentally, socially, and morally in a way that no other single type of activity can. The child who has little chance to play is far less likely to become a well-adjusted adult than is the child who spends most of the day playing.

Benefits of Play to Young Children

Outlet for extra energy

Development of all parts of the body —bones, muscles, and internal organs

Exercise which develops good appetites and healthful sleep

Chance to learn to control the body

Development of many skills that will be useful all through life

Development of ability to keep the mind on the task at hand

Encouragement of creativity

Chance to discover meanings about things in the environment

Way to get rid of anger, fear, jealousy, and grief

Chance to learn how to get along with other children

Chance to learn to be a good sport—a good loser or winner

Chance to learn to follow rules

Play has many values for young children. The most important are outlined above. Note that these values are not limited to one kind of development, such as physical development. Instead, they have to do with *every* kind. It would be hard to find any other single activity that is as useful as play.

Essential Features of Play

If play is to give children the benefits listed in the chart, there are certain features that are essential. These are given and explained in the next chart.

All of these features are needed. Some, though, are needed more than others. Young children, for example,

---

Essential Features of Play

Extra Energy   Children must have more energy than they need for daily living if they are to use it for play. Children who suffer from any physical state that saps energy have little desire to play.

Time   After the everyday activities are over, young children should be free to play in a quiet way, as they wish.

Equipment   Children need some simple play equipment. More important than how much or how new is how suitable the equipment is to the children. The children should not be too old or too young for it. It should be simple enough so that adult help is not needed to use it. There should be enough variety to stimulate different kinds of play. Also, the equipment should not have to be taken out and packed away each time it is used.

Space for Play   Very few play activities young children enjoy can be carried out in tight spaces. The space must be large enough for the equipment they need and for the way they want to play.

Knowledge of How to Play   Young children can learn how to use toys and play equipment by trial and error, by imitating other children, or by being shown. The last method gives the best results.

Playmates   Even though young children really play with others very little, they like to know that there is someone to watch or play with if they want to do so.

must have space for play. However, it is not the amount of space that is most important. It is where the space is and how children are allowed to use it. There may be a large yard behind the house. If most of this yard is given over to flower or vegetable gardens, there will be little space for children to play games.

For Discussion

In the same way, parents may have a large playroom for their children where they are sent to play with toys much of their waking hours. But the children also need playmates with them or parents who will show them how to play with the equipment that is there. Otherwise the children will be limited in how they can play. The benefits they get from the play will also be limited.

Variety and Balance in Play Activities

Early childhood is the time when children try out a large number of different play activities. Young children should be encouraged in this. They have more time to play than they will when they go to school. Also, trying out new activities gives them a chance to discover the satisfaction they can get from various types of play. Later they will have to put their time and energy into those they like best.

A variety of play activities is essential to satisfy young children's different needs. For example, they need physical and restful activities. Different activities also help solve boredom. No matter how much young children may enjoy painting pictures, doing it all the time will bore them. The more activities they have, the easier it is to shift when they lose interest in one.

For Discussion

Young children do not need to spend an equal amount of time on each activity, though. The amount of time they spend too much of their playtime alone, ests, their abilities, and the things their environment offers. Along with variety in play there should also be balance. Children need balance if they are to get the benefits that normally come from play. For example, children should not spend too much of their play time alone, making things with sand, blocks, crayons, and paints. That would leave too little time for the play activities that lead to healthy muscle development. By playing alone they also miss chances to learn to get along with other children.

On the other hand, too much time should not be spent playing with other

Playing quietly after a day of physical activity helps children relax. Sylvia Johnson/Woodfin Camp & Associates

children. Then children would not have enough chance to learn to amuse themselves and meet their own needs.

Imbalance in young children's play may come from a number of causes. The most important are explained in the accompanying chart. Note that each of these causes can be controlled. Parents and other caretakers should know the serious effect imbalance can have on the satisfaction children would otherwise get from play because something can be done about it.

Types of Play

There are so many different types of play suitable for young children that it is helpful to put them into groups. The usual groups are *active play* and *amusement* (or *passive play*). Children get enjoyment from what they *do* in active play. They get enjoyment from *watching or listening* to someone or something else in amusement.

If a young child's play is well balanced, part of the playtime will be used for active play and part for amusements.

Common Causes of Imbalance in Play in Early Childhood

Poor Health Children who are in poor health may not have the energy for any active play.

Lack of Variety in Play Equipment If play gear is mostly for one type of play—such as books and games—children will not be able to be active in play that calls for other kinds of equipment— such as swings, slides, or tricycles.

No Chance to Learn a Variety of Play Activities Even though children may have equipment for many kinds of play activities, it will be of little value if they do not know how to use it.

No Playmates Children with no playmates are limited to play activities that can be done alone.

It is impossible to say just how much time should be spent on each. The amount of time depends on the child. And the interests and needs of every child are different.

A well-balanced play program for young children should not put too much weight on either active play or amusements. Some children enjoy amusements more than active play. Some enjoy active play more. But they should all be encouraged to take part in at least some of both kinds of play each day, if possible.

Active Play

Active play may take many different forms. They all have one trait in common. That is, the satisfaction that children get from them comes from what *they* do rather than from what someone else does.

Exploratory Play. The young child's first interest in toys is exploratory. The child looks at a toy; shakes or pounds it to see what noise it will make; sucks it, smells it, and squeezes or pats it to see how it feels. Young children enjoy these exploratory activities. They also learn things they could get in no other way. This learning satisfies their curiosity about the toy.

Construction. By the time children are 3, they are no longer satisfied with exploring toys. They now want to use the toys to make things, no matter how simple and crude. Instead of throwing or biting blocks, for example, young children use them to build towers, houses, or bridges. Instead of chewing crayons, young children use them to color pictures or to draw pictures of their own.

What they make is not very important to young children. For them, the making is the enjoyable experience. That is plenty of reward for the energy they use.

Playground games give children exercise and help children cooperate with peers. Lew Merrim/Monkmeyer

Dramatic play is basically an exercise of the imagination. At the same time, it can also be a valuable learning experience. David S. Strickler/Monkmeyer

Dramatic Play. At just about the time young children begin to use toys to construct things, they discover that it is fun to dramatize with toys. To young children, a doll is not just a doll. It is a real person. A toy telephone can be used to call and talk with someone. Their room can become a store, a cave, or a house. With the aid of a few articles of clothing, children can quickly turn into people in the make-believe world. Toys can become other players. To add to the enjoyment, children often call on a playmate, a brother, or a sister to play roles. This adds to the realism as well as to the fun.

Family Games. Before babies are 2, they like to play simple games with family members. These games have few rules, are usually played with only one other player, and each player takes a turn. The traditional family games for babies are peekaboo, this-little-pig-went-to-market, and guess-which-hand.

During early childhood, children want to play more complicated games. They also want to play with more family members—parents, brothers and sisters, grandparents, or anyone who is around at the time. These games are usually played indoors. When the weather is warm, however, they can be played outside.

Indoor games may be simple card games (matching cards or collecting certain kinds), guessing games, or more lively games such as Simon says, musical chairs, or find-the-hidden-object. Outdoor family games may be running races, hide-and-seek, or catch.

Family games are good training for play with other children. Through them children learn that they must follow rules, wait their turn, and be good losers as well as pleasant winners.

Sometimes, family members let young children win when they do not deserve to win. If this is done too often, it can be unfair to children. It makes them think they are better players than they really are. They are likely to carry this idea out to play with neighborhood children. They may not want to play with other children when they discover that they cannot always be the winner or that winning is not easy.

Neighborhood Games. By the age of 4 or 5 years, children begin to lose interest in family games. They want to play with children their own age. The games they play at first are very much like those played with family members. However, the rules are tougher and the play a little more complicated. There is also more competition, and the players are all the same age.

The children with whom the child plays come mostly from nearby in the neighborhood. Two or more children, or even a whole group, can play such traditional games as tag, hide-and-seek, follow-the-leader, or statues.

As early childhood draws to a close, children's games begin to copy adult sports such as baseball, football, and basketball. But children do not have the playing skills or the ability to understand complicated rules. So these sports must be greatly changed for children to play them and enjoy them.

Amusements

Children play a passive role in amusements. The enjoyment comes from watching or listening to others.

Amusements are ideal when children are tired and yet need something to keep them from becoming bored, restless, and fretful. Just before meals or bedtime, amusements can fill an important need in the young child's life. However, if children are encouraged or allowed to spend too much time in play of this type, they miss the benefits that come from more active forms of play.

All children should have a chance to experience different forms of amusement. Then, in time, they will be able to choose those that give them the greatest satisfaction.

Watching Others. No matter how simple and repetitious an activity may be, young children are fascinated by watching people do it. They like to watch parents and other adults do things around the house. They like to watch animals, whether household pets, animals on a farm, or zoo animals. And they like to watch other children at play.

Watching others not only gives children enjoyment, but it has great learning value. Children learn how to do things and they learn new meanings about them. Watching a parent fix a broken chair, for example, shows children how it is done. It also teaches

Puppet shows amuse children by bringing to life some of their favorite stories. Mimi Forsyth/ Monkmeyer

them about the use of tools and safe work habits. As they watch other children, they learn how to be social and how to play in a cooperative way.

Looking at Pictures. Bright colored pictures in books, in comics, in magazines, and in newspaper ads have great appeal for young children. They like most of all pictures of simple, everyday settings and of people doing everyday things. Such pictures are easier to understand than pictures of things children have never seen.

Besides the enjoyment young children get from looking at pictures, they may also learn word meanings by talking about the pictures with adults. When they ask "What is this?" or "Why does it do that?" they are learning to associate meanings with words. These words might otherwise have no meaning to them. They also develop an interest in reading. This will help them be ready for school when they reach the school age.

Children enjoy looking at the same pictures over and over again. This has learning value for two reasons. First, it encourages them to focus their thoughts. Second, it encourages them to seek new meanings. Every time children look at the same picture, they may discover something they did not see before.

Listening to Stories. Even before children can understand many words, they like to have stories told or read to them. The story must be one children like and must be told or read so that they can understand it. Otherwise their attention will not be held and they will not enjoy it. The accompanying chart lists story themes that children like.

The storyteller often uses facial expressions to give meaning to the words. To this they add gestures. The storyteller should stress meaningful words, speak slowly so that children have time to grasp what they hear, and use simple words that children know. The more the teller can act out the story, the better children can understand it.

Young children also like poems. The poems should be short and simple. The

---

Themes of Stories That Appeal to Young Children

Stories about homelife

Stories about school life

Stories about children

Stories about people they know outside the home—a mail carrier or a police officer—and what their jobs are

Stories about animals of all kinds

Stories with the child as the main character

Stories about the childhoods of parents, grandparents, and other relatives

Fairy tales, which children around the age of 5 years begin to like

Nonsense stories

Stories with parts that add on ("The House That Jack Built" type)

Stories about people in other countries and how they live, if they have pictures to give the stories meaning

Adventure stories, which begin to be popular as children near the end of early childhood

An imaginative child will find enjoyment with playthings that lend themselves to creative play. Courtesy of Fisher-Price Toys

nursery rhymes that are passed down from parent to child and the more modern poems for children, such as those of A. A. Milne, are the best liked. The more jingle there is to a poem, the better the young child will like it.

For Discussion

How does reading out loud and showing pictures in books, magazines, and newspapers make a young child's vocabulary greater? How does it increase the child's desire to learn to read? Do you feel that this kind of amusement is a good way to prepare for school? Give reasons for your answers.

Looking at Comics. Comics have bright colors and simple drawings that are easy to understand. Because of this, young children like to look at comic books and comic strips. Their en-joyment is greater if, while they look at the pictures, they have someone to read what the people in the comic strip are saying.

As long as the comics are about everyday people and animals doing everyday things or funny nonsense things, they have no unfavorable effects. However, the comics children are allowed to see should be carefully checked by parents or other adults. Otherwise young children may get hold of terror comics from a playmate or from an older brother or sister. Even if the child enjoys looking at the pictures, the fears they cause far outweigh the enjoyment the children experienced.

Listening to Music. Children like music that is simple and has a strong beat. Little children like to sing along with the music. They are not self-conscious about their ability to sing, as many older children are. After hearing a tune several times, children will sing even

274

without music. Common sources of musical enjoyment are family members who play a musical instrument, the radio or television, or the records children can play on a phonograph.

Phonograph records are especially good. The music can be played over and over again if the child likes it. Also, on most children's records the words are said so clearly that the child can understand them. This helps children learn to sing the songs.

Watching Television. Most television stations have shows appropriate for young children. These are on at times of the day when children are likely to be indoors. If the shows are properly chosen for the child's level of development and if the child does not watch for too long a time, television can be educational, relaxing, and enjoyable.

Many television shows are very unsuitable, though. This is especially true of shows that have a great deal of shooting, fighting, and killing. These terrify young children and often lead to sleep problems and nightmares.

Parents should check the television listings very carefully before allowing young children to watch. Parents should try, as well, to make time to watch at least part of the show with the children. In this way parents can check its suitability. They will also be able to explain parts that may be puzzling or tell the children facts they want to know. This adds to the children's enjoyment and to the learning value.

Play Equipment for Children

Children must have equipment to stimulate an interest in play so that they can have a variety of play experiences. Parents realize the importance of playthings for their child. They are often willing to give up many things they want in order to give their children play equipment. However, they often make mistakes in choosing equipment. There are seven mistakes that are very common.

First, parents may get too much—too many toys, too many books, or too much outdoor equipment. Ads and other people often make parents feel they are not good parents unless they give their children many toys. But young children enjoy repetition. They like to play with the same toys over and over again. A favorite stuffed animal, for example, goes everywhere with the child, while other stuffed animals remain unused. Also, young children get as much pleasure, and sometimes even more, from exploring the objects in the home, such as pots and pans, as they get from carefully chosen toys.

Second, far too many parents buy toys they think are cute and interesting. They do not think through what the child will do with it. For example, the child might be bored by the stuffed dog that the parent thought would be a wonderful toy.

Third, many parents put too much money into play equipment. Partly because of high-powered ads, they forget that homemade toys and those bought at sales or in secondhand shops are often favorites. These may meet the child's needs even better than those bought at great cost. A doll's clothes, for example, that are made at home may mean much more to a child than costly ready-made clothes.

275

Fourth, play materials that are too complete offer little chance for constructive or dramatic play. Once children have looked at them, there is little left to do in the way of playing with them. A dollhouse that is complete in every way or a train set with everything needed to make it work like a real train fails to meet children's exploratory or constructive needs.

Fifth, if the children are too old or too young for the equipment, it will not meet their needs. A child may be 4 years old. But that does not mean that all toys for 4-year-olds will be right for that child. A very bright child will find the toy babyish. A child who is not developed enough for it will find it too hard.

Sixth, parents often give children too much equipment for one type of play and none for other types. For example, children may have equipment for outdoor play but none for amusement on rainy days or when they are tired.

The seventh mistake is perhaps the most serious. Far too many parents fail to check play equipment for safety. They think that the factory is responsible and that the government watches out for the buyer. This is not true. Parents should carefully check each toy for safety before buying it.

Equipment That Is "Right" for Young Children

Play equipment that is right for children meets their interests, abilities, and needs at that time. It also stimulates an interest in play of *all* types. Only if parents think about each child's needs, abilities, and interests will they be able to make a wise choice of play equipment for their children.

The following chart lists features of good play equipment for young children. These can be used as a guide in choosing toys and other equipment as long as individual differences are always kept clearly in mind.

Playthings with Appeal

There are certain toys and play equipment that appeal to all young children. Almost all children like stuffed animals that look like real animals and blocks that can be used for building. They also like play equipment that makes it possible for them to climb, to move around more rapidly than they can on foot, or to swing in the air. From these toys and equipment that everyone likes, children choose their favorites.

Parents cannot tell for sure what will appeal most to a young child. But they can get some ideas that will help them in their choice of playthings. This is im-

---

What Makes Play Equipment Right for Young Children

Offers chances for many play activities

Suited to the child's age and development

Can be used without adult help

Safe, no matter how the child uses it

Can be used for play with other children

Appeals to the child's interest in color

Stimulates the child's interest

Stimulates creativity in the child

Playground activities can be dangerous as well as fun. Children should be instructed about the safe use of equipment. Michael Hardy/Woodfin Camp & Associates

portant. It may save parents from buying or making equipment that has little interest for the child.

Two clues have proved to be most helpful. First, watch children at play. See which toys or play equipment they choose most often and the length of time they play with them. Children may try to grab these toys from other children or trade their toys.

Second, take children to a toy store and give them plenty of time to look at the toys. From this parents can get an idea about which toys and equipment the children like most. At first, the children may seem to like everything and want everything they see. But they should be told that they cannot have ev-

erything. They must choose what they like best. This will tell parents much about children's real interests.

However, two warnings are in order. Parents should check prices first. They should not use this method unless they are able to pay for the more costly items in the store. A child may choose one of these. Parents should also bear in mind that toy sellers put most stress on the lastest fashions in toys or those that give them the largest profit. Some old favorites are less flashy and less costly. They may not even be in the store. Or they may be so hard to see that the child will not notice them. So the child's choices in the store are not completely useful as a guide to what the child will like.

Equipment to Stimulate the Young Child's Development

Physical Development Climbing boards, swings, slides, push-and-pull toys, jungle gyms, seesaws, boxes for climbing, wading pools, skates, tricycles, and bicycles

Large Muscle Coordination Roller skates, tricycles, bicycles, jump ropes, doll carriages, balls, jungle gyms, ice skates, garden tools, sandbox toys, and boxes for climbing

Small Muscle Coordination Scissors, crayons, paints, clay, pencils, small blocks, pegboards, weaving sets, jacks, and balls

Intellectual Development Records, picture books, storybooks, TV and radio shows, puzzles, games, comics, and "how-to" toys

Creativity Cast-off clothes and household equipment, dolls, stuffed animals, simple musical instruments (triangles, bells, and tambourines), toy trains, airplanes, trucks, and puppets

Speech Development Pictures in comics and magazines, stories, books, radio, and TV shows

Social Development Anything that can be shared or used in play with other children, such as sleds, sandboxes, wading pools, make-believe play equipment, balls, swings, seesaws, jungle gyms, and jump ropes

Playthings That Stimulate Development

Any activity that young children enjoy can and should stimulate some kind of development without lessening the pleasure they get from the activity. Some types of play stimulate motor coordinations. At the same time they encourage creativity. Other forms of play put more stress on social development. The accompanying chart lists the major areas of development that can be stimulated by play and some of the equipment that is useful.

Highlights of Chapter 20

- ☐ Play differs from work and drudgery in the person's attitude toward the activity.
- ☐ There are many values—physical, emotional, social, and intellectual—young children get from play.
- ☐ If children are to get benefits from play, they must have extra energy, time to play in a relaxed way, enough equipment, space for play, and playmates.
- ☐ A varied program of play is essential, but there must be a balance in this variety.

☐ All play can be divided into two major categories—active play and passive play, which is usually called amusement. In active play the enjoyment comes from what the player does; in amusement, from what others do.

☐ The most common forms of active play are exploring, constructing, dramatizing, and family and neighborhood games. The common forms of amusements are watching others, looking at pictures, listening to stories, looking at comics, listening to music, and watching TV.

☐ Play equipment is right for a child if it meets that child's major needs—physical, mental, and social—at that time.

☐ Play equipment should stimulate young children's physical, social, and mental development.

Suggested Activities

1. Make a list of household tasks that many young children are expected to do. Among these may be picking up their toys, setting the table for a meal, or collecting dirty clothes to be laundered. How could these tasks be made to be play if handled to make them seem enjoyable?

2. Examine the pictures in several new children's books (the librarian can help you choose them) and in several well-liked comic books. What do they have in common? How do they differ?

3. Read the comic strips in your local newspaper for a few days. How many of these do you feel are suitable for young children? Take into account the pictures, the language used, and the stories. Give reasons for your answers.

4. Watch several movies and TV shows that are meant for young children. Watch them from beginning to end. What would young children enjoy about each? What might be frightening? Is there anything else about the shows that you feel is bad for children to watch? In each case, explain why you feel as you do.

Chapter 21

Sex Roles

Some goals of this chapter are:

- ☐ To know the meaning of sex roles and how children learn about them
- ☐ To realize the importance of attitudes toward sex roles, how these attitudes are developed, and how parents can encourage positive ones to develop

---

A role is a pattern of behavior that is approved by the social group. Sex roles are behavior patterns approved for members of the two sexes. Until now, these patterns have been based on the traditional belief that the two sexes were different, not only physically, but also in abilities and temperament. It has also been believed that people should learn the roles that are in keeping with these differences.

Approved sex roles are passed down from parent to child. In time, they become *stereotypes*, or fixed, overly simple ideas, of what members of the two sexes should do. Added to these are approved standards for the way the members of the two sexes look, for their abilities, and for their personalities.

Changing Sex Roles
Socially approved sex roles remained pretty much unchanged for many hundreds of years. In the past, it was easy for parents to know what would

be expected of their children. They knew what abilities and personality traits their children would be expected to develop as well as how they should dress and look. Most people accepted these standards with very little thought.

In the last hundred years or so, the age-old male-female sex roles have proved to cause poor adjustment to modern life. More and more people are realizing that these sex roles are unfair. They keep people from developing and using the possibilities they were born with. As a result, there have been changes in the approved sex roles for both men and women. These changes have been toward less difference in what the two sexes should do, what abilities and personality traits may best prepare them to do well in the world, and even what is appropriate in appearance. Sex roles today are more *egalitarian,* or equal, than the traditional sex roles. The old roles stressed differences between men and women.

Definition of Sex Roles

Traditional

Traditional sex roles are based on the false belief that males are physically and mentally stronger than females. Male and female roles are therefore very different.

Male Role

Gets satisfaction from achievements

Is self-oriented

Is the wage earner; expects to be waited on by females in the home

Is the major decision maker for all matters

Advises and disciplines the children and is the role model for sons

Holds positions of authority in work and in neighborhood groups

Female Role

Not able to fill hard and challenging roles, so must be protected

Gets satisfaction by "proxy"—through relationship with male family members

Is other-oriented

Does no work outside the home unless it is seriously needed, or helps others for no pay

Major responsibility is care of home and children

Egalitarian

Egalitarian sex roles are based on the knowledge that differences between the sexes are much smaller than once believed. These few differences are of little importance in modern life. Male and female roles are more alike than different.

Male

Works with female in a friendly relationship in the home

Does not feel that it is not appropriate to take on home duties

Makes decisions with cooperation of all family members

In business and industry, works with women on an equal level, below them, or as their boss, depending on individual situation

Takes follower as well as leader roles in neighborhood, depending on abilities rather than sex

Female

Becomes more self-oriented than other-oriented

Is free to choose own role and work outside the home

Expects aid from husband in care of home and children

Has position in work depending on abilities

Is free to enter jobs once thought of as for men only

Does not feel it is wrong if she works outside the home

Fills leadership roles in neighborhood groups of men and women, depending on ability

Work and responsibility are not the only things shared in families where all have egalitarian roles. Charles Moore/Black Star

The change to egalitarian sex roles has come about because of changes in life-style. Women go to the same schools men do and are also trained for jobs in business or as professionals. Many women want to use this learning in the work world. They do not want to spend all their time on homemaking and child care. Some women take on both home and outside responsibilities. To make this possible, men take over some of the responsibilities women have always carried alone.

For Discussion

What is meant by saying that men were supposed to be self-oriented and that women were supposed to gain satisfaction by proxy? Give examples to show what is meant by this. Do you think that these sources of satisfaction met the needs of most men and women? Give reasons for your answer.

Children's Awareness of Sex Roles

The young child's first conscious interest in sex is not in sex roles but in where babies come from. This interest largely depends on the child's experiences. If there is a new baby in the family or neighborhood, or if a pet has a litter, the child will want to know where the babies came from.

Most young children, between the ages of 2 and 3 years, have experiences that make them curious about how life begins. They are usually satisfied with any answer. That is why it is so important for parents to be honest. The answers should also be clear, but simple. Children do not need much detail at this age. They need honesty.

By the time they are 3 years old, children begin to notice and talk about differences between females and males. Their first interest is in physical differences. They want to know why boys stand up when they urinate, for example, and girls sit down. They also want to know why the boy's genital organ is different from the girl's. They may ask why women have large breasts while girls, boys, and men are flat in front. They notice that men have hair on their faces while women do not.

While they are discovering sex differences, young children are also learning that certain things are appropriate for girls and women and certain things for boys and men. If egalitarian sex roles are approved, adults will try hard to overcome habits of the past, when only certain kinds of behavior were allowed for each sex. These adults will try to see to it that play groups let both girls and boys take part in all kinds of play without being made fun of.

All these facts—where babies come from, sex differences, sex appropriateness, and how the social group feels about these matters—are not learned overnight. It is a slow learning process. And it only begins when the child becomes aware of sex differences. Before early childhood ends, most American children today have had many experiences having to do with sex roles. They have developed attitudes toward these roles and have learned what people's expectations are.

For Discussion

Many children's books show adults and children in traditional sex roles. How can parents deal with the child's belief that these are the only approved sex roles? Which is likely to carry more weight with a child, what parents do or what books say? Why?

Learning Sex Roles

No one expects a baby to behave like a boy or a girl. However, when babyhood is over, parents believe that the time has come for the child to learn to be a girl or a boy, not just a child. Children learn sex roles in much the same way they learn anything else. The most common methods are by imitation, identification, and training. As a general rule, children learn by all three methods together.

Will young children learn to play a traditional or an egalitarian sex role? This depends on what roles parents play and what roles they think are right for children to play. If the mother works outside the home and the father shares home responsibilities, children will learn patterns of behavior that fit the egalitarian ideas of sex roles. But, children may grow up in a home where parents play traditional roles. Then the children will learn the traditional role for their sex. However, some traditional parents feel that, to be prepared for living in tomorrow's world, all children should learn at least some of the tasks that belong to the egalitarian role. They may, for example, feel that a boy should learn some household jobs. And a girl should learn how to support herself. Such parents may use child-training methods to teach children these things.

The most important part of learning sex roles in early childhood is not learning the activities that make up these roles. It is learning to have healthy attitudes toward them. For example, if a boy is learning to play an egalitarian male role, he should have a favorable attitude toward it and toward himself.

Children love to imitate adult behavior.
Clockwise from upper left: Erika Stone/Peter
Arnold; Landau Mayer/Monkmeyer; Sepp
Seitz/Woodfin Camp & Associates; Michal
Heron/Woodfin Camp & Associates

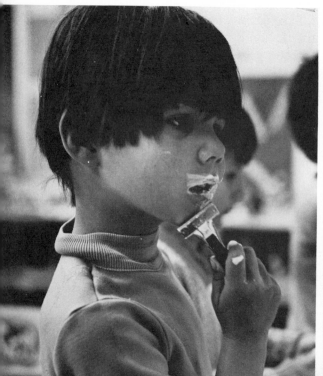

When children enter school, outside pressures will become stronger with each passing year. By that time children need healthy attitudes toward sex roles.

Attitudes toward Sex Roles

Children develop attitudes toward sex roles as they learn the meaning of these roles and how to fill them. At first, young children have the same attitude toward the approved role for both sexes. They accept the roles in an unquestioning, unemotional way.

By the time children are 5 years old, many have well-developed attitudes toward the sex roles. How strong and deeply rooted these attitudes are will greatly depend on how they learned these roles and the pressures put on them to learn to act in an approved way.

If fathers have no hang-ups about doing chores around the home, then neither will their sons. James H. Karales/Peter Arnold

As a general rule, adults have a greater effect on children's attitudes when the children are very young. As children come to spend more time with age-mates, the attitudes of playmates become more important. To make sure they will be accepted in the play group, children usually accept their playmates' attitudes toward sex roles.

For Discussion

Why is it more important for parents and teachers to develop healthy attitudes toward sex roles than to teach children how to play these roles? Give some ideas about how parents and teachers can help children develop healthy attitudes toward male and female sex roles.

War between the Sexes

By the time children are 5 or 6 years old, their attitudes toward sex roles are very fixed. It is now that these attitudes begin to affect the child's behavior. When children feel favorably toward the egalitarian roles, boys and girls go on playing together peacefully, as they did when they were younger. However, children may feel unfavorably toward egalitarian roles. If so, they will want playmates of their own sex.

Soon this preference develops into an unfriendly attitude toward members of the other sex. Boys show it by refusing to play with girls. Girls do the same thing to boys. Instead of ignoring each other, they go out of their way to make fun of each other's interests, activities, and clothes. As a result, the members of the two sexes form their own play groups. There is little or no interaction between them.

All studies of young children point to the fact that dislike of the other sex is started by boys. It begins in the play group rather than in the home. This war between the sexes only begins to appear when early childhood comes to an end. But it usually grows stronger and more widespread as children grow older. Parents should do all they can to keep it from happening. This is far from easy. It means fighting attitudes of age-mates in the neighborhood play group. By so doing, parents are putting blocks in the way of children's acceptance by age-mates.

For Discussion

How do you think unfriendly attitudes toward the other sex affect boys and girls? Does it add to poor personal and social adjustments? Give reasons in each case.

How Parents Can Encourage Positive Attitudes toward Sex Roles

From the way things are going, it is fairly safe to say that in the years ahead egalitarian sex roles will be more widespread. And they will be more favorably accepted than they are today.

Children should be encouraged to play with toys that they find interesting and challenging. Lew Merrim/Monkmeyer

If this proves to be correct, children need to master at least some of the skills of the egalitarian role for their sexes. They will need these if they are to be well prepared to adjust to adult patterns of living. This means that boys should learn many homemaking and child-care tasks. Girls should learn some of the tasks in the home that have always been "men's work."

To be exact, boys should learn to take care of their clothes and rooms. They should help with the work of the home, such as preparing meals, cleaning, and marketing. If there are babies and younger children, boys can learn to help in their care until they are old enough to care for themselves.

There should be no sex-typing of play and playthings in the home. If boys get more enjoyment from a doll than from a train or truck, they should be allowed to play with it. They should not be shamed for doing so by being called

Mother's traditional role can be expanded to include creative, fun outings. Ginger Chih

"sissies." When girls find dolls boring and like mechanical toys, they should be allowed and encouraged to play with them.

Parents should encourage favorable attitudes toward the roles of *both* sexes. This can be best done by pointing out that differences do not mean that either is better than the other. Also point out that there are more differences within a sex group than between the sexes. It may be hard for parents to control dislike of the other sex outside the home. But they can control it within the home. By doing so, they teach young children that speaking badly of a person because of that person's sex is just as wrong as doing that because of race, religion, or cultural background.

One important area in which favorable attitudes can and should be en-couraged is that of attitudes toward future work. Sooner or later, every pre-school child will say, "When I grow up, I want to be a bus driver (or a librarian or a lawyer)."

All children, as they grow older, change work wishes many times. So it is important that they have basically good attitudes toward any work they might like and that they might be able to do well. A girl, for example, might want to be a lawyer. She should be en-couraged to aim for this goal if she has the traits needed. She should not be told that law is man's work. It is not.

The foundations for favorable atti-tudes toward egalitarian sex roles should be laid in early childhood. Then it will be fairly easy for children to learn a role that will fit into their life patterns as they grow older.

288

Highlights of Chapter 21

☐ Sex roles are socially approved standards of behavior for members of the two sexes. They cover abilities, achievements, personalities, and standards of appearance.

☐ There are two kinds of sex roles in today's society. The *traditional* stresses differences in the approved patterns of behavior for the two sexes. The *egalitarian* stresses the ways the roles for the two sexes are alike.

☐ Before children become interested in sex roles, they notice differences between the sexes and social attitudes toward these differences.

☐ Children learn sex roles by imitation, identification, and child-training methods. Each strengthens the other.

☐ Attitudes toward sex roles are developed along with learning the meaning of sex roles and how to play them.

☐ Unfriendly feelings between the sexes, usually started by boys, begin in the play group rather than in the home.

☐ The chances of having a satisfying adult life in modern America are greater if parents prepare children for egalitarian sex roles rather than traditional sex roles.

Suggested Activities

1. Make a list of household tasks young children can be expected to carry out well. Look over the chart on page 236 for some ideas. Which of these tasks were once "girl's work" and which "boy's work"?

2. Find out how adults and teenagers feel about traditional and egalitarian sex roles. Compare the views of each group. Of what value are any of the differences?

3. Listen to the record *Free to Be You and Me.* What social value does it have for children learning sex roles.

4. Plan a bulletin board showing how children learn sex roles by imitation, identification, and child training. Use pictures from comic strips and magazines to show each concept.

5. Watch a group of preschoolers—3- and 4-year-olds are best—and a group of school-age children. Are there any reasons to think that feelings between the sexes are less friendly in the older than in the younger group? If so, what are they?

Chapter 22

The Child in the Family

Some goals of this chapter are:

- [ ] To know in what ways the family is important to young children
- [ ] To realize why a young child's schedule and variations in it are important to the child and to the family
- [ ] To know the causes of the changes in family relationships that usually take place when children leave babyhood and the effect of these changes on all family members
- [ ] To know ways that family relationships can be improved

During childhood, children begin to form new relationships with all family members. These are very different from the relationships they had when they were babies. No longer are the children completely dependent on family members. Parents, brothers, and sisters now expect young children to do some things on their own and to get across their needs and feelings. Young children have to do their share, whether by expressing themselves or by carrying some of the load of home responsibilities. By doing these things, they interact with family members.

This interacting is very important to young children. They are becoming part of the group that does so much for them. (See the chart below.) The more time children spend with family members, the more interaction there will be.

What the Family Does for Young Children

Gives them a feeling of security from being a member of a group

Supplies companionship until children are old enough to form friendships with age-mates

Meets their physical and emotional needs

Helps them solve the problems they must face in their everday adjustments to life

Family outings are more enjoyable for everyone when children participate on an equal basis. George Zimbel/Monkmeyer

The Young Child's Schedule

The first important way young children come to feel part of the family is through a schedule that is like that of the other family members. Being able to eat with the family goes a long way toward making children feel that they are now truly family members.

However, the routine of young children must still be decided mostly by their physical needs. What is easiest for the family or what the children would like is not the first consideration. For example, the family's supper may be set back for some reason. It may be easiest to set back the small child's supper, too. But if the child's meal is set back an hour or more, bedtime will also be delayed. The child will become hungry and overtired. This will often lead to

Suggested Routine for a Young Child

7:00 to 7:30 A.M.	Toilet, clean teeth, wash, dress
7:30 to 8:00	Breakfast
8:00 to 8:10	Toilet
8:10 to 9:30	Help with care of room, quiet play
9:30 to 9:45	Orange juice and cracker
9:45 to 11:45	Play (outdoors when possible)
11:45 to 12:00	Toilet, preparation for meal
12:00 to 12:30 P.M.	Dinner
12:30 to 3:00	Nap or rest period
3:00 to 3:15	Toilet, fruit juice and cracker
3:15 to 5:00	Play (outdoors when possible)
5:00 to 5:30	Bath
5:30 to 6:00	Quiet play
6:00 to 6:30	Meal with family
6:30 to 7:00	Preparation for bed
7:00 P.M. to 7:00 A.M.	Sleep

fretfulness, irritability, and rebellion against eating and going to bed.

The accompanying chart gives a suggested schedule suitable for young children. It may have to be changed to meet the needs of an individual child or family. It will also change as the child grows older.

Children's meal hours may fit closely into a family schedule. But many doctors recommend that for the first year or two the main meal be at noon. A lighter meal should be eaten at night. At the evening meal, children can eat small amounts of the foods prepared for the family. By the time children approach their fifth birthdays, they may be ready for the regular family meals. Then they will have lunch at noon and dinner at night.

Children are also awake more than they were as babies. This gives them the chance to be with family members when they come home from school or work. As the children get older, they can stay up longer and increase the time spent with the others.

For Discussion

Why is it important for a young child's schedule to fit into the family schedule? Is the sample schedule shown above very realistic? In the families you know, do parents try to keep the children on their schedules?

Variations in Routine

A routine is very important to the young child's physical well-being. But a schedule with no variations causes nervous tension and anger. This does not make healthy, happy children. Nor does it lead to a pleasant home climate or pleasant relationships with other family members. But neither does a careless, hit-or-miss manner of handling the young child's daily needs. A child needs a routine. But enough variation to break the day-in and day-out sameness is also needed.

In most cases variations should depend on children's physical and emotional states, not on the pleasure and ease of some member of the family. When children are rested and in good spirits, that is the time to give them a little treat. That is when they can be given more freedom than they are usually allowed. If they are tired and fretful, it is not fair to them or to the rest of the family to upset their usual routines to suit the wants of another family member. However, even this rule must be applied with common sense and good judgment. A very special occasion—such as a rare and short visit from favorite relatives—may be cause enough for changing *everyone's* routine.

One way to break everyday routine, avoid boredom, and help children learn to adjust to variations in the pattern of daily life is to take them to different places. Then they have a chance to see new people and new things and to have new experiences.

Holidays are another way to bring variation into a young child's schedule. Children can be encouraged to share in the preparation for the holiday. They can help decorate the home or prepare some special food. Helping just a little will make them feel that they are a real part of the family group.

One of the chief causes of trouble so far as young children go is the special food traditionally prepared for a holiday. Children are often allowed to eat too much of the wrong things. When accompanied by being excited and tired, this can lead to stomach upsets. These make children fretful and irritable.

Besides variations in food, there are usually variations in the time when food is served. And, there almost always is between-meal eating. Naps, if there are any, and bedtimes are likely to be different from the daily schedule.

Joining in the hustle and bustle of preparing a holiday meal makes a child feel a part of the festivities. Ray Ellis/Rapho/ Photo Researchers

To avoid any bad effects and to encourage the good effects of variations, holiday schedules for young children should be kept as nearly like the schedule for other days as possible. This may take away some of the pleasure for the rest of the family. But this is far better than having the holiday spoiled by a fretful, irritable child or by several days of illness afterward. Also, a party feeling can be had by using special decorations, music, stories, or games. These do not have to affect the child's everyday routine at all.

Changes in Family Relationships

Relationships between people never remain the same. As people change, so do the relationships they have with others. The way family members change in their attitudes and behavior are described in the following chart. The time when the changes are most marked is shortly after the baby's first birthday. With each passing year, the changes become more pronounced and the effects on family relationships greater.

Ways Family Members Change

Young Children

They are bigger, stronger, and older looking than they were as babies.

Their coordination improves and they demand more independence.

Their intellectual development leads to curiosity, which shows up in constant exploring and questioning.

They gradually prefer companions outside the home.

Parents

If there is a new baby, they shift attention to care of the baby.

They gradually go back to doing things they enjoyed before the baby was born.

They use caretakers, which often makes children think that they are being rejected.

Brothers and Sisters

They no longer see the child as a cute doll to play with.

They may feel children are spoiled brats when the children grab their toys and interfere with their play.

They may be angry about having to play with, or care for, the young child all the time.

Relatives

They sometimes change from being loving and permissive to being strict disciplinarians.

They may become critical of normal childish behavior.

If the changes were for the better, and if the relationships with family members improved, it would be all to the good. However, changes are more often for the worse. Friction builds up between the child and members of the family. In such a situation, the home becomes tense and unpleasant for all. This may lead children to feel that they are unloved, unwanted, or rejected by the very people whose love they crave. In this way insecurity replaces the security they enjoyed when they were younger.

A family can work out any negative effects on the relationships that are caused by the changes each member goes through. Parents and older children have much more control in this than do young children and babies. They can help lessen the tensions that arise from changing needs. For example, parents should not expect the older children to play with the younger ones every day after school. This is asking too much. By giving older children freedom to do their own things, parents keep anger from building. Then when parents really need help, the older ones are usually more willing.

For Discussion

What other changes in a family can you think of to add to the chart on page 294? How would these added changes affect the relationships children have with the other family members?

Relationships with Parents

The greatest change in family relationships is between the child and the parents. There are a number of reasons

---

Conditions That Contribute to Changed Parent-Child Relationships

On Parents' Part

Shift from pampering children to making stricter demands on them

Failure to give children the independence they are able to handle

Criticism of children's poor skills and messiness

Failure to realize how limited young children's memories and understanding are, leading parents to think they do not obey on purpose

Anger because children always explore and question

On Child's Part

Anger at getting less affection because of a new baby or a new job

Anger at being criticized for doing things slowly and badly

Anger at having tasks taken away when the child is trying hard to do them

Anger at being turned over to outside caretakers

Anger when parents fail to understand what the child is trying to tell them

Anger at what the child sees as parents' favoritism toward a brother or sister

for this change. Some of these are on the part of the parents, and some are on the part of the child. These reasons are listed in the chart on page 295.

The major blame for the worsening of parent-child relationships rests with the parents. It is true that young children are harder to handle than helpless babies. They often do things that anger or embarrass their parents. But these things are hardly ever done on purpose. The behavior that bothers parents is closely related to the children's level of development and the stages they are going through.

Young children are upset by any breakdown in the parent-child relationship. This can be seen by the fact that most children try to win back their parents' affection. They want to get back the security they once enjoyed. To do this they use unsocial forms of behavior more often than social forms.

No matter how children try to win back parents' affection, it shows how important this affection is to children. When children feel unloved and unwanted by parents, they are unhappy. Their whole outlook on life may show this unhappiness.

Sisters and brothers are more friendly when they have shared interests.
Erika Stone/Peter Arnold

For Discussion

Give reasons for and against both parents working outside the home when children are young. Base your reasons on what has been said in this chapter about parent-child relationships and their effects on the young child's development.

Relationships with Brothers and Sisters

The relationships young children have with brothers and sisters change as the older ones' attitudes toward the young child change. While children were babies, older brothers and sisters could play with them as they played with toys. The older ones were free of any responsibility for the younger ones' care. However, young children outgrow their baby cuteness and become exploring toddlers. Then the older child may come to think of them as pests and treat them as such.

Also, older children may be expected to use some of their playtime to do things for the younger child. They may have to take the younger child out to play with their friends. The older child will show anger by trying to get rid of the younger one. If young children complain to parents about this, they are called tattletales. This widens the gap between older and younger children.

In families with traditional sex roles, the relationships with the most tension are usually those between brothers and sisters. Because of double standards, boys are given more rights and at an earlier age than their sisters. Also, they may not be expected to take on home responsibilities as often as their sisters are. The girls begin to be angered by this unequal treatment of their brothers.

In families where egalitarian sex roles are encouraged, brother-sister tensions are greatly lessened. The double standard does not exist. Brothers and sisters are held equally responsible for home tasks, depending on their age and abilities. They are also given rights as they are deserved.

For Discussion

How can the battles between the sexes be prevented when there are children of the two sexes in a family? Who should be responsible for this control? How are the boys and the girls of the family affected by unequal treatment?

Relationships with Relatives

The kind of relationship there is between young children and their relatives depends largely on how often they see each other. If they live close enough to relatives to see them often, the relationship will be very different from the relationships with relatives who live far away.

The closest relationship young children have with relatives is usually with grandparents. They are the relatives seen most often. Grandmothers, especially, are often called on to help when there is an emergency or when parents want a baby-sitter. There are many roles relatives play in their relationships with young children. The most common are listed in the chart on page 298.

Age is no barrier to the real pleasure of good company! Irene Bayer/Monkmeyer

Roles Played by Relatives of Young Children

Playmate   Relatives play with children as their age-mates, using their toys, telling them stories, playing games with them, or doing whatever the children want to do.

Critic   Relatives always find fault with what children do and how they do it. Praise is rarely given, and children feel that they are not able to do anything right.

Disciplinarian   Relatives may spend much of the time with children telling them what to do.

Caretaker   Relatives take full responsibility for the children's care, for a short or long time, while the parents are out of the home.

Teacher   Relatives help young children learn things appropriate to their age. They may teach children how to dress themselves or how to count to 10.

Good Fairy   Relatives who play the good fairy always have a surprise gift, no matter how small, for children when they are together. They plan little treats that leave children with a pleasant memory of the visit.

Parents often have a say in the roles relatives will play with their children. While an aunt or uncle may be a playmate or caretaker, parents may keep them from being critics or disciplinarians.

Seriousness of Poor Family Relationships

Young children are likely to experience great psychological damage from poor family relationships. The harm will be worse for them than for other family members because their lives are centered in the home. It is the child's one and only means of stability and security. If the home does not give stability and security, the child has nowhere else to turn for them.

There are three common forms of psychological damage to young children that poor family relationships cause. First, they affect children's attitudes toward people outside the home. It also affects the way the children treat them. The young child who develops an angry attitude toward a strict, authoritarian parent is likely to develop an unfavorable attitude toward all adults.

Second, poor relationships with the family result in personality traits that often lead to poor adjustments as children grow older. Feeling unloved and unwanted in the family, for example, may lay the foundations for an inferiority or martyr complex.

Third, unfavorable family relationships make children unhappy. Such children can and often do develop the habit of being unhappy.

As children grow older they have more chance to be with people outside the home. This keeps them from being as upset by unfavorable family relationships as they were when they were younger. However, children are always somewhat affected.

The less children are at home, the more they want the companionship of neighborhood playmates and the stronger is their desire to be popular with them. However, many children who have poor relationships with members of their families are not popular with other children. They tend to carry into the play group many forms of unsocial behavior they learned in their relationships with members of their families. For example, the child who quarrels with an older brother or sister may also quarrel with a playmate.

When a child finds better companionship with friends than with the family, parents are likely to be bothered by the time the child spends with friends. Parents may feel the friends have too much affect on the child. This makes the relationship between the child and the family even worse.

How to Improve Family Relationships

Poor family relationships leave psychological scars on young children's developing personalities. These are serious enough to make it worthwhile to try everything possible to improve such relationships. This effort must come largely from parents.

To reach this goal of good relationships, parents must be both preventive and corrective. Much of the bad feeling in the home can be prevented. To do so, parents must first see to it that

Parents usually provide the basic model of healthy family relationships.
Hanna W. Schreiber/Ralpho/Photo Researchers

the routine of everyone in the family—not just the child—is relaxed. No one should be tired or tense.

A second way to prevent poor relationships is not to expect too much from children. So long as children are trying to do the best they can, what they do should be praised. This is true even if their best is below adult standards.

A third way to prevent strained family relationships is to keep from turning over the care of a young child to older brothers and sisters, except in an emergency. Much quarreling between the children can be avoided if they play together only when they wish. And

then an adult should be present to supervise.

On the corrective side, parents can be on guard to spot any behavior in a child or in themselves that will lead to poor relationships. When such behavior comes up, they should do something about it at once.

The chart on page 302 gives ideas for keeping the home environment happy and secure for all family members. The major responsibility for pleasant relationships is in the hands of parents. But all children must understand that they have some responsibility too. They are expected to add to the happiness of the family. In the case of young children, their help may be more passive than active. It may take the form of not doing things to make the home unpleasant.

As children grow older, they can be expected to learn to help make family relationships pleasant. They can, for example, do their share of the home responsibilities. This may be setting the table for a meal or keeping the bathroom neat by hanging up their towels and washing out the bathtub. These may seem like small things, but they are important. They lay the foundation for a pattern of behavior that can lead to children doing their share in more and more important ways.

It is not realistic for anyone to expect family relationships to be ideal. A

Pleasant family experiences become a part of positive feelings about one's childhood. Gabor Demjen/Stock, Boston

home cannot always be free from any form of unpleasantness. This is especially true in a home where there are young children. Young children are too inexperienced in social relationships to know how to get along in a friendly way with family members at all times. But family relationships can be good most of the time. If the home is more often peaceful than not, that is all one can reasonably expect.

For Discussion

Some families have meetings once or twice a week. At those times family members discuss any problems that have come up in the family and how to solve them. What do these meetings do to improve family relationships? Use an example, such as an older brother's teasing a younger child and making fun of the way the younger child does things.

How to Improve Family Relationships

Set examples of good family relationships for children to imitate.

Show children how to get along pleasantly with other people. Supervise their relationships with others until they learn how to get along.

Curb any sign of unsocial behavior as soon as it appears.

Be on the lookout for unsocial speech and bad feelings about the other sex. Be ready to stop it as soon as it appears.

Keep family members from getting tired or tense by planning children's schedules to suit their development. Then stick closely to their schedules.

Teach children to be understanding of others. Set a model of this for them to imitate.

Explain why certain patterns of behavior must be followed so that children will not think the patterns are unreasonable.

Give children a chance to explain why they did or said an unsocial thing. Then show them a better way to do or say it.

Do not expect adult behavior from young children, but expect them to behave as well as they can.

Make children feel loved and secure even when they are troublesome by stressing that the *acts* were bad, not the *child*.

Make children understand that they have responsibilities to the family, just as other members have. Expect them to fulfill these responsibilities.

Make all members of the family accept their responsibilities for a happy home by not allowing a member who causes unpleasantness to remain with the family group.

Hold family meetings several times a week. Encourage every member to offer ideas about how to keep the home a happy place.

Highlights of Chapter 22

☐ When the helplessness of babyhood ends, young children must do their share to fit into the family pattern. They can no longer expect family members to make all the adjustments.

☐ The family is important to young children. It gives them feelings of security and stability, and it affects the pattern of their development.

☐ Variations in a young child's schedule are essential to good relationships with members of the family and to the child's ability to adjust to people outside the home.

☐ Changes in family relationships during early childhood come from changes in the child as well as changes in the members of the child's family.

☐ Poor family relationships are especially serious during the early childhood years. The family and the home are the chief sources of security for young children.

☐ There are many ways to improve family relationships during early childhood. The most important of these must be put into action and controlled by the parents.

Suggested Activities

1. Make a list of the features of what to your mind is an *ideal* family for young children. How many of the features on your list are reasonable in the American home of today? How many are ideal but impossible to really have?

2. Watch several young children after a weekend trip or a holiday gathering. Then watch the same children whose schedules have been unbroken for several days. Note the changes in their moods and behavior in the two situations.

3. Note how several parents and grandparents treat a baby. Then note how they treat young children. Do you find that they are much less generous and easygoing when dealing with children than when dealing with babies? In what ways?

4. Plan a bulletin board to define the various roles of relatives in their relationships with young children. Use color pictures from magazines or comic strips as examples of the roles in the chart on page 298.

5. Find out what students in the class feel they could do to improve relationships with brothers, sisters, and parents. How do their ideas measure up to the chart on page 302?

Unit Five | GROWING UP

Growing up is never easy. It is also difficult for the adults who are part of children's lives. Parents often find that they are at a loss to know what to do about some of the stages of childhood. The chapters in this unit have been written as guidelines to help adults understand the growing child and the various stages all children go through.

Chapter 23, "Discipline—Good and Bad," discusses the basic purpose of discipline during early childhood. It also points out what types of discipline are suited to the child's level of development and have the most lasting effects on the child's attitudes and behavior.

Chapter 24, "Some Common Problems of Early Childhood," covers the most usual problems children face in going through the stages of growing up. It also gives suggestions for ways parents can help their children deal with these problems.

Chapter 25, "The Child Who Is Different," gives some insight to added problems that are unique to many children. Some suggestions are discussed for ways people can help special children gain self-confidence and independence while making social adjustments.

Chapter 26, "Day-Care Centers and Preschools for Children," describes how these institutions differ and how they share the purpose of contributing to a child's personal, social, and intellectual development.

Chapter 27, "Getting Ready for School," suggests ways parents can help prepare young children for the difficult adjustments they must make when they begin school. It explains how the child can be prepared ahead of time to lessen the tension all first-graders experience.

Chapter 23

Discipline – Good and Bad

Some goals of this chapter are:
- [ ] To know the various kinds of discipline and how they differ from one another
- [ ] To understand the importance of education, reward, and punishment as basic elements of discipline
- [ ] To understand why parents' and children's attitudes toward discipline are greatly different and why children's attitudes are more important
- [ ] To know why it is best to evaluate discipline by the child's attitude toward it

To many people, discipline means punishment. But dictionaries say *discipline* is training in self-control or education. It also means training that molds, strengthens, or perfects. Note that, in its real meaning, stress is on *training* rather than on punishment.

It is true that punishment is often part of discipline. But punishment is not all there is to it. Education is the major feature in the discipline of young children. It is not reasonable or fair to expect children to obey until they know and understand what they are doing.

Elements of Discipline

Education This means teaching children what they should or should not do.

Reward Praise, approval, gifts, or special treats are given to children after they do, or at least try to do, what is expected of them.

Punishment This should only be given for willful wrongdoing.

Discipline could be just a conversation that touches on the difference of knowing right from wrong.   Peter Travers/ Peter Arnold

No matter what the age of the child, good discipline should include three separate but closely related elements. These are given in the accompanying chart. The first and second elements of discipline—education and reward— should be stressed in early childhood. Not until the child is a little older and able to willfully misbehave should any stress be put upon punishment.

The main purpose of discipline is to make children follow the rules laid down by people in authority. In this way, children learn to behave in a socially approved manner. But this is not by any means the only purpose.

Another important purpose of discipline is to get children to want to do what is expected of them and to avoid doing what they know the social group does not approve.

Types of Discipline

In America today there are three common forms of discipline. *Authoritarian discipline* is based on rule by authority rather than by reason. "Spare the rod and spoil the child" is a saying that describes this traditional form of discipline. It has come down through the ages and is widely used among various cultures all over the world.

Permissive discipline is the other extreme of authoritarian discipline. Under it, children are allowed to do pretty much as they choose. *Democratic discipline* takes the best features of the two. It is called "democratic" because it has many of the ideas of democratic government.

The chart on page 308 shows the highlights of each of these three kinds of discipline.   The highlights are

Comparison of Three Common Forms of Discipline

Authoritarian

Education Little or no stress on explanation. Children are expected to accept rules without question because the adult says so.

Reward Not often given, for fear of spoiling children or weakening their motivation to act accordingly when rewards cannot be given.

Punishment Stress on physical punishment for misbehavior. No attempt to find out if misbehavior was willful or not.

Permissive

Education Few rules and little guidance or explanation.

Reward Children are expected to get satisfaction from the social approval their good behavior brings.

Punishment Children learn from results of the act that they have done the wrong thing.

Democratic

Education Stress is on explaining the meaning of rules and the reasons for them and repeating them until children learn them.

Reward Praise freely used for right behavior or attempts by children to do what they know is expected of them. Other rewards given for repeated good behavior.

Punishment Saved for willful misbehavior. Children are given a chance to explain why they misbehaved before any punishment is decided upon. Physical punishment is hardly ever used. Instead, punishment is directly related to the misbehavior.

---

grouped under the three important elements of all discipline: education, reward, and punishment. A careful study will show how different these elements are for the three kinds of discipline. It will also show the ways that these three kinds of discipline are like the three types of outer-directed learning of the same names, which are described in Chapter 10.

All children differ and no two patterns of family life are the same. So no one kind of discipline is best for all children at all times. In general, facts seem to show that democratic discipline is best. Strict authoritarian discipline may produce "good" children. They are no trouble because they are afraid of what will happen if they are not good. But this kind of discipline also causes unfavorable attitudes on a child's part.

Many people who are against permissive discipline say that it is no discipline at all: none of the three essential elements of good discipline are there. However, there are some parents who favor it. They say that it works well with their children.

Whatever type of discipline parents decide to use, it is essential that they use it all the time. They should not change from one to another. The only time it is right to change methods is when it is clear that the discipline the parents decided to use is not working well enough. They may, for example, become certain that permissive discipline is not producing behavior that fits social expectations. It is far better to change to another type of discipline than to stick with one that is clearly not giving the desired results.

For Discussion

How can parents who use baby-sitters, relatives, or neighbors as caretakers for their children be sure that there will be no change in the discipline their children receive?

The Elements of Discipline

To understand good discipline, the three elements of discipline must be understood. It will then be possible to be a better judge of the different kinds of discipline and to decide which form seems best for most children or for a particular child.

Education in Discipline

No one is born with a sense of right and wrong. Everyone must learn what the social group thinks is wrong.

This knowledge, like all knowledge, can be learned in many ways and from many sources. It is the responsibility of parents and teachers to see to it that children have a chance to gain this knowledge. Failure to do so is just as unfair as failure to teach them how to speak.

The most important part of discipline in early childhood is, without question, learning what is right and what is wrong. Young children learn slowly and forget easily. So teaching them right and wrong must be tailored to their intellectual level at that time.

Until children are at least 3 years old, their vocabularies are very small. Explaining the whys and wherefores of good and bad behavior is almost impossible. Therefore, a few well-chosen words to describe right and wrong should be decided upon and used all the time.

For example, when children's behavior is good, the words "good," "fine," or "nice" may be associated with it. In time the young children will learn that their behavior is all right if they hear these words. In the same way, "bad" or "naughty" can be associated with misbehavior and "hurt," with dangerous actions.

As children's comprehension grows, more explanation can be given. When children understand why they are not supposed to do something they want to do, they will be more willing to give it up than they would if they thought their parents were just being mean.

Adults who want to teach children to obey rules should obey all rules themselves to avoid confusion. Erika Stone/Peter Arnold

When explaining to children why they should or should not do something, it is a good idea to keep the following warnings in mind: First, remember at all times how small a young child's vocabulary is. Only simple words that the child knows should be used.

Second, children have too little knowledge to grasp the meaning of any explanation unless it is brief and simple. Third, just because children seem to understand an explanation does not mean that they really do. To make sure that they understand, they can be asked to tell what the explanation means to them. If they have misunderstood, it can then quickly be corrected.

Fourth, children may not remember the rule or the reason for it at a later time. This is especially true if the new situation is not exactly like the old one. For example, children may understand that they must not play or dig in the family vegetable garden because they might kill the plants. But a day or two later, they may dig in a flower garden in another part of the yard. They do not realize that it, too, has plants that could be damaged.

Reward for Good Behavior

Until recently, there was a traditional belief that praise, or any other reward, makes people lazy and encourages them to rest on their achievements. Like many traditional beliefs, this has been proved to be faulty. As a result, strong stress has been placed on the important role of rewards. Rewards motivate learning and, for that reason, make learning easier and more lasting.

Looking at the matter from the child's point of view, one can hardly blame children for not trying to be good when their efforts receive little or no notice. If they are to have any real reason to try to do what is expected of them, it should be made worth their while. This can

310

Rewards for Young Children

Praise   It builds up the self-concept, gives a feeling of personal satisfaction, and adds to feelings of security. When praised, children realize that they have behaved as others expect them to behave. It creates a desire for behaving better at all times so as to get this very pleasant reward again.

Gifts   When children have been good or have tried to be good in situations when it is hard, rewarding them with a small gift as well as with praise will make them feel that the try was worthwhile. The moment for giving the gift is when the child's eagerness for trying is beginning to sag or when the child seems to be discouraged. Such a gift should be simple, cheap, and appropriate to the family's life-style. It should never be flashy and grand.

Treats   Going to the store for an ice-cream cone, having a playmate come over for a meal, or going to a movie—these serve as rewards for good behavior in the same way that gifts do. They work especially well when the child's good behavior or efforts to be good deserve some special notice.

best be done by giving children some type of reward.

Rewards should not be confused with bribes. A *reward* is anything that is given for something a person has done. A *bribe* is a promise of reward given ahead of time to encourage good behavior. When a parent says to a child, "If you are good when we go to see Aunt Mary, I will buy you some ice cream," that is a bribe. On the other hand, after the visit the parent might say, "You

A reward as positive reinforcement for good behavior encourages desired habits. Nancy Hays/Monkmeyer

Hugging and kissing are priceless to all children who need praise and affection.
Ginger Chih

were so good while we were with Aunt Mary that I am going to buy you some ice cream as a special treat." That is a reward.

Bribes certainly make children realize that being good will be in their best interest. But they may learn to depend on bribes for motivation. Some children may not be good unless they have the promise of some reward.

There are many rewards that might be used in the discipline of young children. However, studies of different rewards have shown that three stand out as the best. The rewards and their values are explained in the chart on page 311.

Punishment for Misbehavior

Part of all good discipline is punishment for willful misbehavior. If there is never any punishment, children will not learn the full meaning of wrong behavior.

Of the three elements of discipline, punishment is the hardest to use properly. Far too often it just makes children angry. As a result, it loses its learning value. At the same time, it creates a very bad attitude toward the person who did the punishing. That kills the child's motivation to try to learn to behave the way society expects.

Effective use of punishment, on the other hand, creates a favorable attitude toward the person who does the punishing. However, the children may be angry or upset for a while. More important, effective punishment motivates children to try to meet social expectations in the future. If it is to be used well, punishment must have the following characteristics.

First, punishment should be given only for willful misbehavior. Before punishment is given, there should be proof that the child misbehaved on purpose, not because of poor understanding or too little knowledge.

Second, punishment should never be given because the *child* has been naughty. It should be given because the *behavior* has been wrong. When children are punished because they are naughty, the stress is placed on the faults of the child. The result is a sullen, angry child. If, however, the punishment is given because the behavior is naughty, the child's attention is focused on the behavior. The difference is generally made clear by the adult's words: "Knocking Linda's ice-cream cone out of her hands was something you must never, never do!" *Not* "You're a bad, bad girl!" By turning the stress from the child to the behavior itself, the parent makes it less likely that the child's attitude will be colored by anger.

Third, the punishment should be closely enough connected to the misbehavior that even a child cannot fail to see the relationship. Take the case of spanking as an example. Very few children can say, after they have been spanked, just why their behavior was wrong. In the same way, a child does not connect misbehaving with being locked up in a closet or a dark room. So this method has no learning value—to say nothing of its cruelty.

Fourth, the punishment should come as close after the misbehavior as possible. Then children will know why they were punished. Telling a child, "When we get home you're going to get a good spanking," has no learning value. By the time they arrive home, perhaps an hour later, the child may have forgotten the misdeed.

Fifth, the more severe punishments should be saved for the more serious misbehaviors. This is important to its learning value. The more severe the punishment, the more stress it puts on the seriousness of the misbehavior. If a child is kept from going to a friend's birthday party for breaking a younger brother's toy but is only mildly scolded for hitting the younger brother, the child is likely to think that attacks on people are not nearly as bad as breaking things.

Punishing this child will serve no purpose unless the child understands the nature of the misbehavior. Peggy Kahana/Peter Arnold

Sixth, punishment should be fair. Children will then realize that they deserved it. As a result, they will want to learn to behave in a better way in the future to avoid punishment. When they feel that the punishment is unfair and that they did not deserve it, children develop an unfavorable attitude toward the person who punished them and toward all in authority. Even worse, they have little desire to try to behave in a better way.

Choosing the right punishment for a misbehavior is not as easy as always using the same form, such as spanking. But it pays off in improved behavior and attitudes of the child. The following chart gives a brief description of the common forms of punishment. Some are unsatisfactory. Others are satisfactory because they help correct misbehavior.

For Discussion

When parents try to give reasons for their use of physical punishment, it is not unusual for them to tell the child, "This hurts me more than it hurts you." Does this make the children feel that they are being fairly treated and that they have no one to blame for the punishment but themselves? Why or why not?

Attitudes toward Discipline

Parents' attitudes toward discipline are greatly affected by what parents think a child should be. If they think a child should be "good as gold" and no trouble to other people, especially adults, they will have a very different attitude toward discipline than they would if

Common Forms of Punishment for Young Children

Unsatisfactory

Spanking   Because it puts too much stress on the child as a "bad child" and too little on the wrong act, it leads to unfavorable attitudes.

Other Physical Punishments   The bad points of spanking are equally true of other forms of physical punishment—slapping the face or hands; whipping with a hairbrush, shoe, or strap; and washing out the child's mouth with soap. All physical punishment has the danger of turning into child abuse or causing injury when the adult is really angry. For this reason alone, it should be avoided.

Scolding and Nagging   Scolding is finding fault with a child for misbehaving. Nagging is going over past wrongs. Both scolding and nagging put too much stress on the child and too little on the child's behavior. So they have no learn-ing value. At the same time, they develop an unfavorable attitude toward the discipliner.

Locking Up   Even today, many parents use the old-fashioned method of punishing children by locking them up in a closet or in a dark room. This has no learning value since the misbehavior and the punishment are not related in any way. Further, it can be very frightening and psychologically damaging to the child.

Sending to Bed   Young children are unable to see the way misbehaving and being sent to bed are connected. And, indeed, they usually are not. However, the children are not too young to as-sociate bed with punishment. As a result, they often develop a resistance toward going to bed.

Satisfactory

Making Amends   When children do something wrong or harmful to others, they should have to do something to make up for their misbehavior. This often takes more time and effort than it would have taken just to avoid the unwanted act in the first place. So children soon realize that good behavior is easier than bad.

Isolation   Because young children's misbehavior often harms or bothers someone else, misbehavers should be kept from the pleasure of being with others until they are willing to say they are sorry and promise better behavior in the future.

Depriving Children of Treats   If deprived of a treat, especially when other children are receiving the treat for good behavior, the child can see that there are more benefits to good behavior than to bad.

---

they were more realistic.   Parents should realize that children are not adults. One cannot expect adult behavior from a child.

Parents who believe that children are not able to behave like adults worry less about much misbehavior. They know that children must have time to learn how to behave in an appropriate way. Instead of severe punishment to make children "good," parents try harder to teach the children what good behavior means. They reward children for trying to follow their rules.   And they let children experience disapproval and other unwanted results of willful misbehavior.

Such parents also understand that children forget more quickly than adults and that children are more impulsive. The parents are not too upset if a child sometimes does something the parent is sure the child knows is wrong. Instead of punishing for this slip, they give the child a chance to explain her or his side of the story. If the explanation does not seem to be reason enough for acting badly, this can be pointed out.

The worst parental attitude toward discipline is uncertainty. If parents are upset by what others say about the way they discipline their children and the way their children behave, the parents may become unsure of their disciplinary methods. This encourages them to change to a method recommended by others. This not only mixes up children, but it also makes parents seem unfair.

For Discussion

> Why do parents tend to change their use of discipline? Is this truer of one kind of discipline—authoritarian rather than democratic or permissive, for example—or is it characteristic of any method? Give reasons to back up your answer.

The Child's Attitude

Even though young children are not intellectually mature, they are very aware of fairness in the way they are treated. They are especially aware of fairness in punishment.

Of the three elements of discipline, punishment is the one that is most likely to give rise to unfavorable attitudes on the child's part. To make sure that unhealthy attitudes toward discipline will not develop, children must understand why and how they were at fault. They must realize that the punishment was deserved. It is always wise to explain to children both before and after punishment the reason why it was given. When this is done, there is little chance that the children will not understand why they are punished. Nor will they be likely to think the punishment was not deserved.

Young children's attitudes toward discipline, once formed, are likely to stay with them and affect their whole moral development. For that reason, it is important that foundations be laid for wholesome attitudes when children are still young and when discipline first plays a role of importance in their lives.

For Discussion

> How can you tell if a young child's misbehavior is done on purpose or not? Why is it important to do so before you punish the child? Give reasons for your answer.

Evaluation of Discipline

Most people evaluate discipline in terms of children's behavior. However, just because children's behavior appears good, one should not think that the method used to bring it about must be the best possible method. Nor should one think that it should be used in the discipline of *all* children.

Children who have healthy attitudes toward discipline are anxious to make amends for wrongdoings. Michael Putnam/Peter Arnold

Most children can be made into "good little boys and girls." But it takes harsh treatment and leaves its marks on the child's personality. A child who is naughty every once in a while is more likely to be better adjusted as an adult than one who was perfect during childhood.

A far better way to evaluate discipline is in terms of the child's attitude toward it. The best way to learn how young children feel about discipline is to watch them when they are being disciplined. When attitudes to discipline are favorable, children may cry and show signs of hurt feelings. But they will quickly get over this and return to normal activity.

On the other hand, children may sulk and be angry with the person who has punished them. Or they may blame someone else for their misbehavior. Or they may lie about it. If so, the discipline used is not right for them. In that case, parents will be wise to change their methods of disciplining.

Highlights of Chapter 23

- ☐ While all parents know that young children need discipline, they do not agree on what kind of discipline it should be.
- ☐ Good discipline includes three separate but closely related elements —education, reward, and punishment.
- ☐ There are three kinds of discipline common in America today—authoritarian, permissive, and democratic.
- ☐ During early childhood, the most important element of discipline is teaching children what people feel is right and wrong.
- ☐ The best way to motivate children to behave as the social group expects is to use rewards, not bribes.
- ☐ Punishment should be fair, consistent, immediate, and related to the child's misbehavior. It should be given only when the child misbehaves on purpose.
- ☐ Parents' attitudes toward discipline are greatly affected by two conditions: what parents think a child should be and the attitude of other people toward the way parents are disciplining their children.
- ☐ Children's attitudes toward discipline are more affected by the punishment they receive than by the other elements of discipline.
- ☐ In discipline, children's attitudes are more important than the quality of their behavior.

Suggested Activities

1. Suggest ways of showing children what a rule means before the children can understand words well enough to understand an explanation. For example, how can you show children where in the house or yard they may play and where they may not play?

2. Ask several parents what punishment they use when their children misbehave. Later, not in front of the parents, evaluate these punishments by using the facts given in this chapter. List them in order from most to least favorable.

3. Find out how parents reward their children for good behavior. Later, not in front of the parents, evaluate their rewards using the facts given in this chapter. List the rewards in order from most to least favorable.

4. Watch a family that uses authoritarian discipline, a family that uses democratic discipline, and a family that uses permissive discipline. Then compare how the young children react to discipline in these families. In doing so, take into account education, reward, and punishment and their roles in disciplining.

5. Suggest ways children can make up for three or four misbehaviors, such as breaking another child's toy in a temper tantrum or using a mother's perfume after being told many times not to touch it.

Chapter 24

Some Common Childhood Problems

Some goals of this chapter are:
- [ ] To know the correct meaning of "problem behavior"
- [ ] To be able to list the important groupings of problem behavior and know the most common problems under each
- [ ] To see the various ways parents can help their children overcome problem behavior

In learning to adjust to the world as they grow up, children often develop certain kinds of behavior that bother and embarrass adults. Adults often call such behavior *problem behavior* and try to correct it. In so doing, they often make things worse rather than better.

More often than not, what adults call problem behavior is perfectly normal for children at a certain stage of development. Children do not know what behavior is socially acceptable. So they try to express their natural drives in ways that are not quite acceptable. Many adults may think this is problem behavior because they judge young children by standards meant for older children.

Certain kinds of behavior can be called problems only when they inter-fere with children's happiness and their adjustment to life. Problem behavior is behavior that makes life difficult and unsatisfactory for the child, not for the parents.

Common Types of Problem Behavior

Most young children behave in quite a number of ways that interfere with good adjustments. This is characteristic of their level of development and will change as they become more mature, both physically and mentally. But other forms of behavior, often less troublesome at the time, may stay with them and, in time, become habits. These are the ones that need special attention and guidance to be overcome.

The most common problems of early childhood are divided into four groups according to how they affect the child's well-being. These are explained briefly in the chart below.

For Discussion

What problem behaviors of their children do parents find most bothersome, most embarrassing, and most difficult to deal with? Keep a list of these problem behaviors and analyze each in terms of the meaning of problem behavior given below.

After making this analysis, what do you think about parents' attitudes toward problem behavior?

Parents tend to be more concerned about problems that interfere with the child's physical well-being than with any others. They are thinking of the immediate effects on the child's growth and development instead of the adjustments the child will make growing up. For example, some parents are very concerned when the child does not sleep at nap time or resists going to bed at night. At the same time, they may overlook the child's calling brothers and sisters names or teasing them. Parents blame this unsocial behavior on the child's not having enough sleep. They think that if they can solve the sleep problem, the teasing and name calling will stop by itself. This may be true sometimes, but certainly not always.

Of all problems that affect the physical well-being of young children, those that head the list in most families have to do with eating and sleeping. These problems are often taken more seriously than they need to be. This is because parents do not understand that physical growth is slowing down. Therefore, children need less sleep and need to eat less often than they did during the babyhood years, when growth was more rapid.

Common Behavior Problems in Early Childhood

Behavior That Interferes with Physical Well-Being Any behavior that interferes with children's nutritional and sleep needs and any illness or accident that saps their strength are physically and psychologically damaging to children.

Behavior That Interferes with Efficiency While dawdling and awkwardness are not serious in early childhood when children have few responsibilities and plenty of time, it will sooner or later prove to be a great handicap to them.

Behavior That Interferes with Social Adjustments Being rude, selfish, and thoughtless about the rights and feelings of others will make children disliked by both children and adults.

Behavior That Gets Unfavorable Attention Because being the center of attention is ego satisfying, young children often cut up or do foolish things. Adults often think attention-getters are silly pests, and playmates may think they are show-offs. In an extreme form of trying to get attention, children may keep on doing things they know are wrong, such as lying or taking things that belong to others.

Behavior problems exhibited by children are not always noticed because parents may be involved in a family activity. Richard Nowitz

For Discussion

How does knowing about the usual pattern of a child's growth help parents accept some of the bothersome mealtime and bedtime activities as normal rather than problem behavior?

Eating Problems

There are a number of common eating problems among young children. These may lead to the development of unfavorable attitudes toward meals. Because a child's eating problems often affect the whole family, parents should try to keep such problems from developing. On page 322 there are some ideas as to what parents can do.

Sleeping Problems

Problems connected with sleep are generally not as serious as eating problems. But they are certain to arise at some time. Unless they are dealt with correctly, they can lead to other, more serious problems that may harm the general state of the child's health.

Children's sleep needs vary. Parents who realize this and change the sleep schedule from time to time will do much to correct many sleep problems. Parents should also realize that children go through stages that are not real problems. When, for example, a young child is moved from a crib to a bed, it is normal for the child to want to enjoy the new freedom by getting out of bed and running around. If, on the other

Ways to Prevent Eating Problems

Give children a small amount of food and then let them have more if they ask for it.

Make the child's plate pretty and avoid heaping it with food.

Do not force them to clean their plates, but instead let children eat as much as they want.

If children always eat very little, take them to the doctor to find out why.

Do not encourage overeating.

Avoid giving a child snacks between meals because they make the child less hungry at mealtimes.

Remember that every child needs time to get used to the taste and feel of new foods.

Prevent dawdling by keeping the eating environment free from distractions.

Do not nag about bad table manners. Show the child how to eat in a socially approved way.

---

hand, the child starts running around after having had the bed for several months, it is more likely to be the start of a problem.

Like other problems, those that take place at bedtime are hard to check once they develop. For that reason, every possible effort should be made to keep them from developing. The accompanying chart gives some ways to help do so.

One problem that many children share is bed-wetting. Children cannot be expected to have good enough bladder control to keep dry all night every night much before they are $3^1/_2$ or 4 years old. Even after that, bed-wetting every once in a while is common after an exciting day or some experience that has caused nervous tension. If, however, bed-wetting takes place nightly after the age of 4 years, this suggests that

Ways to Prevent Sleep Problems

Review the sleep schedule with the doctor if children seem to sleep less than the parents think they should.

Prepare children for bed in a relaxed manner.

Avoid exciting games, stories, or TV shows before the nap or evening bedtime.

Give children a warm bath before bedtime if they seem tense.

Ask children if they have everything they want or need—water, going to the toilet, etc.—to discourage calling for attention as soon as they go to bed.

Keep the house as quiet as possible during children's nap time and when they go to bed at night.

Avoid starting a game or reading if it will mean hurrying the child to prepare for bed.

Never put children to bed for being naughty or for not finishing a meal.

Have children help put toys away and remove any distractions from the room.

Encourage children to talk about their fears of the dark. Try to make them see that their fears are only imaginary, not real.

something is wrong. It must be corrected before the habit of *enuresis*—bed-wetting all the time—develops.

Studies have shown that few cases of enuresis have a physical cause. Most have an emotional cause. They come from some psychological disturbance in the child's life. This may be the result of too exciting an environment, jealousy, parental pressures to do more than the child is developmentally able to do, and, most important of all, parental criticism. The accompanying chart gives some ideas for handling the psychological causes of bed-wetting. If there is reason to believe that there may be some physical cause, the doctor should be seen.

Accidents

Accidents in early childhood can be and often are one of the most serious problems that affect the physical well-being of children. This is because the long-term effects are often greater than the

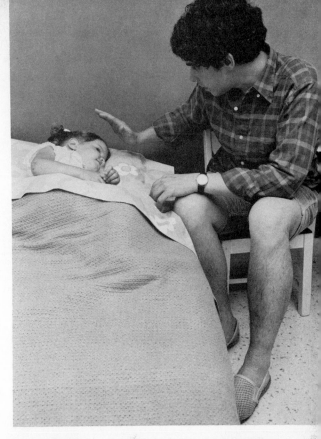

Some children may have problems with sleeping, but an understanding parent can always help the child through this difficulty. Erika Stone/Peter Arnold

---

Ways to Handle Bed-Wetting

Find out why the child is tense and try to take away the cause. Do not put much stress on the bed-wetting itself.

Never scold, or punish, or make fun of the child for wetting the bed.

When children wet the bed, tell them that they will soon be able to keep dry through the night.

Lessen the child's liquid intake about 4 P.M., but be sure that the child gets extra liquids all through the day.

If the child wakens and calls for someone to take him or her to the toilet, do so at once.

Teach the child to go to the toilet alone during the day so this will become a known routine.

When the child has learned to go to the toilet alone during the day, try to establish the same learning process at night.

Put a flashlight by the child's bed and show how to use it to go to the toilet when it is dark.

Go over the path the child is to take when it is dark, using the flashlight, until the child knows it well enough to do it alone.

Injuries to Children up to Four Years Old
Caused by Consumer Products

U.S. Consumer Product Safety Commission/
Bureau of Epidemiology, January 1977

long-term effects of illness. This is especially true when an accident leads to a physical defect.

Young children tend to have more accidents and more serious accidents than babies. The younger they are, the more accidents they are likely to have. The reason for this is that young children are no longer as carefully supervised and protected as they were when they were babies. Nor are young children as aware of possible dangers and as careful as they will be when they grow older.

Accidents can affect any part of the young child's body. By far the most common area hurt is the face. The next most common part is the head. The trunk and legs are least likely to be hurt in accidents. The diagram above gives an idea of how often injuries happen.

Even when accidents have no short-term or lasting physical effect, they could leave psychological scars. After an accident, children tend to become more careful with new people, animals, objects, or places. This, of course, is good because it curbs some of the adventurousness that leads to accidents. But if a child has many accidents, he or she may lose self-confidence in many situations. This can and often does lead to a withdrawn kind of personality that causes problems in making friends and achieving many goals.

Awkwardness

From 2 to 4 years of age, almost all children do things in an awkward manner. They hold eating utensils in a way that makes it almost impossible to keep from spilling food. They drop and break things they are carrying. And they bump into people and furniture when they run and even when they walk.

As long as the child's world is limited almost entirely to the home, awkwardness is a problem that will bother parents. But it will have no lasting effect on parent-child relationships.

This, however, is not true when the child's world begins to expand to the neighborhood play group and perhaps a nursery school or kindergarten. If the child is awkward and clumsy in play with other children, she or he may be left out of the play group. This deprives the child of the fun others are having and also of the chance to learn new skills when others are learning them.

Awkwardness is equally handicapping when children go to school. Much of the activity of the early grades calls for hand skills, for doing such things as writing, painting, or crayoning, and leg skills for running, dancing, and jumping rope. For these reasons, steps should be taken to correct awkwardness. This means being aware of the child's awkward movements and helping the child learn to move in a more coordinated way.

Dawdling

Dawdling means doing something in a slow, lingering way—taking more time to finish the act than is needed. Dawdling may come from awkwardness. But mostly it is due to having the mind wander from the task at hand. Dawdlers are distracted by something else—activities around them or their own thoughts. If an act is so well learned that it can be carried out without thinking about it, there is no serious problem if the mind wanders. But few activities of young children can be done with little or no concentration!

Like awkwardness, dawdling usually shows up first around the age of 2 years. It is very marked in such behavior as self-feeding, self-dressing, and self-bathing. Dawdling may bother parents,

Responding to clumsiness with anger may only confuse the child, who is just trying to be grown-up. Robert Capece

but it is not serious to children until they begin to spend time outside the home. Then they find that dawdling makes them so inefficient that they cannot keep up the pace set by others. Dawdlers are often left behind to play by themselves. The long-term effects are even more serious.

Because dawdling is so common in early childhood, it is important to know how it can be corrected before it becomes a real problem. The chart below gives some ideas that have proved useful. Note that all of them have one basic aim—to improve the child's concentration by controlling conditions that lead to distractions.

For Discussion

Which types of problem behavior do you think are most serious in terms of the child's adjustments to life? Which are least serious? Give reasons for your answer.

Social Adjustment Problems

Children under 4 years of age cannot be expected to behave in a truly social manner. They will push, grab, and fight, and refuse to share their things with others. However, by the time they are 5 years old, children should have overcome some of this behavior.

Children who still behave in an unsocial way after other children of the same age have developed more socially acceptable patterns will find that they have no one to play with. This is especially true if they boast and criticize others, tease and bully smaller children, or tattle to adults.

Many parents overlook unsocial behavior in young children, thinking that the children will outgrow it. Some of it, without a doubt, will be left behind when children realize what a handicap such behavior is. But if children fail to realize that it is their unsocial behavior that is making people dislike them, they will not have the reason needed to change.

Ways to Overcome Dawdling

Watch the child carrying out a task, such as self-dressing, and guess about how long it takes.

Study how the child carries out a task to see when dawdling begins and what causes it.

If dawdling comes from poorly developed skills that make the task unusually hard for the child, work on improving the skills.

If dawdling comes from distractions, keep the environment as free from them as possible.

Play "Beat the Clock" with children who dawdle to give them a reason to do a task quickly. Set a kitchen timer to go off when the task should be completed. Because children enjoy winning, this will help them to keep their mind on the task.

Each time the child finishes before the bell rings, a reward like praise or a simple treat should be given.

What may appear to be dawdling could really be curiosity. Young children are fascinated by the simplest things! Jean-Claude Lejeune/Stock, Boston

Unsocial behavior should be checked as soon as it appears. At that time, patterns of social behavior should be developed to take its place. Pages 257–259 discuss in detail ways in which parents and other caretakers can help young children learn patterns of social behavior that will help them to make more friends.

Attracting Unfavorable Attention

Young children usually want to be the center of attention. Some achieve this goal with behavior that wins favorable attention. Unfortunately, behavior that should win favorable attention is often overlooked, while undesirable behavior puts the child in center stage. For example, a child who does a good job of self-feeding at the family dinner table will not get the attention that a child who throws bread or makes funny faces gets. This often happens in many other situations as well.

It is not surprising that when children feel they are being overlooked they soon discover what the best way to get the attention they want is. They do things that attract unfavorable attention. The following chart lists some common ways children attract attention to themselves. Note that almost all of them attract unfavorable, not favorable, attention.

327

Problem behavior that comes from the desire to win attention can be dealt with in two ways. One way is to ignore such behavior or to show quiet disapproval of it. The disapproval must *not* cause a big stir. When children discover that their behavior is not giving them the attention they want, they will have less desire to repeat it.

The other way to deal with problem behavior is far more important. Socially approved behavior should be given attention. If children gain the attention they crave when they do the right thing, they will have a strong desire to repeat such behavior. Children who are praised for good table manners and encouraged to take part in the family conversation will be far less likely to cut up and carry on at the dinner table than children who feel that they are being overlooked.

Occasional conflicts between children are a common part of growing up. It only becomes a problem if children enjoy the unfavorable attention they attract through these spats. Sam Falk/Monkmeyer

Prevention or Correction of Childhood Problems

Ideally, parents and other caretakers should watch for the first signs of possible problem behavior. They should be ready to keep it from developing more. By so doing, they avoid the need to correct it later when it has developed into a habit which will handicap the child's adjustments.

As we know, patterns of behavior are learned, not inherited. It is just as easy for children to learn to behave in a manner that will make adjustments to life easy and pleasant as in a way that will make adjustments hard and unpleasant for them. However, children are too inexperienced to know what behavior will hinder them and what behavior will help them. Getting satisfaction from the behavior is all that matters.

Children need guidance to ensure that they will learn the most useful and desirable patterns of behavior. This is important, not only for the immediate present, but also for the future. Later, social expectations will be greater and more strictly enforced than they are for preschoolers.

The following chart gives some ideas for guiding children in overcoming problem behavior. Most of these ideas are based on principles of learning. A learned activity that has proved to be a handicap can be replaced by one that will prove to be an aid.

For Discussion

Of the six ideas for overcoming problem behavior given in the chart below, which one do you think is the easiest to use? Which is the hardest? Give reasons to back up your answer.

Ways to Overcome Problem Behavior

Find out why children cling to a form of behavior that is proving to be harmful to adjustment. If they are satisfying some need by behavior that will lead to poorer and poorer adjustments, then a new means of satisfying this need must be found.

Help children become fully aware of what they are doing and why it would be better to behave in a more acceptable way.

Encourage children to want to change the behavior that will be a handicap as they grow older. If children understand the reason for change, they will be more willing to try.

Encourage children to replace troublesome behavior with behavior that will be of more help to them and give them equal satisfaction. Praising the new behavior will strengthen its satisfaction.

Don't overlook setbacks. Each one strengthens the very behavior children want to stop. This, in turn, makes the job harder and more discouraging.

Encourage children to be active. Children who are active in play drain off much of the energy that might otherwise be turned into troublesome behavior. When energy is pent up, it is far too often let out in the form of misdirected, undesirable behavior.

Highlights of Chapter 24

☐ Adults tend to call any childish behavior that bothers or embarrasses them problem behavior.

☐ Correctly used, the term "problem behavior" is behavior that makes life hard and unsatisfactory for the child, not for the parent.

☐ Problem behavior in childhood can be divided into four major groups: behavior that interferes with physical well-being, behavior that interferes with efficiency, behavior that interferes with social adjustments, behavior that attracts unfavorable attention.

☐ The three most common forms of behavior problems that interfere with physical well-being are eating problems, sleep problems, and accidents.

☐ Awkwardness and dawdling are the most common problems that lead to inefficiency in early childhood.

☐ Unsocial behavior and behavior that attracts unfavorable attention not only interfere with social adjustments in childhood, but also tend to stay with children and lead to serious social adjustment problems as children grow older.

☐ Keeping problem behavior from happening is more important than correcting it. Once such behavior has developed, it can be corrected but with some difficulty.

Suggested Activities

1. Watch the speed at which several children eat different foods. Do you see any relationship between the speed and the child's dislike for the food?

2. Go over some of the traditional children's stories, such as *Little Red Riding Hood* and *Snow White and the Seven Dwarfs*, for any terror elements that might cause bedtime fears or nightmares among young children. Do the same with some Walt Disney stories that have been written in the last few years. Are there many terror elements in them?

3. Study a dawdler. (Dawdling is such a common problem among young children that you should have no trouble in finding one.) When you do, try out some of the ideas for overcoming dawdling given in the chart on page 326.

4. Think back to when you developed a pattern of behavior which you now find to be a problem, such as dawdling. Did you, your parents, or your teachers try to correct this behavior? What was done? Do you find that you dawdle less now than you did as a young child?

Chapter 25

The Child
Who Is Different

Some goals of this chapter are:

☐ To understand why children who are different from other children their age have special problems in growing up

☐ To be aware of what parents can do to help children who are different adjust to the problems associated with being different

☐ To realize that parents and caretakers need to try to change the widespread attitude that being different is being inferior

All children are different from one another. Some, however, are so different from their age-mates that they stand out. This makes the problem of growing up more difficult for them than for other children. They must deal with the problems that come from being different as well as with the problems that usually come with growing up.

Some children are different from their playmates because of physical or psychological traits. Others are different because of situations in their lives. Most often the makeup of their families or the pattern of living of their homes is different. Few, if any, of these causes of differences are within the child's control. But all have an effect on the child's

---

Factors Influencing the Effects of Being Different

How noticeable the difference is

How parents and other adults react to the difference

How age-mates react to the difference

How being different affects personal and social adjustments

How being different affects doing what others do

How being different affects the child's self-concept

What meaning the child puts on being different

Children who have special problems can develop physically, mentally, emotionally, and socially just as any other child when given the chance.
Michael Hardy/Woodfin Camp & Associates

personal and social development, especially during the foundation years.

How greatly does the realization of being different affect children? And how will this add to problems of growing up? This will depend on a number of factors. The most common and most important of these are described in the chart on page 331.

A careful study of this chart strengthens the view that there is nothing about being different, by itself, that is damaging to children. Only the attitude that being different is being inferior is damaging. It follows that one of the major responsibilities of parents and all other child caretakers is to try to get rid of this attitude. Parents should teach their children—especially those who are *not* very different in any way—never to make fun of, tease, leave out, or be mean to children who are different. Parents must show by their own example that a friendly, accepting,

For Discussion

When is being different from other children the biggest handicap to the child's school adjustments—in nursery school, in kindergarten, or in first grade? On what grounds do you base your judgment?

and kind attitude toward the person who appears different may open the door to a satisfying friendship.

The Very Bright Child

Attitudes towards brightness are usually favorable. So most bright children think well of themselves. In spite of favorable social attitudes, very bright children feel that their difference puts them out of step with children their own age. They often find little enjoyment in playing or talking with age-mates. They then go off by themselves, liking their own interests better than being with other children.

The more time children spend by themselves, the more out of place they will feel in a group. And the more damaging this will be to their personal and social adjustments.

One good solution to the problem is to try to find other children whose intellectual development is the same, or nearly so. Then the bright child can have friendly playmates. Even one playmate helps solve the problem of loneliness and helps work against the feeling of difference.

For Discussion

How would you, as a parent, treat a very bright child to keep that child from becoming overly self-satisfied and angering other children? Is there anything a parent can do to keep relatives and other people outside the home from making a very bright child intolerant toward those who are less bright? If so, what can be done?

The Slow Learner

Slow-learning children find it impossible to keep up with the pace set in play by their brighter age-mates. They soon find themselves left out or rejected as playmates. Sometimes, in a desire to join in the fun other children are having, slow learners try to force themselves into the group. Then they are often told with harsh frankness that they are not wanted.

Like all rejected people, slow-learning children may soon develop feelings of inferiority. They may also feel they are being treated unfairly. This not only makes them unhappy, but it also badly damages their personal and social adjustments.

To keep this from happening, parents can help slow learners find playmates whose level of development is like their children's, even if they are younger. This is better than being with children their own age who reject them.

In every play group and, later, in every school class, there are some slow learners. These children should be encouraged, when they first start to play with children outside the home, to seek the friendship of children of their own intellectual level. Then they will not be psychologically damaged by feeling that they are "different."

Parents can also join with other parents and neighbors to try to create an open and accepting feeling in their neighborhood play groups. Then slow learners, as well as other children who are different, will feel welcome. This is possible if parents work with their children to encourage friendly and understanding attitudes.

The Physically Handicapped Child

Early childhood is an active age. Children who have some physical defect will be held back when they try to be as active as their playmates. The playmates may then think that the physically handicapped children are inferior. The normal children have to be taught otherwise by adults.

Physically handicapped children, like all young children, want to be independent. They may become rebellious and angry when they have to rely on others to do things for them. This also gives them the feeling that they are inferior to other children, who are able to become independent.

A physical defect that takes away from the appearance of a child is not too serious a problem in early childhood. It will be a worse one when children reach the self-conscious stage of adolescence. However, any physical defect that others will notice is a possible source of inferiority feelings for young children. This is because young children have little tact. They may very well ask pointed questions about anything that attracts their attention or makes them curious. They may, for example, notice something in a deaf child's ear and ask what it is for. If, in a thoughtless way, they say that they can hear without having something in their ear, it will make the deaf child feel self-conscious and, perhaps, inferior.

Parents know that physical defects are both physical and psychological handicaps to a child. So they seek medical aid and are willing to give up a great many things in order to pay for any treatment that may correct or lessen the severity of the handicap. However, there are other things they can do to help children overcome some of the feelings of inferiority that defects may cause. Ideas of things to do are given in

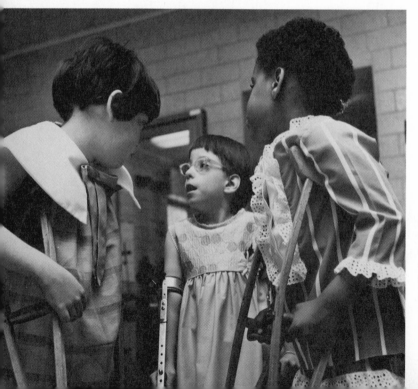

Handicapped children who socialize with others who have similar handicaps have the chance to realize that they are not so "different" after all. The National Foundation—March of Dimes

How to Deal with Problems Caused by Physical Defects

Try to make any physical defect that other children will speak about unfavorably less noticeable. However, if the efforts make the child look strange or overdressed, it may be better to allow the defect to show and the child to look natural otherwise.

Pay special attention to the child's clothes so the child can feel at ease and satisfied about his or her appearance.

Encourage and teach the child as many independence skills as she or he can learn.

Encourage and teach as many social-help skills as the child is able to carry out.

Be sure that the child gets the exercise needed for normal physical growth, even if this means setting up exercises.

Encourage the child to watch other children at play and take part as much as the handicap will allow.

Teach the child to play those games that can be played in spite of the handicap. Encourage some playmates to learn these games to play with the child.

---

the above chart. Note that the stress is on teaching and encouraging children to do as much as the handicap will allow, not on showing concern and pity because the children are handicapped.

The Child with a Special Ability

Some children have such marked special talents that they show up even before babyhood ends. The child with musical ability, for example, may show an awareness of rhythm during babyhood that is not usually found at that age. The child may listen carefully to music and try to copy rhythms.

The major problems associated with special talents are those caused by parents. They put too much stress on developing the ability. The best method of dealing with these problems is to encourage a well-rounded development. For example, parents should not only give a young child play equipment that is closely related to his or her talent. The parents should also give the child plenty of equipment for *all*

kinds of play and should encourage and show the child how to use it.

In the same way, the parents should not encourage the child's preference for playing alone. Adults should instead encourage the child to engage in a wide range of activities, especially those in which other people take part. If the child is also encouraged to use her or his special ability to give enjoyment to others, the child is likely to become a welcome and valued member of any group.

The Child in a One-Parent Home

Many more children today live in a one-parent home than did so in the past. Death of a young parent today is less common than in the past, but there are more and more families broken by divorce. And many children are being born to parents who have never married.

The parent in a one-parent family in our society today is usually the mother.

Encourage children to develop special talents, but not at the expense of their developing a well-rounded personality. Michael Hardy/Woodfin Camp & Associates

Factors Affecting Child's Adjustment in a One-Parent Family

Attitudes of relatives and family friends, as shown by their comments and advice to the parent.

Attitudes of other children, as shown in their comments about the one-parent family.

Social attitudes toward cause of single parenthood: Death of a parent leads to feelings of pity. Divorce in some communities may still be received badly.

Home duties the child must take on to help the parent.

Care the child gets while the parent works and how the child feels about the caretaker.

The child's feeling about the fun and good times the family has (such as on hol-idays or vacations), as compared with other families.

Economic state of the family, as judged by the earning power of the single parent.

How well the parent deals with own problems and how much the parent is able to keep from being either too protective or neglectful.

Whether or not there is a role model of the other sex from the parent so that children may be close to an adult of that sex, too. (Sometimes an aunt or uncle, grandparent, or family friend may take part in family activities for this purpose.)

There are, however, some one-parent families where the father is in charge of the home. The number of such families is growing.

One-parent families are still unusual enough in some areas to attract attention. This is truer of small towns or rural areas than of large urban or suburban centers.

When one-parent children begin to play with other children, they realize that the pattern of their homelife is somewhat different from that of other families. Children in one-parent families may adjust well or poorly to their pattern of life, depending on a number of factors. The most important of these are listed in the accompanying chart.

There is no doubt that a great many one-parent families are satisfactory places for the child to grow up in. The children in such families can be happy and well adjusted. However, some single parents feel that it would be better for the child to have a second parent. Besides, they may be lonely for a partner. Therefore, they remarry and bring a stepparent into the home to replace the missing parent.

The Child with a Stepparent

Very young children generally accept a stepparent gladly. The stepparent gives stability and security to the home which was lacking when the family was broken by death or divorce. Later, as they grow older and play with other children, they may begin to feel that having a stepparent makes them different. This is mostly true in a neighborhood where there are few or no other children with stepparents. But such neighborhoods are becoming unusual.

Second marriages are very common in America today. So the child with a

Children in a single-parent family are happy and well adjusted when they feel comfortable with their situation. Leonard Nadel/McGraw-Hill

stepparent is really not very different from other children. The feeling of being different is not often a major problem. The relationship between the child and the stepparent, however, *is* of major importance. It can have a marked effect on the child's development. The accompanying chart lists a number of factors that help judge whether the child has a good or a poor relationship with the stepparent.

Children of divorced parents, both of whom remarry, may feel different from other children. They now have four parents. Their friends have only two. Feelings of difference are complicated by adjustment problems. The child

who does not have stepparents does not have to deal with these types of problems.

Children of divorced parents, for example, live with one of their real parents. After a visit with the other real parent and the other stepparent, these children often find adjustment to the parent and the stepparent with whom they usually live very difficult. Suppose a child lives with the father and stepmother and visits the mother and stepfather. The child is likely to be treated as an honored guest in the mother's home rather than as a family member. This is treatment the child thoroughly enjoys.

Factors Affecting Child's Relationship with Stepparent

How the stepparent treats the child—kindly or as a bother.

How the stepparent's discipline compares with the discipline the child is used to.

Whether the stepparent shows a preference for, and favoritism toward, own children. If so, the child will resent the stepparent and the stepparent's children.

Whether the grandparents and other relatives like the stepparent. If they do, it will encourage the child to do so as well.

How playmates react to the stepparent

—pitying the child or feeling that he or she is lucky. (Often they will have no reaction.)

The way stepparents are shown in mass media, especially in comics and on TV.

Whether stepparent replaces a parent who is dead or divorced.

Social or religious beliefs about remarriage after death or divorce. These affect relatives' and neighbors' attitudes.

How much the stepparent adds to the economic well-being and stability of the home.

Parents with children sometimes remarry and combine families. They can help their children adjust favorably to the situation by treating each child as their own. Charles Moore/Black Star

When the child returns home, the father and stepmother expect the child to go back to the routine pattern of life. Next to the treatment in the mother's home, this is less enjoyable. The result may be rebellion on the child's part and reminders all the time to the father of how much fun the child was allowed to have on visits to the mother.

Such experiences stress the need for divorced parents and stepparents to speak with one another about the needs and behavior of the child for whom they all care. The child has to be able to build good relationships with both sets of parents and not become confused or insecure by moving between them. To do so, a great deal of tact, sensitivity, and willingness to compromise are needed. Both sets of parents should put the needs and feelings of the child ahead of their wishes.

The Adopted Child

Until recently, adopted children were matched as closely as possible to the adoptive parents in physical traits, race, intellectual level, religion, and socioeconomic status. The belief behind this match principle was that the adopted child would not have to deal with the problem of being different besides the other problems that often accompany adoption.

Today, fewer children of American parents are being put up for adoption. So it has become more and more common for Americans to adopt children from foreign countries, especially the war orphans from various Asian countries, such as Korea and Vietnam. There are also more white parents who adopt black and other minority children.

Because of the differences in appearance between the children and their adoptive parents, the children now need to deal with an added problem. That is the problem of being different. The child is different, not only from the adoptive parents, but also from the children of the neighborhood.

The following chart lists some of the factors that give rise to problems of adjustment that all adopted children must deal with.

One problem is that of understanding why they are not with their natural parents, as other children are. The

---

Factors Affecting the Adjustment of Adopted Children

Social attitudes toward adoption

The way in which adoption is explained to the child

The way relatives, neighbors, and friends of the family feel about adoption and about children who are adopted

How other children react to adoption and how different they think this makes the child

How the natural-born children in the family feel about the adopted child and how they treat her or him

How curious the adopted child is about his or her natural parents

The source from which the child learns about the adoption—parents or outsiders

Adoption satisfies a universal human need for love and acceptance. Arthur Grace/Stock, Boston

adoptive parents may be able to tell them truthfully that their real parents are dead and that there were no relatives who were able to take care of them. If, on the other hand, they tell the adopted children that their natural parents did not want them, the children may fear that their adoptive parents may someday reject them too. This fear undermines the feelings of security that are so essential to all children and especially to those who are adopted.

To work against this feeling of insecurity, some adoptive parents bend over backward to show adopted children how much they are loved. This, in turn, may lead to pampering, as well as a false idea about love.

There is a better way of dealing with children's questions about why they were adopted. Instead of stressing or trying to explain why the natural parents did not want them, the stress should be laid on how much the adoptive parents *did* want them—how they waited for them and chose them. Instead of feeling rejected, adopted children can be made to feel that they are *chosen* children.

Another problem that may arise comes from the way relatives feel about adoption and the way this affects their relationship with the adopted children. Relatives who feel uneasy or disapproving may not treat the adopted child the same way they do the other children of the family. The adopted child quickly sees and resents this.

A less common problem arises when the attitudes of neighborhood children are unfavorable to the adopted child. These attitudes generally mirror their parents' attitudes. They are important only when these parents have some

341

reason to make an issue of the fact of the adoption. Usually, playmates accept and pay little attention to the fact of adoption after some curiosity.

A fourth problem is that of the adopted child's relationship with the natural child or children of the family. If natural children feel that their parents show a preference for the adopted child, they will resent him or her. They will react to the adopted child as children always react to a child they see as the parents' pet—with jealousy and anger. This, in turn, leads to problems between the adopted child and the parents' natural-born children.

Because of the adjustment problems that go with adoption, most parents are advised by adoption agencies to tell children they are adopted as soon as the children can understand what it means. This, the agencies stress, is to avoid any shock children might experience if they learn of their adoption from outsiders.

It is best to consider adopted children exactly the same as their parents' natural children. They should be treated as the other children in the family are treated. Any show of favoritism toward the adopted child or the natural-born child is always serious. It gives rise to jealousies and anger.

For Discussion

> At what age would you explain to a child that he or she was adopted? How would you do it? Do you feel that this explanation would be enough to make the adopted child feel that she or he was really a member of the family? Give reasons for your answers.

Highlights of Chapter 25

☐ Some children, because of physical or psychological characteristics or patterns of family life, are very different from others.

☐ Being different becomes a problem for young children only when they become aware of this because of the comments and behavior of others.

☐ Children who are different because they are brighter or learn more slowly than other children can be protected against the psychological damage of being different by helping them find friends of their own intellectual levels and by encouraging them to add what they can to the enjoyment of their age-mates.

☐ Parents and other caretakers of children can do much to help their own and other children's adjustments by trying to change the attitude that being different means being inferior. They can teach children that this is not true and can help to create an accepting, friendly feeling in neighborhood groups.

☐ Physical handicaps and special abilities need not make children different from their friends if parents help children add to the play of other children.

☐ Growing up in a one-parent home or a home with a stepparent may make children somewhat different from others. However, this difference is rapidly fading as such homes become more common.

☐ Even though most adopted children feel secure and happy, adoption sometimes gives rise to adjustment problems. Among these are feelings of being different from other children.

Suggested Activities

1. The chart on page 335 gives ideas about how to deal with problems arising from physical defects during the early childhood years. List these, putting the ones that best meet the problems first. Explain your reasons for your order.

2. Find a one-parent family with either the mother or the father in charge of the children. Note the duties and responsibilities all children in the family are expected to take on. How does this family pattern differ from family patterns where there are two parents in the home?

3. Get in touch with an adoption agency in your area. If there is none, your doctor or school counselor can give you the address of one in another area. Ask for their printed material about requirements for adoption. Study this to see what people must do to adopt a child.

4. Make a list of descriptions of stepparents—stepmothers and stepfathers—in stories, in movies, in TV programs, and in such fairy tales as *Cinderella*. Study how these stepparents are shown. Is there any reason why children might get an unfavorable attitude toward stepparents from these sources? Give examples to back up your finding.

Chapter 26

Day-Care Centers and Preschools for Children

Some goals of this chapter are:
- [ ] To understand how day-care centers and preschools differ
- [ ] To be aware of the ways day-care centers and preschools help a child's personal, social, and intellectual development

The feeling of independence that children seek during the early childhood years is often shared by parents. A mother who gave up her job when the baby was born may decide to return to work when she feels the child is able to adjust to the care and attention of someone else. Sometimes, parents realize that their money situation calls for both of them to work. Many single-parent families may never have had a choice about who would care for their children while they worked.

Such situations are so common that day-care centers and preschools have taken on new responsibilities to children. To meet these new responsibilities, people are specially trained in child care and in early childhood education. The centers and preschools try to meet the needs a child may have. Sev-

eral teachers supervise and guide the children in their play and social activities, and aides help teachers make the attention more individual. Above all, these people generally enjoy working with children. Attention, affection, and understanding are freely given to try to help children make adjustments to their environment.

Functions of Day-Care Centers and Preschools

The purposes of day-care centers are different from those of preschools. Young children are sent to a day-care center because there is no one to take care of them at home. Children usually attend preschools to gain companionship with other children and to learn to adjust to people outside the home.

Day-care centers and preschools are often the first opportunity for children to experience interaction with others outside the family.
Sepp Seitz/Woodfin Camp & Associates

Some Ways Day-Care Centers and Preschools Help the Young Child's Development

Good Health   By balancing activity and rest and making sure that all children have medical checkups and are immunized against certain diseases

Skills   By improving skills already learned and teaching new ones under the teacher's guidance and supervision

Speech   By making children's vocabularies larger and widening their interests

Emotions   By teaching children to express their emotions in socially approved ways

Social Behavior   By teaching socially approved behavior patterns

Social Attitudes   By teaching children to be tolerant of those who are different, to add to the group, and to be good sports, good followers, and good leaders

Creativity   By encouraging children to express their creativity in ways that will please them

Discipline   By teaching children, through consistent and fair discipline, to obey rules and respect those in authority

Self-Concept   By stressing self-confidence, and feelings of self-worth

Easier Adjustment to School   By teaching skills that are basic to schoolwork

For many people, working with children is a tremendously rewarding experience! Top: David S. Strickler/Monkmeyer; bottom: Elaine Wickens, Bank Street College; facing page, left: Christopher Marrow/Stock, Boston; right: David S. Strickler/Monkmeyer

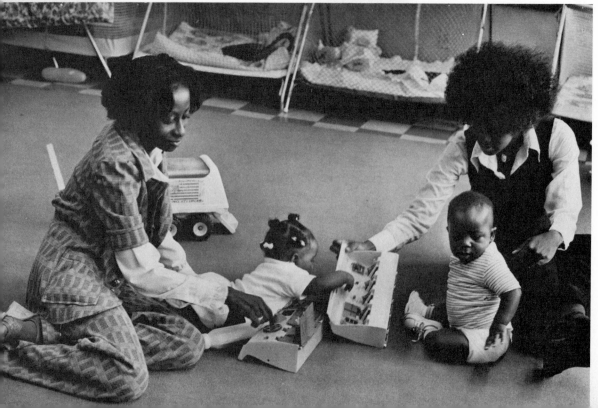

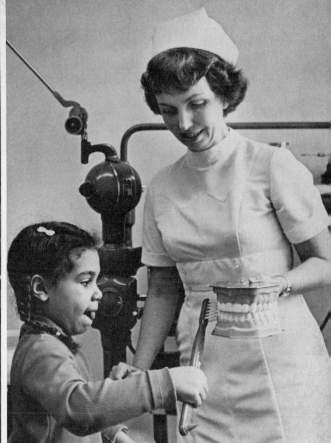

In day-care centers, taking care of the children's physical needs is a major concern. Often young children receive most of their toilet training in the day-care center. They also learn many of their self-help skills, such as self-dressing and self-feeding.

Day-care centers and preschools do share some common goals. The chart on page 345 shows how they help with the children's personal, social, and intellectual development.

Day-Care Centers

Day-care centers can be thought of as second homes for children. The caretakers can be thought of as substitute parents. Children go to the centers from early morning until early evening five days a week. They are usually taken there each morning as parents are on their way to work. Parents trust the caretakers at the center with the child. The child's basic physical and psychological needs are taken care of by people other than parents.

Physically, children thrive in well-run day-care centers. Many children eat two or three meals there. They are given the right food for their age and level of development. Since the children are there all day, they eat, rest, and play according to a schedule that meets their needs. There are safe places for and supervision of activities. As a result, accidents are rare. Centers are usually well equipped for indoor and outdoor play. Medical attention is on hand in case a child has an accident or is ill.

Socially, children learn to deal with people outside the family, especially other children. They have a chance to share toys, play games, and take part in activities. They learn how to cooperate with each other. When caretakers are specially trained in early childhood education, they guide and encourage children in their learning experiences. This helps develop the child's intellectual abilities.

Choosing a Day-Care Center

Ideally, children's basic needs are met in well-managed day-care centers. Unfortunately, not all centers are well managed. It is a good idea for parents to look into centers before choosing one for their child. They will need to use both their own judgment and the advice of other, more experienced people before making a decision.

For Discussion

Look back at the chart, *What Caretakers Do*, on page 131 in Chapter 9. How do teachers and aides in day-care centers and preschools do these jobs? For example, how do they encourage the development of a child's physical and mental abilities?

When parents decide that they want to send their child to a day-care center, they may first seek advice from their doctor. If there are several centers in the neighborhood, the doctor may be able to recommend one over another. There may be long waiting lists, but sometimes the doctor can help place the child. In any case, children need a medical checkup before being accepted in a center.

However, not every doctor knows about the day-care centers in a neighborhood. Parents may get more useful

What Parents Should Think About When Choosing Day-Care Centers

Is the center licensed and regularly checked by government authorities?

What is the cost for each child?

How old is the child? Are there other children the same age for companionship?

Is the center near enough to the parents' place of work so it could be quickly reached in an emergency?

Is it well equipped for activities?

Do those who manage and work at the center like their jobs? Do they act as though their task is just to baby-sit, or do they encourage the physical and psychological development of the children?

Are there enough teachers and aides to give each child individual attention?

Is there careful supervision of all children at all times?

Is the food well prepared, of good quality, and suited to the age of the children?

Is the environment relaxed and happy? Or do the children seem bored and irritable?

Children attending preschool play most of the time, but at the same time they are learning to work cooperatively in a group.
Irene Bayer/Monkmeyer

advice from other parents, teachers, clergy, or social service agencies. These sources may know more about the child-care centers in the area and can give parents needed facts.

It may also be helpful for parents to visit the different day-care centers. Before deciding which one is best for their child, parents should give some thought to the ideas listed in the accompanying chart.

In some cases, it may be helpful to send the child to the center for a few weeks as a trial period. This gives the child time to adjust to the new environment. It also gives the parents time to make changes if they are needed.

For Discussion

In choosing a day-care center for their child, what do you think is the most important thing parents should think about? Give reasons for your answers.

Preschools

Nursery schools and kindergartens are preschools. In general, children from 2 through 4 years of age go to nursery school, and 5-year-olds go to kindergarten. Usually, children go to preschools for only a few hours in the morning or afternoon.

In spite of the fact that most people think of preschools as play schools, they are far more than that. They do provide equipment, encouragement, and guidance in learning a wide variety of play skills. But they also stress self-help skills, social-help skills, and learning how to get along with other people. In these ways, preschools try to lay the basis for a well-rounded development and to prepare children for the first grade.

Highlights of Chapter 26

☐ Day-care centers and preschools try to add to children's personal, social, and intellectual development.

☐ Day-care centers may be thought of as second homes for children and the teachers there as substitute parents.

☐ Before choosing a day-care center, parents may visit several and also seek advice from people who know more about them.

☐ Preschools help children get used to being away from home and being with other children as preparation for school.

Suggested Activities

1. Find out about and report on the background needed to become teachers or aides in day-care centers, nursery schools, and kindergartens.

2. Visit two or three day-care centers in your neighborhood and compare them. Here are some points to look for in each: How many children are there for each teacher and aide? How old are the children in the centers? Are they divided into groups for activities? Does each child seem to be receiving enough individual attention? How do the teachers or aides deal with behavior problems?

3. Ask the parents in your neighborhood if their children attend preschool. Ask some children what they like best about going to nursery school or kindergarten. If they do not like going, ask them why.

4. Make a chart for a bulletin board to show how day-care centers and preschools add to children's personal, social, and intellectual development.

Chapter 27

Getting Ready for School

Some goals of this chapter are:
- [ ] To realize the importance of early school experiences in forming children's attitudes toward school
- [ ] To understand why beginning school is a major adjustment for children, even for those who have had preschool experience
- [ ] To be aware of the adjustments children must make in skills, relationships, discipline, and learning when they begin first grade

As early childhood draws to a close, the time comes for children to go to school. All physically and mentally normal children must go to school when they are 6 years old. For those who are physically or mentally handicapped, many areas offer special classes to meet their needs.

While parents have no choice about whether their children enter school, they can and should prepare their children for this new experience. Even children who have gone to nursery school and kindergarten need some preparation.

Young Children's Attitudes toward School

To young children, going to school means growing up. And because they want to grow up and have the independence that being grown-up brings, they look forward eagerly to going to school. Children whose older brothers or sisters go to school every morning are especially eager to join the ranks of school children. They also want to share the experiences they hear their brothers and sisters talk about at home.

However, when the time comes for them to begin school, their eagerness may change to fear. They may dread leaving the security of the home to enter the unknown world of school. Even children who have attended and liked preschool may fear going to first grade. The reason for this is that the break between the home and school environments is not as great in nursery school and kindergarten as it is in first grade.

351

On the other hand, children who have had preschool experience usually make easier and quicker adjustments to first grade than those who have not. But because of the difference between pre-school and elementary school, even those children have to make adjustments.

Early School Experiences Affect Attitudes

How children feel about school depends largely on their early experiences in school. If these are pleasant, they will like school and want to learn. If, on the other hand, they find school unpleasant or even terrifying, they will not only dislike school but will try to use every means they can to keep from going to school. There are many factors that form children's attitudes toward school. These are explained in the accompanying chart. Being prepared for what will be expected of them in school will make children's attitudes more favorable toward learning.

Studies of children who work below their intellectual abilities and of children who actually "hate" school have traced such problems to the children's early experiences in school. Even though problems may not show up until later grades, there are plenty of facts to suggest that the start of the trouble was in the first grade. More often than not, these children had unpleasant experiences instead of the pleasant ones they looked forward to during their pre-school years.

Going to School Is a Major Adjustment

Starting first grade calls for many adjustments. For children who have not had preschool experience, going to school is their first real break with home. This may be the first time such children are faced with new people, new surroundings, and new patterns of behavior. They are taking a major step in growing up.

An informal preschool atmosphere helps children develop a more positive attitude toward learning. Sepp Seitz/Woodfin Camp & Associates

Common Things That Affect Early School Experiences

Preschool Experiences Whether children like or dislike nursery school or kindergarten will affect their attitudes toward the first grade. Children who like preschool usually enjoy first grade and find the work rewarding. It is also easier for these children to make social adjustments with the other children.

Preparation for School If children have a false idea about school, they may not like the real thing. They may also feel unprepared and unable to do what is expected of them.

Social Acceptance Being liked by classmates makes early school experiences pleasant for children. Feelings of rejection or neglect by others make children not want to be at school.

Communicating with Others Being able to communicate with others helps children build up social contacts in school. When children are unable to communicate, for any reason, they are cut off from their classmates and feel lonely. It is only natural for children to dislike the situation that makes them lonely.

Learning Success Keeping up with the rest of the class in what they are learning makes early school experiences pleasant. Not being able to read or write like the others makes children feel inferior. A desire often develops in these children to escape from the situation in which they feel they have failed.

The ability to make adjustments to new situations depends partly on intelligence. The brighter the child, the more quickly the adjustments will be made. Also, the less upsetting they will be.

Making adjustments depends more, however, on experience in dealing with different situations than it does on intelligence. Many young children have had little chance to adjust to new situations and even less guidance in learning how to do so.

A child's poor adjustment to school has long-lasting effects. It can be prevented, and every effort should be made to do so. Parents can guide and prepare children for the adjustments they will be expected to make in the first grade.

Before children are 3 years old, they are likely to be upset if there is any change in their routine activities. After that, however, children actually welcome changes. This, then, is when children are ready to learn to make adjustments to new people and new situations. Parents who are aware of this can make use of the children's "readiness." They can gradually introduce children to new people and new situations. Children will find the new experiences stimulating and enjoyable, not frightening. This will help cushion the shock that so often happens when children go to school for the first time.

There are a number of other ways in which young children can get experience in making adjustments. These will lessen the adjustment problems they face when beginning school. Some of the most important of these appear on the next page in the accompanying chart.

A child's initial nervousness about going to school may be lessened if a familiar person brings them to and from school. David S. Strickler/Monkmeyer

The more time children have to learn to make adjustments, the easier it will be for them to do so. Concentrated training, in the last three to six months before entering first grade, for example, rarely produces the good results of gradual training over a longer period of time. A good time to begin preparing for school is when children turn 5.

For Discussion

The chart on page 353 lists some of the things that affect early school experiences. Study the list carefully, and then discuss the importance of each item to the child's school adjustments. Are some factors more important than others? Give reasons for your answer.

Ways to Lessen School Adjustment Problems

Children can attend nursery school, kindergarten, or a child-care center.

Children can belong to a neighborhood play group supervised by adults.

Children can visit a school with a parent to get an idea of what going to school means.

Parents of preschoolers can talk with parents of first-graders about what is expected of their children and what problems the children may have faced. By doing this, parents can be ready to help their children avoid such problems.

They should be able to put on and take off outdoor clothes—coat, cap, mittens, rubbers, and boots.

They should know when to go to the toilet without waiting to be told.

They should be able to wash their hands and face and comb their hair.

They should be able to feed themselves, using knives and forks, in case they eat lunch in school.

They should be able to keep their belongings neatly in the space given to them.

Some Important Areas of Adjustment

Though schools differ from one to another, they have enough in common for parents to know what will be expected of children beginning the first grade. Children should be ready to learn how to read and write when they begin school. But they should also be able to take care of their own basic needs and get along reasonably well with classmates.

Mastering Skills. For about a year before children start school, parents should see to it that they have a chance to learn, with help, skills they will be expected to have when they enter school. The important skills young children should master are divided into four groups—self-help skills, social-help skills, play skills, and work skills. These are described in detail on pages 173–177.

Of all the skills, the self-help skills will be of most value to children in their school adjustments. The accompanying chart points out what children should be able to do for themselves before going to school.

During the early grades, creativity is stressed. A great deal of time is spent on play skills and on making things. All through early childhood, children should be encouraged to be creative, not just to copy models made by someone else. Parents can help children develop this creativity by not being too critical of what children make, no matter how strange it may be. Children

A self-help skill such as dressing for school should be encouraged by parents. Robert Capece

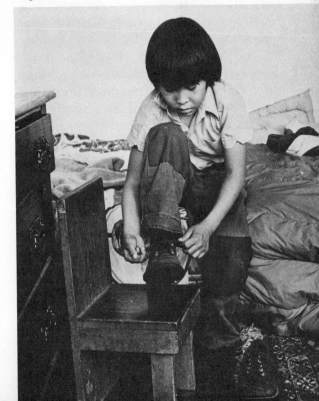

need help in getting the results of their efforts close to what they want. But this help should be given without stifling their creativity.

One of the important skills learned in first grade is writing. Some preschools help children master this skill. By the time children reach first grade, many can form numbers and letters. Many children who have not had preschool experience feel inadequate when they compare their early attempts at writing with those of children who have already learned to form letters and numbers.

At home, parents can prepare young children for this adjustment by encouraging the child to draw. After children have learned to do this, they can learn to hold a pencil and form letters and numbers. Few things make children feel prouder than saying they can write their names even before they enter first grade!

Social-help skills, or doing things to help others, are also very important to healthy adjustment to school. Children will be asked to perform little duties for the teacher, such as putting away paints or erasing the blackboard. And they will be held responsible for doing these duties. It will be helpful to children's school adjustment, therefore, for them to have experience at home in doing such tasks.

Making Good Social Adjustments. Children's attitudes toward school will be strongly affected by the way they are treated there by both adults and other children. Since most of the children will be strangers, they will all have to learn to adjust to one another. Unlike preschools and day-care centers, there will be little adult supervision of the children's social relationships when they begin first grade. Children are now more on their own in learning to get along with other children. They are concerned about who their new friends will be and whether they will be accepted by their classmates. One way to help children make good social adjustments is through their appearance.

First-graders are not aware of style, but they are aware of difference. They are concerned if their clothes are very different from those of their classmates. To help children feel comfortable with the others, it is wise to put off buying most of the child's school clothes until the child actually starts school. Seeing the other first-graders will help parents and children decide what kind of clothes to buy.

Neatness and good grooming are also important to making favorable impressions on others. By the time children are ready to enter school, they should know basic grooming skills, such as washing their hands, combing their hair, and making themselves look neat.

Another social adjustment children will be faced with in first grade is their relationships with teachers. Children may expect the same amount of attention from their teacher that they are used to getting from other adults they know. With one teacher for twenty or more students, children will soon find that they must share time, attention, and affection with many more children than they ever had to before.

To ease the task of making satisfactory social adjustments, there are certain things parents can do to help children before they begin school.

One good result of favorable social adjustment to school is that children learn to work together cooperatively. Susan Anderson/Monkmeyer

These are listed in the accompanying chart.

The way a child is trained in the home has a huge effect on social adjustments. Children's attitudes toward others and the kind of relationships they have with others are formed in the home. Where democratic training is used, children easily learn to give and take. In permissive homes, however, children are encouraged to be too individualistic. This may result in their becoming self-centered and uncooperative. Authoritarian training may encourage being like others. But it may also encourage children to rebel and

---

How Parents Can Help Children Make Social Adjustments in School

Give children a chance to be with people of all types, ages, and home backgrounds.

Let children visit in homes of playmates, relatives, and friends of the family.

Encourage children to notice the appearance and behavior of other children.

Encourage children to cooperate with family members, whether in household tasks or in playing games.

Encourage children to follow the wishes of the majority, first in the home and later in the play group.

Help children to curb unsocial behavior patterns and replace them with behavior that will lead to social acceptance.

Teach children the play skills that other children like as well as the play activities the child likes best.

Encourage children to talk to and be kind to others.

take a negative attitude toward all suggestions from either classmates or teachers.

Adjusting to School Discipline. One of the common reasons many young children have a hard time adjusting to school centers around discipline. Children who have had inconsistent discipline in the home will find it hard to adjust to school discipline. In school, teachers try to be fair to all the children. If one child is allowed to disobey the rules, it is not fair to the others.

To help children adjust to school discipline, it would be wise for parents to take a good, hard look at the way they discipline. This should be done at least six months before the child is to enter school. A year before is even better. When parents do this, they will discover soft spots and gaps between their ideals of discipline and the methods they use. Parents should then try to be consistent and to discipline children firmly but fairly. If parents do

this, they will find that their child will adjust to school far more easily than many children do.

Making Intellectual Adjustments. In spite of the fact that intellectual abilities develop rapidly during the early years of childhood, many parents do very little to help their children learn to use intellectual abilities. This is mostly because parents feel that this is the chief function of school and partly because they are concerned with other responsibilities.

There are three mental abilities that play important roles in early school adjustments. Parents can do much in helping children develop these abilities.

The first is being able to concentrate. All school activities call for concentration of attention. This is a hard adjustment for most children. Many do not know how to concentrate before they enter school. Young children have few experiences that really show them how to concentrate. For example, if the

Completing puzzles and playing games to the end help children develop the ability to concentrate. Norm Hurst/Stock, Boston

child's attention wanders while a story is being read, the adult usually stops reading or reads another story of the child's choosing.

Too little interest is at the root of poor attention. So the first step in improving concentration is to try to increase interest. For example, if children become bored with making sand cakes after a few minutes, parents can increase the children's interest by suggesting ways to decorate the cakes. Or they can encourage the children to tell stories about the cakes and who they are for.

Memorizing is the second mental ability that is new and hard to learn. Children are expected to memorize the words of songs, of poems, and of other writings. They must also learn basic number combinations and how to spell simple words.

To help children develop the skill of memorizing, simple games of counting, learning names of objects, and spelling simple words can be played at home with all family members taking part. This training will be of great value as preparation for school. It will also be fun, because it is part of a game.

The third important mental ability that the school expects of children is the ability to reason. In the early school years, only very simple reasoning is needed to do well. It mostly calls for making decisions in fairly easy situations or in easy subjects. However, some young children have had most of their decisions made for them by adults. These children will find this a hard task.

Young children should be given plenty of chance at home to make decisions. They can decide, for example, which of three or four shirts they want to wear, whether to plant petunias or geraniums in the window garden, whether to go to a friend's house or stay home and help make cookies, and so on.

For Discussion

What might you do to help children develop concentration, memory, and decision-making skills? When reading to children, how would asking questions about the characters in a story help children learn to concentrate? How would teaching children simple poems help them learn to memorize? What can parents do to help children learn to make decisions?

Learning to Read. Reading is one of the most important skills learned in first grade. It plays a deciding role in the child's attitude toward school and learning. Children who read well usually like school better than those who have trouble reading. Being embarrassed, first for having to stand up before the class, then for reading poorly, and then for not understanding what she or he just read, makes the child want to stay away from school and reading altogether.

For Discussion

How might watching television affect children's ability to learn to read? Some teachers say that television helps children learn to read. Others say that watching TV is the major reason for low reading levels. Give examples of why you think the teachers feel as they do.

Most teachers would rather that parents do not teach their children how to read before starting school. The reason for this is that the method of teaching that parents use may be different from that used by the school. This will only confuse children. Also, most children are not really ready to learn to read until they are in school. When parents try to teach their children to read, they may be adding uncalled-for stress.

However, parents should do all they can to encourage their children to be *interested* in reading. Parents can encourage children to follow words when they read and show children a word that is associated with a picture on the same page. They can also ask the children to point out a certain word after it has been read several times. This will help children become familiar with it.

A very important way to encourage young children to want to learn to read is by having reading periods in the home. During this time, every member of the family may read. Associating reading with being grown-up is one of the easiest and quickest ways to get a young child to want to learn to read. While children may not be able to read, they should be given the chance to look at and "read" a favorite book. Sometimes children "read" by telling the story in their own words.

Early exposure to fun books promotes interest and curiosity for good future reading habits. Jean-Claude Lejeune/Stock, Boston

Happy birthday.... happy school days! Rosemarie Hausherr

For Action

Watch several TV shows made for preschool children to see how they may help prepare children for school. Which shows encourage an interest in reading by showing words with pictures? This gives the children a chance to associate printed words with the objects that they stand for.

Testing Readiness for School
No matter how parents try to prepare their children for school, they are never sure if they have done enough until the children go to school. However, it is possible to get a clue as to how good the preparation is even before children enter school by testing children's present behavior in a simple way.

The questions in the following chart will serve as a guide to judge whether there has been enough preparation for school. If most of these questions can be answered as shown at the end of each question, the child is well prepared for school. If, however, only a few of the questions can be answered as shown, there are weaknesses in the preparation. The more correct answers there are, the more certain parents can be that the child is ready for school and that the child's adjustment to school will not be too hard an experience. Wrong answers tell parents where their child needs help.

Is the Child Ready for School?

1. Can the child take care of his or her own needs, such as sneezing into a tissue and going to the bathroom? (Yes)

2. Can the child put on her or his coat, snowsuit, gloves, cap, and rubbers or boots without help? (Yes)

3. Does the child eat meals without complaining about the food and without being helped or urged? (Yes)

4. Can the child color an outline picture without going outside the lines more than once in a while? (Yes)

5. Can the child cut well enough with blunt scissors to be able to cut out large figures? (Yes)

6. Can the child paste pictures on pieces of paper? (Yes)

7. Can the child handle paint without too much smearing? (Yes)

8. Can the child throw, catch, and bounce large balls? (Yes)

9. Can the child ride a tricycle or bicycle, roller skate, and jump rope? (Yes)

10. Does the child get along with other children? (Yes)

11. Does the child want to play with other children rather than just watch a group at play? (Yes)

12. Does the child prefer to be with other children rather than with adults? (Yes)

13. Does the child adjust quickly to new adults and new children? (Yes)

14. Does the child get along better with children the same age than with older or younger children? (Yes)

15. Does the child willingly carry out any task given? (Yes)

16. Does the child do little tasks for others without being asked? (Yes)

17. Does the child have any responsibilities at home? (Yes)

18. Does the child carry out responsibilities without being reminded all the time? (Yes)

19. Is the child obedient most of the time? (Yes)

20. Does the child often put up an argument when told to do something or when scolded for wrongdoing? (No)

21. Does the child try to shift the blame onto others to avoid punishment? (No)

22. Does the child react favorably to discipline? (Yes)

23. Does the child try at all to concentrate on a subject, even though not interested in it? (Yes)

24. Does the child's attention wander easily from the task at hand? (No)

25. Does the child ask questions about stories that are read aloud? (Yes)

26. Does the child make decisions rather than rely on someone else to make them? (Yes)

27. Does the child study the pictures in books and tell their meanings? (Yes)

28. Does the child follow the printed words on the page while being read to? (Yes)

Highlights of Chapter 27

- [ ] Going to school, even for those who have had preschool experience, is a major adjustment for children.

- [ ] Early school experiences often affect children's attitudes toward school for many years.

- [ ] Parents can ease the adjustment problems all young children experience when going to school by preparing children during the year before starting school.

- [ ] Learning self-help, play, and social-help skills at home helps in making a good adjustment to first grade.

- [ ] Helping children make social adjustments to people of all ages makes the change from home to school easier for young children.

- [ ] Parents and caretakers can, through games and home activities, help children learn to concentrate, memorize, and make decisions. These are aids to children's adjustments to school studies.

- [ ] It is wise to encourage children to be interested in reading, though children do not have to be taught to read before they begin school.

- [ ] The test for school readiness, suggested in this chapter, gives parents some ideas about weaknesses or oversights in preparing their children for starting first grade.

Suggested Activities

1. Find out what activities are part of a preschool program to help young children prepare for school. Using the material in this chapter, which activities would be most helpful in preparing children for the first grade?

2. Ask the parents of several first-graders about the adjustments their children had to make going to school. Do the children face certain adjustment problems more than others? Which ones? Why do you think this is so?

3. Study the coloring, clay modeling, and drawing of preschool children. Make a list of the different ways children express creativity. How do people react to children's creativity? How do their reactions affect children's desires to be creative? How will this affect their adjustment to school?

4. Watch the Saturday morning children's shows on TV. Make a list of the ways they may help children learn to concentrate, memorize, and make decisions. Which of the shows are *educational* in that they help prepare children for school?

Bibliography

Books

Ames, L. B., and J. A. Chase: *Don't Push Your Preschooler*, Harper & Row, New York, 1974.

Ames, L. B., and F. L. Ilg: *Your Two Year Old: Terrible or Tender*, Delacorte Press, New York, 1976.

Ames, L. B., and F. L. Ilg: *Your Three Year Old: Friend or Enemy*, Delacorte Press, New York, 1976.

Ames, L. B., and F. L. Ilg: *Your Four Year Old: Wild or Wonderful*, Delacorte Press, New York, 1976.

Apgar, V., and J. Beck: *Is My Baby All Right?*, Trident, New York, 1973.

Arnstein, H. S.: *The Roots of Love: Helping Your Child to Love in the First Three Years*, Bobbs-Merrill, New York, 1975.

Baker, K. R., and X. F. Fane: *Understanding and Guiding Young Children*, Prentice-Hall, Englewood Cliffs, N. J., 1975.

Biller, H., and D. Meredith: *Father Power*, Archer Books/Doubleday, Garden City, N. Y., 1975.

Brazelton, T. B.: *Doctor and Child*, Delacorte Press, New York, 1976.

Brazelton, T. B.: *Toddlers and Parents: A Declaration of Independence*, Delacorte Press, New York, 1974.

Brenner, E., and S. Schimin: *A New Baby! A New Life! From Birth to One Year through Words and Pictures*, McGraw-Hill, New York, 1973.

Broadribb, V., and H. F. Lee: *The Modern Parents' Guide to Baby and Child Care*, Lippincott, Philadelphia, 1973.

Caplan, F. (ed.): *The First Twelve Months of Life: Your Baby's Growth Month by Month*, Grossett and Dunlap, New York, 1973.

Cass, J. E.: *Helping Children Grow through Play*, Schocken Books, New York, 1973.

Child Study Association of America: *What to Tell Your Child about Sex*, Child Study Press, New York, 1974.

Church, J.: *Understanding Your Child from Birth to Three: A Guide to Your Child's Psychological Development*, Random House, New York, 1973.

Corsini, R. J., and G. Painter: *The Practical Parent: ABC's of Child Discipline*, Harper & Row, New York, 1975.

Davis, A.: *Let's Have Healthy Children*, Harcourt Brace Jovanovich, New York, 1972.

Denzin, N. K. (ed.): *Children and Their Caretakers*, Dutton, New York, 1973.

Dreikurs, R., and V. Stoltz: *Children: The Challenge*, Hawthorn, New York, 1976.

Fein, G. G., and A. C. Stewart: *Day Care in Context*, Wiley, New York, 1973.

Gilbert, S. D.: *What's a Father For? A Father's Guide to the Pleasures and Problems of Parenthood with Advice from the Experts*, Parents' Magazine Press, New York, 1975.

Ginott, H.: *Between Parent and Child*, Avon Books, New York, 1973.

Gottlieb, D. (ed.): *Children's Liberation*, Prentice-Hall, Englewood Cliffs, N. J., 1973.

Graubard, P.S.: *Positive Parenthood: Solv-*

ing *Parent-Child Conflicts*, Bobbs-Merrill, New York, 1977.

Green, M.: *Fathering*, McGraw-Hill, New York, 1976.

Grey, L.: *Discipline without Tyranny: Child Training during the First Five Years*, Hawthorn Books, New York, 1972.

Hechinger, F., and G. Hechinger: *Growing Up in America*, McGraw-Hill, New York, 1975.

Highberger, R., and C. Schramm: *Child Development for Day Care Workers*, Houghton Mifflin, Boston, 1976.

Hoover, M. B.: *The Responsive Parent: Meeting the Realities of Parenthood Today*, Parents' Magazine Press, New York, 1972.

James, H.: *The Little Victims: How America Treats Its Children*, McKay, New York, 1975.

Jenkins, G. G., and H. S. Shacter: *These Are Your Children*, 4th ed., Scott Foresman, Glenview, Ill., 1975.

Kalb, J., and D. Viscott: *What Every Kid Should Know*, Houghton Mifflin, Boston, 1976.

Kappelman, M.: *Raising the Only Child*, Dutton, New York, 1975.

Kaye, E.: *The Family Guide to Children's Television: What to Watch, What to Miss, What to Change and How to Do It*, Pantheon Books, New York, 1974.

Koschnick, K. (ed.): *Having a Baby*, New Readers Press, Syracuse, N. Y., 1975.

Langford, L., and H. Y. Rand: *Guidance of the Young Child*, 2d ed., Wiley, New York, 1975.

Leach, P.: *Babyhood*, Knopf, New York, 1976.

LeMasters, E. E.: *Parents in Modern America*, rev. ed., Dorsey, Homewood, Ill., 1974.

Lesowitz, R. J.: *Rules for Raising Kids*, Charles C. Thomas, Springfield, Ill., 1974.

Levine, J. A.: *Who Will Raise the Children?*

New *Options for Fathers (and Mothers)*, Lippincott, Philadelphia, 1976.

Levy, J.: *The Baby Exercise Book*, Pantheon, New York, 1974.

Lynn, D. B.: *The Father: His Role in Child Development*, Brooks/Cole, Monterey, Calif., 1974.

Maynard, F.: *Guiding Your Child to a More Creative Life*, Doubleday, Garden City, N. Y., 1973.

McDiarmid, N. J., M. A. Peterson, and J. R. Sutherland: *Loving and Learning: Interaction with Your Child from Birth to Three*, Harcourt Brace Jovanovich, New York, 1975.

Moyer, K. E.: *You and Your Child: A Primer for Parents*, Nelson-Hall, Chicago, Ill., 1974.

Neisser, E. G.: *Primer for Parents of Preschoolers*, Parents' Magazine Press, New York, 1972.

Nilsson, L.: *How Was I Born?*, Delacorte Press, New York, 1975.

Painter, G.: *Teach Your Baby*, Simon and Schuster, New York, 1976.

Peairs, L., and R. Peairs: *What Every Child Needs*, Harper & Row; New York, 1974.

Pomeranz, V. E., and D. Schultz: *The First Five Years: A Relaxed Approach to Child Care*, Doubleday, Garden City, N. Y., 1973.

Pringle, M. K.: *The Needs of Children*, Schocken Books, New York, 1975.

Robertiello, R. C.: *Hold Them Close, Then Let Them Go: How to Be an Authentic Parent*, Dial Press, New York, 1975.

Salk, L.: *Preparing for Parenthood: Understanding Your Feelings about Pregnancy, Childbirth, and Your Baby*, McKay, New York, 1974.

Salk, L.: *What Every Child Would Like His Parents to Know to Help Him with the Emotional Problems of His Everyday Life*, McKay, New York, 1972.

Shiller, J. G.: *Childhood Illness: A Common*

Sense Approach, Stein & Day, New York, 1972.

Smith, C. T.: *The Parent Disciplines the Child*, Dorrance & Company, Philadelphia, 1976.

Smith, L. H.: *New Wives' Tales: Conversations with Parents about Today's Pediatrics*, Prentice-Hall, Englewood Cliffs, N. J., 1974.

Sparkman, B., and A. Carmichael: *Blueprint for a Brighter Child*, McGraw-Hill, New York, 1973.

Spock, B. McL.: *Baby and Child Care*, Pocket Books, New York, 1976.

Spock, B. McL.: *Raising Children in a Difficult Time*, Norton, New York, 1974.

Stein, S.: *The Childkeeper*, Harcourt Brace Jovanovich, New York, 1975.

Stenfels, M. O'B.: *Day Care in the U.S.A.*, Simon and Schuster, New York, 1973.

Tough, J.: *Talking, Thinking, Growing: Language with the Young Child*, Schocken Books, New York, 1974.

Weisberger, E.: *Your Young Child and You: How to Manage Growing-Up Problems in the Years from One to Five*, Dutton, New York, 1975.

White, B. L.: *The First Three Years of Life*, Prentice-Hall, Englewood Cliffs, N. J., 1975.

White, B. L., J. C. Watts, and I. C. Barnett: *Experience and Environment: Major Influences on the Development of the Young Child*, Prentice-Hall, Englewood Cliffs, N. J., 1973.

Winick, M. P.: *Before the 3 R's*, McKay, New York, 1972.

Pampflets

American Medical Association
535 North Dearborn Street
Chicago, Ill. 60610

A Child in the Family   OP–030

The Miracle of Life   OP–004

Parents' Responsibility   OP–057

What to Do before Your Baby Comes
      OP–193

What to Do after Your Baby Comes
      OP–353

Johnson & Johnson
Consumer and Professional Services
501 George Street
New Brunswick, N. J. 08901

A Baby Is Born

Birth Atlas

For the Expectant Father

Newborn Baby

Nutrition and Birth

Preparation for Childbearing

Public Affairs Pamphlets
Public Affairs Committee, Inc.
387 Park Avenue South
New York, N. Y. 10016

Abortion: Public Issue, Private Decision
      527

Breastfeeding   353S

To Combat Child Abuse and Neglect
      508

Index

1 2 3 4 5 6 7 8 9 10 VHVH 86 85 84 83 82 81 80 79 78 77